미국 장로교 선교사 박숭현 · 신혜정 선교 편지

LETTERS from the MISSION FIELD

미국 장로교 선교사 박숭현·신혜정 선교 편지
LETTERS from the MISSION FIELD

2020년 1월 2일 초판 1쇄 인쇄
2020년 1월 9일 초판 1쇄 발행

지은이 | 박숭현, 신혜정
발행처 | 한남대학교 인돈학술원
펴낸곳 | 도서출판 동연
주 소 | 서울시 마포구 월드컵로 163-3
전 화 | (02) 335-2630
전 송 | (02) 335-2640
이메일 | yh4321@gmail.com

ISBN 978-89-6447-544-7 03040

인돈학술총서 4

미국 장로교 선교사 **박숭현·신혜정** 선교 편지

LETTERS from the MISSION FIELD

| 박숭현 · 신혜정 지음 |

 한남대학교 인돈학술원   **동연**

　박숭현, 신혜정 선교사님의 선교 편지를 인돈학술총서로 발간하게 되어 기쁘게 생각합니다. 두 분은 한국계 미국인으로서 안정된 미국대학 교수의 삶을 내려놓고 미국장로교(PCUSA) 선교사로 부름을 받아 아프리카 콩고와 네팔과 한국에서 15년간 선교 사역을 감당하고 은퇴하셨습니다. 전문인 선교사로서 회계학과 컨설팅의 전문성을 활용하여 미국장로교가 동역하는 현지 교단과 기독교 기관과 협력하면서 그들이 하나님 나라의 확장에 기여하는 본연의 사명을 감당할 수 있도록 돕는 역할을 충실하게 수행하였습니다.

　주인공이 아니라 조연으로서, 지배하고 가르치는 존재가 아니라 섬기고 협력하는 존재로서 선교사의 정체성을 인식하고, 힘과 물질을 앞세워 현지인들을 선교사들에게 종속시키는 제국주의 선교를 넘어서 그리스도의 증인과 섬기는 종의 삶을 살아가는 성육신적 선교를 실천하고자 부단히 노력하였습니다. 이러한 내려놓음, 낮아짐, 동행, 섬김의 모습이 선교 기간 내내 이어진 삶 속에서 때로는 기쁨으로, 때로는 고통으로, 회한과 회의로, 감사와 찬양으로 새겨져 있고, 그 증언들이 그분들이 남긴 선교 편지 속에 생생하게 증언되고 있습니다. 그래서 이 서신들은 자신들의 삶을 미화하기 위한 글도 아니고, 자신들의 업적과 성취를 자랑하기 위한 성과보고도 아닌, 선교 현장에서 만난 사람들과 친구가 되어 어울려 지내며 경험하고 느낀 자신들의 진솔한 삶의 이야기, 감사와 절망이 어우러져 있는, 그래서 투박하고 날 것 그대로의 삶의 이야기를 우리에게 전달해주고 있습니다. 선교사 부부가 낯선 환경과 전혀 다른 문화권에서, 또는 익숙하지만 이질적인 삶의 환경 속에서 어떻게 생각하고 느꼈는지, 그리스도의 증인으로서 살아가기 위해 고뇌하면서 어떻게 판단하고 실천하였는지 보여줌으로써 우리들 자신의 삶과 행동을 돌아보게 한다는 점에서 이들의 증언은 우리에게도 유용하고 유익한 교훈이 된다고 생각합니다.

인돈학술원은 1892년부터 한국 선교를 담당해 온 미국 남장로회가 1956년에 대전에 설립한 한남대학교 부설연구원으로서 대학의 창학정신을 계승하고 발전하기 위해서 대학 설립자인 미국남장로회의 선교 역사에 관한 자료를 수집, 보존, 연구하고 중요 자료를 발간하는 학술사업을 꾸준히 진행하고 있습니다. 박숭현, 신혜정 선교사님은 미국장로교 선교동역자로 한국에 계실 때, 한남대학교 오정동 캠퍼스에 있는 선교사촌에 거주하시며, 대학 구성원들과 돈독한 우정을 나누었고, 그분들의 소박하고 진지한 삶을 통해 기독교 정신과 선교적 삶이 무엇인지 귀감이 되어 주셨습니다. 또한 한남대학교가 미국장로교와 깊은 유대와 협력을 지속할 수 있도록 중요한 연결통로가 되어 주셨고, 한남대학교의 기독교 정체성의 계승과 발전에 있어서 소중한 역할을 감당하셨습니다. 선교사들은 은퇴하고 떠났지만, 우리에게 이어지고 있는 선교와 교육의 사명을 지속적으로 발전시키기 위해서 우리는 그들의 삶과 사역을 되돌아보고, 우리 자신을 성찰하면서, 하나님 나라 확장과 그리스도의 증인된 사명을 감당하는 일에 부단한 노력을 기울여야 할 것이라 봅니다.

　이러한 측면에서 이번에 인돈학술총서로 발간하는 박숭현, 신혜정 선교사님의 선교편지는 우리들의 노력과 성찰에 유익한 교훈을 줄 것이라 생각합니다. 영어로 된 글을 현장의 생생함과 원문의 내용을 가감 없이 전달하기 위해 따로 번역하지 않았습니다. 이글이 사람들 사이에서 읽히며 숙성이 되고 필요와 요청이 있다면, 자연스럽게 번역출간이 될 것이라 기대합니다.

　아무쪼록 이글을 통해 많은 유익과 교훈을 얻으실 수 있기를 바랍니다.

2019년 10월

인돈학술원장 최영근

머리말

　이 책은 우리가 1998년부터 2013년까지 미국 장로교단 파송 선교사로 지내며 쓴 편지들을 모아서 만든 것입니다. 이 이야기들은 우리 부부의 매일의 삶, 이웃과의 삶, 맡겨진 일을 하며 느낀 실망, 기쁨, 회의 등 영적인 여정을 식구들과 친지들에게 보내서 같이 삶을 나눈 것들입니다.

　어디에 갔었냐고요?

　아프리카 콩고가 첫 선교지였고 그리고 네팔, 한국. 한국에서는 한남대학교 교정에 있는 선교사 촌에 살았으며 중간중간 여러 곳에 단기 사역을 위해 보내지기도 했습니다. 은퇴하기 얼마 전에는 북한 평양 과기대에 6주간 갔었고 돌아와서 보고서 형식으로 쓴 편지도 이 책에 포함시켰습니다.

　어떤 계기로 선교사의 길을 선택했는지 궁금하시죠?

　박숭현 선교사는 고등학교를 마치고 곧 미국 유학길을 갔고, 신혜정 선교사는 한국에서 대학까지 마치고 미국에 갔습니다. 1974년 박숭현 선교사가 박사 과정을 하고 있는 아이오와 대학 교정에 있는 자그마한 채플에서 결혼해 가정을 이루었고 그후 23년 동안 아들 둘을 낳고 키우며 나름대로 말씀 따라 살려고 노력했습니다. 그러는 중 몇 번 가라는 주님의 명령에 순종하여 옮겨 가며 살았지만 이 세상의

유혹을 뿌리치지 못해 온전히 우리의 삶을 다 맡기지 못하고 돌아온 경험도 있습니다.

아이들이 집을 떠나 대학에 갔을 때 우리는 좀 더 뜻 있게 같이 걸어갈 길을 모색했고 엄마로서 아이들 키우는 데만 전념하던 나와 학교에서 교수로 또 컨설턴트로 열심히 살았던 남편이 어떻게 같이 할 수 있는 일이 있을까 고민하고 기도했습니다. 그러던 중에 1990년 초반에 싱가폴 오차드장로교회에서 만난 호주 출신 선교사에게서 자기가 사역하는 아프리카 가나만이 아니라 여러 곳에 회계 및 행정 전문 선교사가 많이 필요하다는 이야기를 듣고 우리도 아이들이 크고 나면 선교사로 살면 좋겠다는 이야기를 나눈 기억이 났고 그 길을 찾기 시작했습니다. 그러던 중 그 당시 다니던 덴버 교회의 두 분 목사님이 미국 장로교단에서 남아프리카공화국에 바로 저와 같은 재능을 가진 사람을 파견하려고 한다는 광고를 전하며 속히 접촉하라고 해서 우리는 그것이 하나님의 뜻이라 생각하고 추진했습니다.

1997년 말에는 집도 팔고 선교지에 가지고 갈 물건만 챙겨 1998년 첫 월요일에 오리엔테이션을 받으러 산타페로 갔습니다. 그러기 전에 보스톤에 있는 큰아들과 캐나다 토론토에 있는 둘째 아들도 보고, 친구들도 만나서 우리들의 새로 시작하는 삶의 이야기도 나누었습니다. 이전에 우리가 여러 곳을 옮겨 갈 때는 대강 어떤 곳인지, 무엇을 할 것인지를 알고 갔지만, 이번에는 새로운 지역만이 아니라 언어, 풍습, 생활 여건 그리고 동료들 모두 생소한 상태에서 무지의 세계를 보내는 분을 믿고 가는 길이었습니다. 하지만 두려움 가운데도 나는 사회 경험이 많은 남편이 같이 가고 우리의 삶을 주관하시는 주님이 늘 함께해 주실 것이라는 생각으로 마음의 평안을 찾았습니다.

3주짜리 오리엔테이션을 받는 중 모든 선교사들이 같은 마음이고, 아이들을 떼어 놓고 떠나는 부모의 마음을 같이 나누면서 울며 기도했습니다. 그런데 우리가 가기로 한 남아프리카 교단연합회에서 우리가 필요하지 않다고 연락을 해와서 첫 번째 사역은 가기도 전에 막혀 버렸습니다. 너무도 불확실한 길이기에 그만 접고 이전 생활로 돌아갈까도 생각했지만 교단 본부에서는 본부가 있는 켄터키주 루이빌에 와서 같이 일하며 다른 사역지를 모색하자고 해서 선교지로 가 보기도 전에 루이빌신학교 안에 있는 선교사들의 안식년 사택에서 살게 되었습니다.

3개월이 지나도록 뚜렷한 진전이 없이 기다리던 중 신학교에서 재정, 운영 담당 부총장을 찾는다는 광고물을 보았습니다. 학교 측과 상의하여 우선 인터뷰를 하자고 해서 면접 일자를 받았는데, 바로 그 날 아침에 콩고에 있는 선한 목자 병원에서 초청이 왔고 우리는 면접을 취소하고 콩고에서의 초청을 받아들였습니다. 콩고에 가기 위해서는 그곳의 공통 언어인 프랑스어를 배워야 하기에, 캐나다 북쪽 퀘벡주의 작은 동네 종퀘어로 갔습니다. 적도에 있는 콩고에 갈 선교사가 영하 40도까지 떨어지는 추운 곳에서 훈련받게 하시는 하나님의 유머 때문에 북극에서 사는 삶도 체험했습니다.

50대의 부부가 새로운 언어를 배우는 것이 너무 힘들어 매일 오늘 하루만 견딜 수 있게 해 달라고 기도하며 9개월을 채웠습니다. 수업을 다 마치고 너무 감사해 울며 짐을 싸고 다음날 새벽에 떠나 남쪽으로 내려왔습니다. 교회의 동료들이 "너희 떠날 때 하나님 안에 불가능은 없다"고 말하고 갔는데 이제 불어는 유창하냐고 물어와, "하나님 안에 불가능은 거의 없다"라고 자신 있게 답했습니다.

그래도 9개월 배워서 콩고에서 병원을 운영하고 또 현지인들과 살아갈 것을 생각하니 이것이 주님 안에서의 기적이고, 성령의 은사라고 생각되었습니다.

콩고에서의 편지가 쓰이기 전에 있었던 우리의 삶입니다. 한가지 더 말씀드리고 싶은 것은 우리의 편지들은 우리가 구체적으로 어떠한 일을 했는지 등은 가능한 한 피했습니다. 사역지와 동료들의 안선에 대한 신중성도 있지만, 우리의 편지는 주로 선교나 교회에 대한 관심보다 우리의 삶과 건강에 관심이 있는 식구, 친지들에게 보낸 것들이기 때문입니다.

그러나 15년간 선교사의 삶을 살면서 얻은 지혜나 느낀 점을 나누라면

- 우리의 선교는 무엇을 했다기보다는, 현지의 (하나님의) 자녀들과 같이 지냈다는 것입니다.
- 선교 사역은 힘있는 기선을 운행하는 것이 아니라, 돛단배를 목적지까지 가게 서로 협조하는 것입니다.
- 선교사의 삶은 계속 주님의 진리를 추구하는 것이지, 진리의 수호자로서 다른 사람들에게 내가 아는 진리를 가르치는 것이 아니라는 것입니다.

선교사는 사역의 주인, 혹은 머리로서 현지 동료들을 지시하고 관리하는 것이 아니라 그들이 가진 각자의 달란트와 책임을 같이 나누고 협조하여 성령이 주시는 힘으로 하나님께 같이 걸어가는 삶이라 생각됩니다. 선교지를 떠난 지금도 우리는 매일 성령이 인도하시는 대로 이웃과 어울려 살려고 노력합니다. 그런데 그런 삶은 우리의 자

연적인 본성이 아니므로 매일 기도로 도움을 간구하며 살고 있습니다.

우리의 편지들을 한남대학교 인돈학술원에서 학술총서로 발간해 주심을 감사드립니다. 소박한 우리의 삶의 이야기가 나누어져 많은 분들이 재미있게 읽으시고 간혹 유익한 재료가 되기를 소망합니다.

2019년 10월

신혜정 선교사

Table of Contents

1998~2013 Mission service with the Presbyterian Church(USA)

This book is a collection of the letters we sent from the field during our service while in appointment with the Presbyterian Church(USA). The stories we shared with our friends and family are mostly about our daily life, lives of our neighbors, our work in general and the struggles, joys, doubts and our spiritual journey. We think it would be helpful to share some contextual information about the letters for easier and better understanding.

Where did you serve?

Our bases were in DR Congo, Nepal, USA and South Korea. We were also sent to many places where the Church needed us in short term assignments.

One of the final visits we made while in mission service was to North Korea to teach at the Pyongyang University of Science and Technology. You can read about our experience there in a separate series of letters.

What was the life like before you went into mission service?

Haejung and Simon exchanged their wedding vows in December 1974 at a chapel on the snow-covered grounds of the University of Iowa where Simon was in his doctoral program in Business Administration. By the summer of 1976 they moved to Champaign, Illinois to begin Simon's teaching career at the University of Illinois. During the next twenty-two years, together with our two sons, we lived in many places while continuing in academic and consulting profession. While we lived in many different communities, we always tried to live as committed Christians, in words and deeds. Yet, each time we tried to reach beyond our own lives to obey Christ's commands, we fell short due to the fear of difficulties and the pull of worldly temptations.

What led you to a life of mission service?

When our children left home for college, we put our heads together to seek a meaningful path for us to walk as a team in personal and professional endeavors; a partnership beyond homemaker and wage earner roles in traditional Korean culture.

While exploring different ways of working together, we continued to study the scripture and prayed for God's guidance. Among the writings we used to help us in our discernment was the book by Dietrich Bonhoeffer, Life Together (HarperOne 1954), in which he writes:

> We must be ready to allow ourselves to be interrupted by God. God will be constantly crossing our paths and canceling our plans by sending us people with claims and petitions. We may pass them by, preoccupied with our own more important tasks···, perhaps- reading the Bible(p.99).

We realized then, that we have been trying to meet Jesus at a time and place of our choosing, and the Jesus of our imagination, not necessarily in His truth. That realization led us to be more open to all possibilities including radical departures from our past lives. We shared this with the pastor at our church and some close friends. Within a short time we learned that our denominational office was looking for a person to work with the Council of Churches in South Africa to manage and account for financial resources, much of which were contributions from partner churches around the world for their struggle against the apartheid and to uphold the wholeness of all God's children. We were told that God is calling us to use our gifts for management and consulting skills for the church. We agreed and so did our national office and we were told to be ready for departure in January of 1998.

Stories leading up to the letters from D.R. Congo

By the end of 1997, we sold our house and possessions in preparation for reporting to work on first Monday in 1998.

We managed to visit our sons and friends in preparation for a new life journey. It would be a lie to say that we did not have any fear of entering into a new life-unknown. Up to this point, whenever we moved or entered into a new job, either the profession or the living arrangements were already familiar, but this move was new work in new area with the people we never met. Somehow, we found courage or stubbornness to enter into the unknown.

How exciting it was to be a part of a great awakening of the great people of South Africa under the leadership of Nelson Mandela! God is calling us to use us in great things. We are worthy to be in His army, we believed.

Nothing goes according to our plan

To start our service we arrived in Santa Fe, New Mexico for three-week orientation after which we will leave for Johannesburg, South Africa at the end of January. We entered into a community of angels who were all going into new communities to share their God given gifts with God's children. It was a spiritual and fulfilling experience.

One week into the orientation, we learned that our host in South Africa had withdrawn the invitation for us to come and work with them. Well, so much for great ideas and plans. Did we mishear or just heard what we wanted to hear? We wanted to work under supervision of an institution we trust, the Presbyterian Church, precisely to avoid making mistakes because of our personal ignorance or arrogance. What happened, should not have the Church known better? We were ready to go back to the previous life and start over but understandably were very disappointed. However, the denominational leadership asked us to stay in the system and search for another opportunity to serve in God's mission.

Three months passed without progress and we were quite discouraged. The Louisville Presbyterian Theological Seminary, on whose grounds we were staying, advertised that they were looking for a Vice President of Finance and Administration and invited Simon for an interview. Only a few hours before the scheduled interview, the invitation from the Good Shepherd Hospital in DR Congo, a mission hospital, came and we accepted that invitation.

We went to Jonquière Quebec Canada to study French, going to arctic circle to prepare for a service in the sub-Saharan equatorial region of Africa! Little did we know then how prophetic that experience was for the journeys to come.

That is the story leading to our letters from Congo.

We should inform the readers of this book that the letters are mostly about our personal experiences and we tried to stay away from the specifics of the work, not necessarily because they are confidential but because of little interest to friends and family who are not in the Church or in mission circles. While the communications we've had with our partners and the colleagues at the Church had and continue to occupy importance places in our growth and faith journey, they are not included in this book.

Now that you have been away from the field for some time, what are the lessons that remain with you?

As we reflect what we learned though our varied experiences in the mission field, we think the following two points are universal across all mission projects and communities in which we participated.

1. God's mission is like a sailboat, NOT a power boat.
2. We must remain "truth seekers", NOT "truth keepers".

Missionaries are not the captain of a powerboat who knows the right path and commands all to follow orders for a journey to the correct destination. Rather, it is the people working together, each according to their own capabilities and responsibilities for a common journey to lift all lives, fueled by the Holy Spirit.

In order for the sailboat analogy to work we all must admit that we do NOT have monopoly over the TRUTH and we are continually seeking the true will of God. Once we take the posture of "truth keeper", we lack the humility to learn and the confidence to listen to others. Ergo, become slaves to our own dogma.

Of course, we continue to pray to be earnest truth seekers daily for we do not have the wisdom, humility and love in our sinful nature.

chapter I

Letters
from D.R. Congo

Dear family and friends:

Today is June 26, and we have been here in Kinshasa for six days. We wanted to wait to write our first letter from Congo from the village of Tshikasi in Occidental Kasai, our final destination—but it looks like we will be here in Kinshasa for some time.

We returned to Louisville in early May after a month-long wait in Cameroon, not knowing whether we would ever get to work in Congo. We were tired and lacked confidence that God did indeed want us to go and serve in Congo. We spent many hours in discussions with colleagues in Louisville and at Good Shepherd Hospital in Congo. We also spent many hours asking Him and listening to Him.

Shortly after our return to the States, we received the word that Tshikaji was very calm and people were anxiously waiting for us to come. We made plans to make another attempt to enter as soon as possible, before the situation in Congo changed and before our desire to serve in Congo diminished. Bags packed, tickets in hand, and the original visa still valid, we were ready to travel. We even managed to get physical check-ups while we were waiting.

But then three days before our departure, Simon's lab results came back with strong indications of diabetes. On doctor's orders, we unpacked our bags, canceled our plane reservations, and let the visas expire.

When all the delays were happening due to others' actions or inaction, we felt frustrated and angry, but when the delay was due to myself, I felt shame, disappointment at myself, concern about becoming a burden to colleagues and to the church, and sorrow for disappointing Haejung. Haejung and everyone around us encouraged me with true compassion, without annoyance or an accusing attitude. Their care and concern allowed me to concentrate on the treatment rather than the newly "obtained" chronic disease.

God used my own weakness to teach us the proper attitude towards those in need. How North American it is to place blame and responsibility upon those who are suffering! All the tests of vital organs came back normal and the glucose level came down rapidly with minimal medicine usage. Four weeks later, I received the doctor's permission to travel.

There is no postal service to and from Congo, so whoever travels to Congo hand-carries letters going to our partner churches and other missionaries. The volume for us to carry spoke loudly of our delays: they have been waiting for a few months. Our arrival was absolutely uneventful. The Presbyterian Church of Kinshasa had worked out all airport formalities in advance, so all we had to do was to sit in the VIP lounge and wait for our passports. Given all our travel struggles, this was anti-climactic.

Our first week in Congo has been a period of training and being cared for. We are trying to cope with our very limited French, while everyone is trying to help us with their (in some cases) very limited English. All have been eager to help, perhaps because we are inadequate, and helping those in need is very satisfying. We feel like "beta version" missionaries. For those of you not familiar with computer software terminology, a beta version is a product that is not ready for release in the general market but deemed useful enough to be tested by real-world usage. God has put us in Kinshasa to be tested and trained in a real mission field, where others can fix my mistakes and share their experiences with us. We met Pasteur Kim, from the Korean Presbyterian Church, who has had to learn and work single-handedly for the past nine years through several evacuations. His family has adopted us as older but innocent newcomers and has provided us with more Korean food than we had in Louisville, Kentucky.

Our original plan was to leave Kinshasa this weekend for Tshikaji. Well, we should have known by now that things don't work that way: foreigners who live and work in the countryside need several documents. First, we need to change the entry visa to a residency visa and then get a permit to travel to a mining zone (interior part of the county experiencing armed conflict), a work permit, and a residency certificate in Tshikaji. It

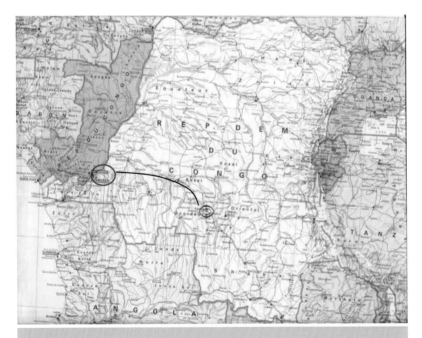

Our final destination is the village of Tshikaji near Kananga, Occidental Kasai, D.R. Congo.

will likely take four to six weeks, so we are staying at a church-run hostel, learning more about Congo and her people, trying to assist the Christian Medical Institute of the Kasai (IMCK) with its affairs in Kinshasa, and being tested as beta version missionaries. We are healthy and remain grateful for the opportunity God has given us. We know every difficulty we face now is to equip us for better service in the future.

Please pray that we would continue to grow in our trust in God, sharing Jesus's compassion, and for a deeper relationship with the people of Congo. If you would like to write us through snail mail (slow snail): c/o Doug Welch, 100 Witherspoon Street, Louisville, KY 40202.

Please send letters and cards only. The letters will be accumulated in the church office and hand-carried when someone travels to this country. If you have an urgent message, e-mail is best. We are attaching a short "how to" for sending messages to Congo.

Will write next month, hopefully from Tshikaji.

With grateful hearts,

Haejung & Simon

Dear Friends

We have been here in Tshikaji for exactly one month. We are beginning to settle in. Simon has been collecting keys to various offices and combination lock numbers to safes and warehouses. We are enjoying life in a village far removed from paved streets and television, and thought we would share a few things while they still seemed like novelties.

Commuting: We live on the station, and we live in house number one. It is probably the closest one to the hospital among the staff houses. It takes three to five minutes to walk to the office. Simon comes home for lunch because it is easy to come back and because there is no other place to eat.

Nature: When the sun goes down, around 6:45 p.m., animal and children noise quiet down, and we are in absolute quiet except for distant drums praying on some evenings. We normally go to bed before ten o'clock. We get up to the sound of cocks and children, who seem to get up about the same time, before 6:00. It is just as well, since the hospital opens at 7:30.

Hope: Hope is the product of faith. We find Tshikaji very much like the Korean countryside when we were growing up. That was quite a few years ago and Korea was poor. People were hungry, but they had hope, and they were working hard for their children's future. When things look impossible, hope and faith give us new energy and conviction. At various places in the hospital we gather for morning worship before work to pray, praise, and hope for a day in the Lord's work. Pray for us and the people of Congo with hope.

Clothes: We have a washing machine, but not a dryer. Line drying is fine, except for the "mango worm." If the clothes do not get completely dry, the eggs can stay on the clothing and the maggot grows under the skin. So, we iron all underwear. It is one necessary luxury.

Weather: We have been hearing from friends in the States how hot it has been this summer. We came here prepared to suffer through the same climate as Singapore, 88 degrees and 88 percent humidity. What a pleasant surprise it has been. Admittedly, we are still in the cooler dry season, but mornings and evenings are in the 70s and during the day it gets very hot, but it is quite comfortable in the shade. We do not have air conditioning at home or in the hospital, but we manage quite well with fans.

Email: We have electricity, running water, and email. The email system is very precious to us, especially since we have no phone or (working) postal service. We send our emails through a VHS radio system to an "email post office" in one of our buildings. The message is coded into radio signals by a computer. The "email PO" in turn communicates with the hub in Kinshasa, about 600 miles away, via high frequency radio. The messages then enter the Internet system from Kinshasa. Your messages have been the most wonderful gift for us. Some of you said that you are keeping the messages short so as not to run up the bill for us. Don't worry. Write as much as you would like. We were simply asking not to repeat our own messages in your reply. Your messages are so dear to us we read them many times.

Birth: We were walking back to the hospital when we saw a gathering of well-dressed ladies just outside the gate. As we got near, the ladies started to dance, sing, and rattle their rattles. In the midst of them were a slightly embarrassed mother holding a newborn baby in her arms. We quietly said a prayer for a healthy life.

Death: It was especially difficult to see a mother whose child died before being admitted to the hospital. Unfortunately, the pediatric wing has the highest death rate in our hospital. When the economy is bad, the parents wait until the last minute to bring the children to hospital. More than half of admissions are for malaria. As a Christian hospital, we should do more.

Wealth: There is a church on the station, with a proper building, chairs, and a pastor. We visited poorer churches in the villages. Last Sunday we worshiped at the only Presbyterian church in the village. They seem to have started with a proper tin roof and stonewall on three sides, but the construction stopped years ago. Instead of benches, there are logs placed on two rocks. We wanted to sit with them, but the logs would not stay still. Mercifully, someone went home and brought two chairs for us. We can probably make a personal gift to finish the fourth side and get a few benches. But is this the best thing we can do? They lament the fact there are not many missionaries left in the village, thus the source of help has dried up. Should the missionaries be the main source of financial resources? What would Jesus have done? What would you do if you were in our shoes?

Inflation: When we arrived here in Tshikaji four weeks ago, the rate of exchange was 9.80 Franc Congolese (FC) per dollar. Today it is 12.00 FC to a dollar, a 20 percent increase in four weeks. We find the prices changing every week in the market. People do not want to save money; we don't blame them in this kind of inflation. At the hospital, salaries are pegged to the dollar. The trouble is we collect fees at lower exchange rates during the month and pay salary at a higher rate at the end of the month. We are thankful that we can share the burden this small way.

Water: We expected good water with no pollution and free of parasites. Unfortunately, we get water from the river and it must be boiled and filtered before we can drink it. We use a ceramic filter to filter out the mud and bacteria. The filter must be cleaned weekly—the water flow slows down considerably when the impurities clog up the filters.

Pews at the village church

Chairs for visiting missionaries. A child ran home and brought these for us.

Food: We have consumed two chickens since our arrival. They are quite expensive, given the local economy. About $10 for a live one. They were so healthy they must have trained for triathlon events. If you have a good set of teeth, you do not have to worry about too much fat. Potatoes, tiny ones, are even more expensive. We just paid $17 for about ten pounds. But mangos and bananas are five cents each. One gallon of diesel fuel is about $5 each, but a bag (about ten pounds) of wood charcoal is $1. Papayas grow on a tree in our backyard.

Time: We have been advised to go to church about thirty minutes after the starting time. Since we live within earshot of the church bell (actually an old wheel from a truck), it is very difficult to sit and drink coffee when the bell tolls at 10:00. We went at 10:30 only to find a few children. At 10:50 the invited choir, a family, arrived and the service began. The sound of the choir was the "real" church bell! People who live on the station started to come at the end of the first anthem. They repeated the same anthem later during the service since a few others and we were the only ones who heard it the first time.

Thanks to the current business manager who takes care of daily needs, we can take time settling in and learning the ropes. We have time to notice things. We are healthy, sometimes lonely but holding up quite well.

In His service,

Haejung and Simon

Dear Friends,

We are completing our second month in Tshikaji. We have been here long enough to remember some names, to begin to have likes and dislikes, and to have begun some work.

We will begin with a bit of update from last month. We now have hot water. Real hot! There are two hot water faucets in the house, the bath (not the bathroom, only the bathtub) and the kitchen. The rainy season has begun, a bit warmer and a bit more humid—and daily rain. The rain falls for about an hour or less in the afternoon. Rarely does it rain all day.

The rainy season also means that we can collect rain water. We are finally able to filter the water without having to boil it first. Also, it is a joy to have ice cubes without the reddish-brown core. We have had circuit breakers trip frequently and have finally understood that we can use only one of the three appliances (water heater, oven and washing machine) at

any given time. Now we are better at planning the wash, cooking, and the shower in a staggered time schedule.

We began to harvest from the gar-den we put in just after our arrival. We have enough Chinese cabbage, just the green leaves, to make kim-chee, blanch and freeze, and give away. They are now growing faster than the bugs can eat them. We plant-

ed zucchini plants and have tasted the first yield. Cucumbers are growing also. As yet, the yield is quite meager, and we identify each zucchini and cucumber and give them individual names. We hope that in a couple of weeks we will have enough to share.

Tomatoes and corn are not edible yet. The lettuce patch is open to the neighborhood, and the green onion is finally visible. One thing though, as described in Barbara Kingsolver's novel, The Poisonwood Bible, many plants flower beautifully but fail to pollinate and bear fruit. I guess the insects here do not like to sample unfamiliar flowers.

We also buy mushrooms from the market. We bought a mushroom that weighed one and a half pounds—yes, a single mushroom, and tried all sorts of cooking methods. Finally, we concluded that we don't enjoy eating building materials.

Simon found out that much of the children's medicine goes unused because the nurses and doctors are used to portioning adult medicine for children rather than using children's. So, Simon sent out a memo urging the staff to use the available medicine for children whenever possible. Simon also sent a memo to Haejung urging her to use more black pepper in her

cooking whenever possible, as we seem to have brought more black pepper than other spices.

Around here everything seems to get promoted to a higher call of duty. A can of Spam takes the place of rib eye steak, while a can of corned beef takes a slightly less distinguished place, only because it is locally available while Spam is not. Other promotions are also necessary. Our Mr. Whipple's certified Charmin TP sits prominently atop our dining table and coffee table as substitute Kleenex. Since our NordicTrack is in a warehouse in Denver, a children's stool serves as Simon's aerobic exercise machine for use while watching video tapes—remember no broadcast TV. We already ran out of tapes, so we watched the "Informational Video for RYOBI Pressure Washer Plus" during yesterday's exercise session. We don't think we will watch that tape again though. Everything gets called to a higher service! That made us wonder whether we were called to higher duty than we are capable of. Well, we probably were, but in God anything is possible.

Just a few days ago, hospital staff went to town to buy rice, oxygen and other supplies. They were supposed to return by 4:00 p.m. When they did not return by 5:00, I went home and returned to the hospital at 6:00 just to make sure that they had returned. One of the doctors found me and gave me a message that the truck ran out of fuel and was stuck about three miles from the station. Since all the service workers have gone home, I armed myself with a water hose and took off on a rescue mission. Many on the road got very angry when I did not stop to give them a ride into town. When I eventually got to the truck, which blocked the one lane road, we found the driver did not have the key to the padlock on the fuel tank. We disassembled the fuel line and found a hole large enough to put the water hose in.

Next came the task of siphoning the fuel from my pick-up to the truck. The difficult part was to find someone with a large enough lung capacity to get all the air out of the long water hose. After about two hours, and after

◀ *Harvesting time. Leaf vegetables grow well, and we are happy to share them with bugs.*

▼ *Clean potable water is a precious thing, learning to be thankful for "rain water" is a blessing in itself.*

providing entertainment to the enjoyment of the village children, we returned to the hospital just in time to miss the downpour, (Simon with another notch on his belt as a roadside mechanic). Now Simon even sports a keychain which goes over the belt with retractable line, a certified gatekeeper, if you will.

A friend in the States offered to pay for the materials to build simple benches for the three-walled church we mentioned in our last newsletter. We pray that if we are a bit more comfortable sitting, we can have more joyful worship. For two-hour services, a flat surface to sit on would be a great help.

The Nursing and Medical Technology school and the primary school at the station are both open. "Mutoke (white person), donnez moi une Bic (pen)" is the standard greeting. Either they are color blind, or Tshiluba does not have a word that separates Haejung and Simon apart from other PC(USA) missionaries. Or simply they have greater success rate with "mutoke."

On a more somber note, we continue to deal with death. One difficulty the hospital faces is that when a patient dies, most of the time the family refuses to pay the hospital bills. They may be partly blaming the hospital for the death, but it is simply not culturally acceptable to demand payment at a time of grief. The hospital staff is extremely reluctant even to present the bill. A clash of culture between Western institution and the local custom. Last year, the loss of revenue due to death was more than one month's payroll for the entire hospital.

Our son John just completed his first trip to Thailand as a missionary and is now back in Florida for a while, and Kevin started his school year at the University of Toronto earlier this month. We appreciate your prayers and encouragement. Thank you for so many wonderful messages. We get e-mail around noon each day from the States, and Simon comes home to check the mail first, then to have lunch. We enjoy being kept in e-touch.

Grace and Peace,

Haejung and Simon

Dear Friends,

It has not been quite a month yet since we wrote to you. Hope you don't mind getting another message from us this soon. Every month, after we write our report, we start keeping a list of things for the next month. This month our notes grew quite rapidly, so rather than waiting until the end of the month, we want to make it this weekend's project.

Update:

We talked to you about being called to a higher service:

Weak Kool-Aid, too weak to know which flavor, is served as communion wine. All the ladies cover their heads when they come to church; the well-dressed lady who sat in front of us had on a colorful vinyl shower cap. And Simon serves as a general maintenance man for all administrative equipment.

What we do on weekends:

Since there is no TV or newspaper, we create our own entertainment. We roast peanuts, bake two loaves of bread, clean out water filters, defrost the refrigerator (remember that kind?) and take malaria prophylaxis. Twice a week we sweep the floors to get rid of all dead bugs.

Getting settled in:

We have been here long enough for the excitement and novelty to wear off, but not long enough to appreciate local culture and relationships, in a limbo state. We are not surprised to see babies being breastfed in public, but still mildly embarrassed. At the end of each day, we are quite tired for having survived in an unfamiliar environment.

Dr. Mvita's family, who live across the street from us, prepared a feast of local cuisine for us. Since it was too much for two of us, we invited them to eat with us at our home. There were special dishes that they could not afford to prepare for themselves. We were so glad that we had the wisdom to share.... dried eel, green vegetables and caterpillars, pigeon, manioc, and a few mystery dishes. Haejung picked around and went through the motion of eating, while Simon had to bear the burden of actually consuming generous portions. The evening meal was followed by a few cups of very strong coffee.

Maintenance:

On Monday of this week, Simon had to perform emergency maintenance work on the Gestetner duplicating machine at the hospital. With no maintenance or cleaning for three years, it is a miracle it stood up that long. It turned out we had to disassemble many internal parts and clean them well. It works now. That experience got us wondering "What about the maintenance of our heads (professional knowledge) and hearts (faith and spirit)?" What would our faith and relationship with God be like, if we put it into heavy duty use for three years without regular maintenance?

Many of our friends tell us that they envy the strength of our faith and spirit filled life. We try to gain strength from the encouraging comments and letters. The truth is, our daily work is not really spiritually fulfilling. Request for fuel, authority to spend money, request to fix broken machines, worrying about salary payments, people at the door wanting to sell us things, people with hardships needing help, the list goes on. We do not have a large enough English-speaking community to have proper worship and support each other in our spiritual health, our Tshiluba knows four words, and French worship is not readily available and difficult to understand.

When we made decisions to enter into mission service and to come to Congo, it was a commitment of faith, and we look to God at times of difficulty, but we do need regular maintenance of our faith life. Sometimes, it gets very lonely emotionally and spiritually. We are determined to cry out to our Lord, to have mercy on us and fill us with His spirit. We started our weekly prayer meeting and bible study, just two families. We will pray for our children, our obedience to Him and His ministry at L'hopital du Bon Berger. Pray for us, especially for our spiritual nourishment, without which our work here is only a very difficult job. It may be disappointing to hear that our life is not always filled with joy and victory, but then we wouldn't need Him, would we?

Many of you also asked about Simon's diabetic condition. The glucose level is mostly within the doctor prescribed range. What we do not know is whether Simon's glucose level is really under control, or Simon has been careful as to when to examine his blood sugar. By avoiding peak times, he can record good results. Out of guilt once in a while, he measures at a time he knows it will be high. We wonder whether this is similar to our desire to pick and choose the time and place to meet our God and savior, when our life would look halfway decent. In the past, we probably have written to you only about the sunny side of missionary work. In the future we will try to be more truthful and more complete.

We have not sent you much economic news, so we will send you our shopping list and prices. We were told that we might experience some food shortages, so we bought a few items. Some are very cheap, some similar to the States, some outrageously expensive. (Average salary for fully employed is about $50 per month).

Shopping list: Note what we buy and what we do not (not available)

Green vegetables: Chinese cabbage, Zucchini, Cucumber

Garden Compost: $1 for 2 cubic feet

Gardener: $40 per month plus benefits

Harvest Labor: Simon & Haejung

Garden tools: Wheelbarrow $120, Shovel $10, Coup Coup $2, Machete $3,

Water hose: Borrowed

Fruits: Mango: $.04, Banana: $.03, Pineapple: $.40, Papaya: Backyard, Avocado: $.08

Meat: Red meat: not available unless one is fond of goat meat. We buy canned corned beef and on special occasions bring out a can of spam.

Fish: We bought a large fish with white meat for $14. We buy canned sardines in tomato sauce.

Chicken: Whole live one: $10

Goat: Adult (live): $65 (vegetarian diet is not too bad!)

Staples: Rice-10 lbs: $11, Flour-110 lbs: $35, Table salt-one pound: $3 (yes $3), Sugar:-11lbs: $4

Powdered milk: 4 lbs: $11

Dairy food: Cheese-gouda $5/lb if purchased in Kinshasa (7/99)

Fuel: Diesel: $4.30 per gallon, Gasoline: $6.45 gallon, Methane gas: $150 per 40lbs if one can find it (we use it for stir fry only). Personal use of hospital vehicle: $0.40 per km/$.64 per mile

REQUEST:

Anyone has about two hundred umbrellas you would like to donate? Imagine, your organization's name being displayed all over Central Congo! We are into our rainy season. Fortunately, it does not rain in the mornings, but when it does the workers do not come to work until the rain stops, each having their own definition of when it stops. Last week the workers' commuting truck did not come in until 10:30, three hours late. All because of want of umbrellas. We will take all types, even Coors and Budweiser promotional ones. You will need to ship them to Baltimore Maryland, but we will arrange for shipping from there. If you have some laying around, please...

So goes another report. John finished his trip to Thailand and was excited to come to Zambia this month until the Jesus Film project decided that it is too dangerous to work in Congo at this time. He looks forward to a trip to Kenya next month. Unfortunately, for us to travel to neigh- boring Kenya is more expensive and difficult than a trip to the States, so we will not be able to see John

Nightly visitors. Already they do not bother us, just a part of living in Tshikaji.

when he is in Kenya. Kevin is in Toronto, working hard on his school work, we pray.

Until next month, God's blessings to you all.

Haejung and Simon Park

Dear friends and family,

The second half of November has already begun. Halloween is over and Thanksgiving is here. We imagine the stores in the United States waiting anxiously for the Christmas shopping season to start. We heard about the passing of Walter Payton and Payne Stewart. It seems so far removed, yet we can imagine the TV stories and how people react to such stories. We have had several passing of "mothers" around us during the month. This morning I read that the worth of a life is measured not by its "duration" but by its "donation."

From our last note we found out that a bit of whining brings results. We received many messages from friends who were concerned about our life here. Many prayers came our way and we prayed more also. We only wanted to be honest and let you know—those of you without many missionary friends—that the romanticized version of missionary life is not the total story. We hope we are sharing our Christian life through mundane daily chores, whether at the hospital, at home, or amidst village life.

Meanwhile, in the village, the season for ant-hunting has begun. Children weave a small basket with elephant grass blades and go hunting for large ants, a good source for protein. It is very interesting to watch children insert a long blade of grass into an ant hole and eat the ants clinging to the blade. Yes, live ones, not chocolate-covered or dirt washed off, but the whole thing—a good candidate for an Alka-Seltzer commercial.

Mama Agnes, Mrs. Mvita, had a surgery and was hospitalized for a few days. Shortly after she came home, our alarm clock disappeared. It turned out Mama Agnes ate our alarm clock. We are seeing future alarm clocks in her yard these days.

In our own backyard, the first harvest of our vegetable garden is just about over. We had good crops of zucchini, cucumbers, Chinese cabbage, and tomatoes. The turnips yielded a lot of healthy turnip greens, but the turnips themselves turned out to be miniature boots. We prepared the soil bed with about five inches of loosened soil, with good nutrients, and underneath that was a very hard, sandy soil.

They grew well for a few inches then they ran into very hard soil, so they grew sideways and twisted in search of softer soil. So, we had fifty or so turnips, with two very distinct textures and tastes, in each turnip. That experience made us wonder whether there is a parallel in "personality development." We don't mean to reopen the "nature or nurture" debate. We just want to know: does our faith mature when faced with difficulties, or do they just add a bitter bump?

Certainly, many people here have had to endure in tough soils.

When we hear of the North Korean famine, one of the most devastating pieces of news was that most of the toddlers there had never known a full stomach in their lifetime, since the famine started before their birth. When we first came here, we thought people here would have enough to eat since the growing season is so long and fruits seem to grow in the wild. Yet at the hospital we get about one hundred children per year with malnutrition so severe it requires hospitalization. Many of these children also have malaria and tuberculosis.

Almost all of the families live in poverty, so they cannot afford hospitalization. Seeing it in pictures is certainly different from looking directly into their vacant eyes. Seeing the stunted growth, bloated stomachs, and low body weights, we can't help but think about their future and the future of this country. We can almost see the future in their bodies. Oswald Chambers said that "We are sent by Jesus to witness. Human needs are great, but it should not mask our main task." So, we try to be brave and march to the order of our master.

During the past five years or so, when we were asked to work in many countries, we thought we were delivering "value." Otherwise, why would the people here spend so much money for our services? But these days the same people only remember and mention our small acts of kindness, including admonitions given with genuine care. Perhaps it's because we were well paid for the official tasks, they think the reward was given. But when we give our time and when we give from our hearts freely, they remember. Perhaps they also remember the times that we were too busy to give our time and attention, but God will forgive us and forget. We are learning not to hang our hats on great accomplishments here. We pray that our presence and work here encourage other Christian brothers and sisters in their struggle and at times lightens their load enough for them to catch a breath. So, we find each day worthwhile when we can think of an encounter where a smile appeared.

During the period of preparation and when we first came here, we thought we knew what a proper Christian posture would be. We heard enough sermons and talked about it and even thought about them from many different angles in Bible studies, prayer groups and in church socials. As missionaries, we enjoy the luxury of relative security, material affluence, and freedom (detachment) from cultural obligations.

Our biggest struggle is trying to hold onto our sense of values and ethics in the midst of chaos. Is it a true Christian posture or a simple arrogance? Do we have any right to insist on an island of Presbyterian Church (USA) code-of-conduct in this soil of war and struggle for subsistence? So, if we bend a little to accept the practices as they exist, are we being culturally sensitive or are we simply taking an easy way out? We are certain this is a question faced by all missionaries working in difficult situations. Local folks argue that "it may not be 'right' according to 'your rules', but we have to eat." Pray for us so that we can speak the TRUTH, but with LOVE and COMPASSION. God will help us to see the suffering humanity beneath the greed and selfishness.

While we will not be together with our children on this Thanksgiving Day, we thank God for his guidance and care, especially for John and Kevin. John is in Benin now and Kevin should be getting near to finishing his first half of this school year. Please remember them in your prayers.

À la prochaine!

Dear Friends,

Can't believe that we have been in Congo for six months already, our French is still as if we arrived yesterday. While the time has passed so quickly, we have seen many changes, and we must have changed a lot also. We have to clear up a few things from our November letter. Mama Agnes is the next-door neighbor and when she came home from her surgery, she ate the family rooster, who had been waking us up at dawn each morning. Many friends asked us why we named a goat, who will eat anything, "Mama Agnes." Clear now?

Now we are truly into the rainy season, mosquitoes are out in force. The hospital is built in an open architecture and gives free access to mosquitoes. Now Simon remembers to carry a can of insect spray whenever he goes to the bathroom. It is very difficult to defend against an army of mosquitoes while using the facilities.

We are amazed to find uncanny similarities between Korea of 40 years ago and the Congo now. Not only in the state of the economy, but in daily lives and relationships. It would not have been possible to have any exchange of culture between the two societies at that time. Our Korean friends will appreciate seeing a toddler playing in the dirt dressed in nothing but a large rubber band around the waist. For those who have never seen it, it is to hang the diapers. Haejung was so surprised to hear a parent teasing a child by saying, "She is not your real mother, we found you under the bridge and brought you home." How is it possible that cultures at two opposite ends of the earth can be so similar? The only way we can figure is that God made us all in His image and gave us souls.

Thanks to Dr. & Mrs. Fletcher, the only other missionary family here, we had our Thanksgiving turkey dinner. It was a Brazilian turkey, purchased in Kinshasa and flown to Tshikaji, served with margarine from Holland. We also had bread baked with flour from Yemen, Pakistani rice, and lemonade made with local citron sweetened with America's own NutraSweet. We were thankful for many things, but especially for the opportunity to get close to God and our Savior Jesus.

On Advent Sunday, the choir from the village church was performing at another village five miles from here. We were all set to walk but it rained when we had to leave. So, we waited and took a pick-up truck instead. We were glad that we did because after three-and-a-half-hour service it would not have been easy to walk back five miles in the rain.

At 3:00 p.m. the entire hospital had to jump into action. At a Catholic orphanage 16 miles from here, they were feeding the street children, and a child helper used the scoop for pesticide to scoop milk powder. Everyone who drank the milk became very sick. Fifty-one children and two adults came to the hospital for emergency care. All the doctors and nurses who

Home grown and homemade!! Haejung made these loaves of bread from scratch in an oven with only on-off control, pictured is a rare success case.

live in the station and the nursing students all rushed to the hospital to help. Simon was called because he is the keeper of keys to the warehouses.

Only a couple of days earlier, we were wondering what we are doing here, whether a hospital like ours is truly needed in rural Congo, and other difficult questions such as whether we have any right to insist on higher standard of care than what other medical institutions in the area provide. What a way to find out why we are here!

The Dutch priest from the orphanage prayed with us and praised God for placing His servants at this place to care for His children. While it was a sad event, it was a time of affirmation also. All 53 left the hospital in good health after one to three days of hospitalization. We were able to send a pack of medicine for further care. The bill for all came to be slightly less than $1,000. What a bargain! The Catholic mission was able to pay slightly over half and Institute Medical Chretienne du Kasai (IMCK) took responsibility for the remainder. The next day we received the news that Ed and Edyth Johnson (Central Presbyterian Church, Denver) gave some money for our work here. A portion of it went directly to cover the charity care. Thanks Ed and Edyth. Thank you, God.

We (IMCK) have set up a charity fund at the hospital to intentionally reach out to the population without proper medical care, especially poor women and children. We will strive for good care starting with family planning, prenatal care, vaccination, nutrition, and hygienic living. You could make a Christmas gift to this fund through the Presbyterian Church. A tax-deductible receipt will be sent to you. Checks should be made out to Presbyterian Church (U.S.A.) with notation of "IMCK—(ECO 320202)" and sent to Central Receiving Service, 100 Witherspoon Street, Louisville, KY 40202.

Many friends in the States and in Singapore wanted to know how they could send the umbrellas. Thank you all. The friends at the Korean Presbyterian Church of Champaign-Urbana collected funds for more than two-thirds of the total and another friend in Illinois donated the rest. We were able to find a local source to buy 200 umbrellas as a Christmas gift from you all to the workers at IMCK. Thank you, friends. Thank you, God. We hope the rain will no longer keep the hospital from opening on time, but we know better. A nice Christmas gift, nevertheless.

When we visited Seoul in 1997 to say goodbye to friends for a while, a couple gave us some money to use in our ministry. We waited until we found an occasion, we know they would approve of. We found out there are two primary schools in the village, one public (Ecole Primaire Musasa Kumi) and one at the station (Complex Scolaire Bon Berger). At Musasa

Kumi there are 415 students in one building, actually one large hall with several half partitions, 158 in the first grade and 22 in the 6th grade. Students have to pay about $.50 per three-month term. By the end of the school year the number of students will be reduced to half due to the parents' inability to pay. That is one reason why the number of students get reduced to 50 percent of the previous grade. 1st-158, 2nd-80, 3rd-68, 4th-56, 5th-31, and 6th-22.

At the CSBB, which has 208 students (half of them the children of IMCK workers) the situation is quite similar. 1st-62, 2nd-42, 3rd-30, 4th-25, 5th-25, 6th-17. They will get down to about 60 percent at the end of the year. The school fee is about $1.00 per month here. Myers Park Presbyterian Church built a very proper school building for the community on the IMCK station, but the operating expenses are the responsibility of the parents. The first term ends for both schools on December 18, and we decided to give each student and the teachers a notebook and a pencil as a Christmas gift, but also to encourage all of them to return to school. The Lees do not have much money, but lots of love. Thank you, friends. Thank you, God.

Friends, we are happy and thankful that we can assist you in your ministries in a small way.

December 21 of this year is our twenty-fifth wedding anniversary. Simon promised Haejung that for the 25th anniversary, he will take her, just her without the children, to a very exotic place to which only a few people have traveled. How can you get more remote than Tshikaji! God's sense of humor is always the tops. It takes a while to sink in. We will spend a quiet and reflective anniversary, Christmas and New Year's Day. John and Gwenda Fletcher went back to the States for the memorial service of John's mother, who was called home in November. She and Dr. Archie Fletcher were both born in Korea to missionary families many years ago.

We counted the gifts out by the grade and stacked them, the piles served as a bar graph of the enrollment and attrition rate. Top row for CSBB and the bottom one for Musasa Kumi.

John and Gwenda will be back in early January.

It certainly has been a challenging and action-packed year. We think we grew a bit in our dependence on Him. John and Kevin had to mature in a hurry. We thank them and thank God for their lives.

It will likely be the year two thousand before we send another report. We talk a lot about the Y2K bug, but we know it is the same faithful God who cares for us and we serve. We are grateful to be a small outpost of His ministry among His children.

May you all have a great holiday season filled with spirit and love.

Haejung & Simon Park

Dear Friends and Family,

This past Christmas and the New Year must have been very special in the "connected" world. Many friends wrote about the special events marking the passing of the year, century and the millennium. We had a very reflective holiday season—we looked at each other a lot. The e-mail system being down for a few days around Christmas was a blessing in disguise as well.

However, the Advent season was a very special one; it would have been very special in anyone's standard. Friends at Central Presbyterian Church in Denver assigned one person a day to send us an Advent message every day. It was better than the gifts for the twelve days of Christmas. Some friends talked about their admiration for us, having heard the clear call from God and answering it. Honestly, we have to admit that we didn't hear our call as much as overhear the conversation between God and His servants and think that maybe we could sneak in too. You give us too much credit. Had we thought about it thoroughly, we probably would not have committed ourselves to this line of work, because it is way beyond our capacity of love and wisdom. We continue based on the trust that God will lead us, even if we started on ignorant and misguided courage.

We had a chance to read the book of Jonah recently. We found he really was not a bad or cowardly person at all. Compared to us, he seems like a person of courage, with a sense of righteousness. We don't blame him for running away from an impossible and unreasonable assignment. We do rejoice in the fact that we find ourselves in a similar situation. It must be a

sign that His commands are a little more focused on us than the conversation we overheard, n'est-ce pas?

Here at Tshikaji, Christmas was celebrated much like it would have been before commercialization. We were not completely free of gift-giving though. A special meal was served to the patients at the hospital, and we managed to put a TV-video in the patients' waiting room, showing the Jesus film and other appropriate movies. With something to watch, waiting for the lab results is not nearly as long for the patients. Outside, the village children put their chins on the windowsills to watch the TV images.

In the town of Kananga, meanwhile, the government gave running water for two days as a New Year's gift. It was a scene similar to mid-summer in the inner cities. Rather than forceful fire hydrants, water was running out of smaller faucets, but the children were very happy. We pray that during the next year we can have many "flowing water" days in Kananga, in Congo and in all of Africa. It's been 40 years since the independence of this country. Had they started in the desert crossing then, now is the time to enter the Canaan. We pray the period of answered prayers and kept promises will start soon. So, each day we wish for a Happy New Day, and pray to be faithful for one more day, as tomorrow will take care of tomorrow.

Fruit-wise, we are enjoying (only Simon) the exotic fruits from our yard, goyave (guava) and jilakuji (passion fruit). There are many goyave trees in the village, but ours are the only ones giving good fruits. It is not because the trees are special, but our fenced in yard allows the fruits to ripen and fall on their own when the time comes. With all other trees, the children pick them before their time and end up with green fruits with poor taste—makes us wonder in how many other areas of our lives we fail to wait for His time and end up with a mess.

Jesus taught in parables. We are trying to discern the real meaning of the parables of "life experiences" God is giving us. We pray to wait for His revelation, not our own premature interpretation. We planted bananas and pineapples for future occupants of our house. We discovered that frozen pineapples and bananas make good substitutes for sherbet. Two grown-ups eating frozen pineapples like popsicles is a sight to behold. We can't wait until next mango season. We will freeze several hundred mangos.

When Simon came home for lunch one day, Haejung very cautiously told him that the e-mail bill for the month of December was $565. Normally they run under $100. We sent off a note to MAF asking for an investigation. The response came back that one or two of you—we don't know who—sent two very large messages (pictures, sound or animation file) that never got delivered to us. MAF was good enough to reduce our bill by $460. So, in the future if you would like to send us a large file like that, please consider sending us $230 instead. We do not have access to the internet either, so we didn't get to see the several greeting cards you posted for us. Thanks just the same.

PC(USA) missionaries in Africa are having a retreat in early February at Victoria Falls in Zimbabwe, on the border with Zambia. Kananga to Victoria Falls is not very far in distance, but the trip will take almost a week in each direction, as we need to go to Kinshasa, then to Nairobi, Kenya and Harare, Zimbabwe, then finally to Victoria Falls. We look forward to our first trip since arriving here in July. As is the case with all travels in Africa, we will be trying to do some pressing work for the hospital while in Kinshasa, such as buying medicines and straightening out problems with our vendors and freight forwarders. Pray for a safe trip and restored spirits for us.

Supports from the friends continue for our work. We just received the report from Louisville (PCUSA) that someone has anonymously given $10,000 to care for the poor. We are just as thankful for $20 gifts. Sometimes the affirmation that there are brothers and sisters who believe in our work here encourages us.

The political and economic situation has gone downhill for the past several decades. The standard joke is "for the past XX years, we have said that it can't get any worse, but it does." While it is not safe enough for expat workers to work with USAID office in Kananga, the work continues. Yesterday, January 15, the U.S. ambassador and the USAID administrator for Africa were in town for a visit along with their staff. The governor of Kasai province invited the entire American community in Kananga to a reception. So, four of us, who are the American community, had a quick visit with the ambassador. It is heart-warming to see many people continue to work and hope in hopeless situations.

◀ *We also have a good papaya tree that gives us a ripened fruit every three days. It is important to let the fruit ripen and not take several at a time.*

▼ *Mama Haejung has the best swing in the village, wait the only swing!*

Thus, went our first Christmas in Congo. We felt bad for not having a home for John and Kevin to come to. But they report that they had a good visit with each other in Boston over the holidays. We thank all of you who remembered our children and us and prayed for us. Please continue to do so during the year 2000.

Happy New Day.

Haejung & Simon Park

(If you e-mail us, please don't send attachments. We have to pay by the byte, around $100 per Megabyte)

Dear Family and Friends

We thought we would have a lot to tell when we came back from our retreat at Victoria Falls. The most important story is that we did come back to Tshikaji. We have too much to tell you everything, but not enough important things to devote a monthly letter.

We left on January 26 to go to Kinshasa for a few days of shopping for the hospital. When we arrived at Kinshasa after seven months in Tshikaji, it seemed like we have arrived at a metropolitan city. Parts of the streets were paved, there were lots of cars and stores that sold "real food stuff." We decided right then and there that we would eat all the food we craved. Money was no object.

It was a busy week, making new contacts and purchasing medicines, car parts and the cars themselves. We arrived at the Nairobi (Kenya) airport around midnight because of a three-hour wait for jet fuel at the Kinshasa airport. The taxi ride back to the airport early the next morning revealed a bustling city; signs of all the familiar brand names shocked us. "This is not Africa!" we told each other.

We felt guilty when we checked in at the Bronte Hotel in Harare, Zimbabwe. It was a very well-kept garden-style hotel with a good dining room. Is it okay to enjoy this much luxury? We've never seen a better sixty-five-dollars-a-night hotel. After two nights, we finally gathered at the Kingdom resort at Victoria Falls. We started the retreat with an inspiring worship and rededication.

Each morning we opened the day with a worship service and Bible study. By now, we had already eaten all the rich food that we craved and were looking for a simple, light lunch. While we were stuffed with good food the evening before, by next morning we were hungry again. The only thing that remained with us were the uncomfortable effects of over-indulgence. But, as we got into regular worship and the study of Scripture, we got hungry for more. We realized how much we missed the regular worship and the community to study the Word together. Could this be the difference between the "living water" and the water from Jacob's well?

It was also a great time of seeing old friends and making new ones. We did not forget to take a trip to the Chobe Game Reserve in Botswana. We are no longer impressed with any herd of elephants less than one hundred and farther than ten yards away. Imagine 50,000 elephants in one park. We also visited Victoria Falls. The main fall is deeper than Niagara Falls, and one can see it much closer because the river is narrower than the banks of the lake at Niagara, almost too close for a panoramic view. One can never cease to marvel at the wonders of nature.

Too soon, it was time to bid "till next time" to friends and start on the return trip. It would be less than honest to say that we were fully charged, ready to face any challenges that may come our way. In some sense, we got a real taste of what we were yearning for and to return to "reality" was difficult. But the real world awaited us, and albeit reluctantly we went to Harare for an overnight stay.

We had an opportunity to do some souvenir shopping and to look at the downtown shops. We saw what escaped us the first time. Twenty years after independence, the buildings and the basic system remain, but the country's economic and social system were not well maintained. We saw the vast gap between the well-kept stores, hotels and restaurants that cater to foreign visitors and the rich, and the everyday life of the ordinary people. We wondered whether our spiritual health will likewise keep up the outward appearance but be bankrupt within. Pray for us that we would be continually restored. Also pray for the Worldwide Ministries Division staff in Louisville. They are the invisible servants who get blamed whenever anything goes wrong, regardless of the source.

We spent a few days in Nairobi with Tim and Sue Anne Fairman, who work with the students at Daystar University in a servant leadership program. Besides hitting Japanese and Korean restaurants, we had two memorable experiences. On Sunday we went to Nairobi Chapel in downtown Nairobi. When we got there at 9:40 for a 10:00 service, the earlier service was still going on with more than a hundred worshipers sitting on benches set on the perimeters of the sanctuary and another hundred or so waiting in line to get seats in the next service. It looked like an Olive Garden restaurant on a Friday night. It was an inspiring experience. Next time we go to the States and are waiting in line for a table, we will say "It's just like the Nairobi chapel!" Let's pray that we will be able to say "It's just like xxx Presbyterian church!".

The following Wednesday was Sue Anne Fairman's Mother Teresa's Home day in a Nairobi slum. It was a large compound caring for broken and abandoned people of all ages. We spent most of our few hours with the crippled children and the abandoned ones. At first, we could only see the broken bodies. As we overcame our hesitancy and held them and talked to them, we were able to see the soul and humanity, with joys and sorrows in them. It would be presumptuous to say that we were able to see it all in just a few hours. However, the effect on us was unmistakable. Once we were able to go beyond the initial barrier, we found a whole new world that always existed but to which we were blind.

We want to share with you the struggle we have had for the past few months. As we look back, our "ministry" was to put our, and your, resources to good use. In practical terms, we had to work hard to keep our medicines, fuel, food stuff and money from being stolen and misused. In a sense our mission is that of warehouse guards. How can we witness Jesus Christ while trying to protect our resources from the very people we are to serve? What sort of missionaries are we? Through the retreat and other experiences during the trip, we learned that we have the opportunity to deal with people at their raw and basic needs, ugly as well as good. Perhaps, a true witnessing can take place at this naked relationship. Pray for us that we would be able to witness our Lord in our daily dealings with the people.

We did not forget to bring back good coffee from Kenya and food items from Kinshasa, including a 50 kilogram sack of Italian rice. We will be all set until we go to the States in June for a medical check-up. We have been back in Tshikaji for almost a week. Based on the number of people knocking on our door with problems, we can tell things are back to normal. That's how our second month of the year or the millennium went.

Love to you all,

Haejung & Simon Park

Dear Friends and Family

It is the second half of March already. It is still hot, but some leaves are falling as if it were autumn. In fact, it is the beginning of autumn in this southern hemisphere. We really do not have four seasons, just two: rainy and dry seasons. We have not had rain for a while, and we have used up all the rain water and are now boiling and filtering the river water. We realize once again how precious the water from heaven is.

After receiving three Toyota Land Cruisers (African version—diesel, no radio, no air-conditioning), Simon told the sentries at the hospital how it happens in the United States that whenever we wash cars it rains immediately after. When the rain finally came, Simon was surprised to find the workers washing cars in earnest. In response to Simon's inquiry, the chief sentry replied, "You told us to wash the cars whenever it rains." We are not sure whether it was Simon's French or the ingrained idea to conserve water whenever possible.

We are also getting used to the rationing of water. It seems now the entire village has found a way to tap into the hospital water supply, and our pump capacity is not enough to support unlimited consumption. Since we do not charge for water, there is no incentive to save water. Our examination of the Ten Worst Offending Leaks account found ninety-three 55-gallon drums a day. Imagine what it would take to draw that much water from the river, one pot at a time. If they had to pay personally for the waste, they would not let the leaks go unfixed. Could it be that we are treating the gift of salvation the same way? Simon thinks it is symptomatic of the ministry of "simply giving."

We have been having another clash of cultures lately. We have a large avocado tree in our front yard. Knowing that we could not eat them all ourselves, we asked our gardener to harvest the fruit and share them with all the neighbors. There are a few left on the hard-to-reach limbs. The village children use the traditional method of throwing rocks and tree branches, hoping to fell the fruits. The only problem was that the rocks began to hit the house. Wanting to be good neighbors, we picked some fruits from our backyard and gave them to the children, asking them not to throw rocks at the tree in the front yard. Alas, now we have two groups, those scaling the fence to get the fruits from the back yard and the gang who continues to throw rocks in the front. The way it is explained to us is that they, the children, now know that we are willing to share the fruits with them—and those who help themselves have the better chance to get some—so they feel free to continue. In a larger scale, the resources of the hospital are treated the same way, as are the national resources.

Since November of 1999 we have been experiencing a large increase of new tuberculosis cases at our clinic. We ran out of medicines and the caregivers were overwhelmed by their workload. It took a crisis for us to examine the situation carefully. When we did so, we found that all the government-run clinics in the area were closed due to lack of medicines and the patients were redirected to us. Our patient-load doubled during the past three months, and we expect a four-fold increase eventually. One major concern is that the hospital charges less than 30 percent of our cost for the treatment. At the moment, we charge $11 for an eight-month treatment regime for adults and $7 for the six-month regime for children. Average cost for the medicines to the hospital is about $35 per patient. This doesn't include the cost of X-ray and other tests nor the salaries and administrative overhead. We also provide malaria medicines and painkillers as part of the treatment. An increase of 600 new cases translates to about extra $15,000 to $18,000 for the medicines alone. It is such an important public health ministry we must continue, but what cuts should we make in order to support this ministry?

Another consideration is whether our actions will cause the government programs to shut down permanently. We are considering selling medicines to the government clinics at well below our cost. One concern is when we sell the drugs at such a low price, will they get to the patients or will they end up in the hands of local merchants for their profit? We wanted to share with you a glimpse of the decisions we have to make in your ministry through us. In the future, we will share with you the continuing developments in this area. We are making a special appeal to friends for an emergency care fund. If you are interested to know about more details, just drop us a line (e-mail), we will get the report and the appeal to you.

For this season of Lent, we yearn for a community to worship and pray together. The churches here do not seem to follow the church calendar very closely. It could be because of our inability to understand the Tshiluba language. We are reading the writings by Oswald Chambers for morning devotions. We want to share a passage from today's reading:

Living a life of faith means never knowing where you are being led. But it does mean loving and knowing the One who is leading. It is literally a life of faith, not of understanding and reason....

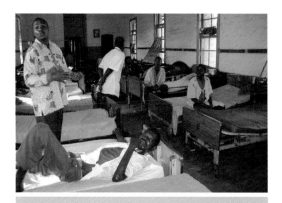

Setting priorities to allocate resources for most benefit to the community is never an easy task. Tuberculosis and malnutrition vs. HIV-AIDS for example.

We feel a bit better for being uncertain and at times confused. Through this period of darkness, we pray our eyes will be opened to see His glory, and to see His children through new eyes. Pray for us.

Our trip to the States is pretty much set. We will first go to Denver for a week (May 26 through June 4), then to Louisville for our medical exams and to discuss things with the staff at PC(USA). We will make a short visit to Champaign-Urbana, Illinois, to thank our supporters (financial and spiritual). We will return to Congo on July 4. We look forward to seeing friends and of course John and Kevin. When and where, we do not know yet. See you again at Easter.

Simon and Haejung Park

Dear Friends

Once abundant avocados are all gone, so are the village children waiting for an opportunity to get fruits from the tree. Whenever the wind would blow before a rainstorm, our front yard would fill with children circling the tree, waiting for the fruits to fall. It is not very different from the freshly unloaded plane passengers waiting for their luggage to appear at the carrousel. Anyway, the fruits have all fallen and we notice the hopeful glances of the children as they pass.

We reported earlier that unless an area is clearly blocked off physically, one is free to roam anywhere, including our front yard. People often cut across our yard to save two steps. If this country ever gets the postal service going, they should have an ample source of letter carriers who already know how to cut across lawns. The concept of open access is granted to animals as well, evidenced by a family of goats who regularly enjoy our front porch. We just wish they would not leave their calling cards at our front door.

Yesterday evening we had a yard full of children again. Apparently, termites built a nest near the trunk of a large tree in our front yard. One of the older boys built a trap.

Right over the termite mound, he built a lattice work of bamboo strips, which he then covered with a flour sack sealing off all sides except one small mouth. He placed a plastic bag at the mouth to catch the termites flying out of the nest. He sealed small gaps in his contraption with dirt. We do not know exactly what he did, but by the time we went out to investigate

the excitement, termites were flying out of their nest in droves.

Right at the mouth was the boy actively protecting his property from the poachers, many younger children in the fringes concentrating on catching the stray termites and putting them directly into their mouths, complete with wings and the ground dirt. Several chickens were risking their lives by jumping in the middle and pecking away at the insects.

Rather quickly, the bamboo and flour structure could not stand all the activities and gaps began to appear. His cry for help was heard and a boy came running with a very large leaf from the nearby field. The leaf and a fistful of dirt repaired structural damage and the boy with the leaf was well rewarded with a fistful of termites from the plastic bag at the mouth of the trap. Before he took three steps, they were all in his mouth, some of them only partially in. Simon caught a couple of termites and offered the freshest source of protein to Haejung. Suffice it to say that the act of generosity was refused. During our trip to the States, we will get a video camera so

that we can record this next year.

Along with our December mail, which arrived this month, we received some vegetable seeds. Among them were some yellow zucchini seeds. They sprouted well, flowered well and zucchinied well. We did not want to wait until the bugs got to them, so we picked them when they were only six inches or so. What you know?! While the outside is perfect, the bugs were inside and eating away already. It seems they get into the flowers and find a place for themselves as the vegetable is formed. Perhaps sin is like that, ever present in our inner being, no matter what we do to clean up our actions and outer behaviors.

On Palm Sunday all the parishioners supplied their own palm leaves. Many thought just the plain palm fronds, often used as brush or broom, was not good enough for Jesus. So, some laced the leaf with colorful flowers. All came with their own leaves to welcome the King. Haejung is having a very spiritual and awakening Lenten period. We yearned for the Ash Wednesday service and Lenten study activities at Central. But this year, we had to try to get closer to God on our own. God is faithful and guided us through the period. Through reading, praying, and life experience, we are beginning to realize that the journey with Jesus is the ultimate joy and responsibility of Christians. As we live and work here, we are beginning to realize that our romanticized version of missionary work was simply a myth. Perhaps God allowed us to have the misguided vision to encourage us, but He is giving us a taste of reality now.

We were often confused and angry as we questioned the purpose of our presence here, and we wanted to search for more meaningful service. As we read and prayed together, God spoke to us, saying that our only responsibility is to stand ready to hear the voice and respond. The period of confusion and pain is the necessary process of growing and maturing in faith. We are beginning to realize that our efforts to become better Christians and do more things is just a way to avoid the growing pains. Oswald Chambers said that perseverance is marching forward with clear conviction that the promised future lies ahead, while endurance is simply trying to survive the difficult time. We pray that we always persevere in our Lord Jesus.

For Simon, it is an extremely busy period, working with auditors for financial examination, preparing for the annual board meeting, while trying to put the operations of the hospital on a sounder footing. Haejung visits patients at the hospital as well as in the village, learning firsthand the sufferings people have in this difficult period.

Another cease-fire agreement went into effect a few days ago, but no one seems to be holding their breath. The economy continues to decline to a level not thought possible. Our regional medical officer from the government was to come to our hospital for inspection. While we were waiting, we got a message from the local World Health Organization office asking us to donate fuel so that the officer could come out and see us. We have had a false report saying that the rebels took control of Kananga. As we got over that problem, the depot at Kinshasa airport blew up, disrupting air traffic. We pray that traffic will be restored soon.

Nonetheless, we look forward to our trip to the States in late May. We will be seeing many of you in person.

Haejung and Simon

Blessed are the poor in spirit!

D'où vient mon aide, mais du Seigneur ? Que devons-nous faire d'autre que de craindre Dieu et d'obéir à Ses commandements...? Psaume 121

We will be out of email contact shortly until we reach the States in June. So, our May report comes to you a couple of weeks earlier than planned. We will participate in the IMCK Board meeting in Kinshasa during the week of May 15. The meeting had to be moved because the PC(USA) representatives could not obtain permits to travel up country to Kasai. After a few days, we will leave for Denver via Brussels to start our annual visit and medical exams. Beginning May 14, we will be out of e-mail contact until we get to Denver. We hope to have the e-mail back by June 1.

We will finish the first half of our term here in Congo in just about two weeks and wanted to look back the year and to look forward with you. We believe God put us here not only to work with our Congolese colleagues but to share with you, praying and rooting for us back home, some of our experiences. Some of you responded positively to our earlier sharing of our growing pains, some of you encouraged us and some even admonished us for our weaknesses. But we wanted to share with you a glimpse of our conversation with God. If it makes you uncomfortable or bored, please just ignore.

Dear faithful and righteous one, thank you for blessing us with your ways in spite of our stubbornness, selfishness and arrogance. We ask for your forgiveness for claiming to make sacrifices FOR you and your people. Forgive us also for expecting an instant reward of spiritual joy and peace and relationships of harmony with all your children on this earth.

But Lord, we need to vent a little. We ask for your forgiveness in advance. It was truly unfair to leave all of our old problems unsolved and to add new ones. Didn't you say that the tired and heavily burdened ones should come to you and you will give us rest? Never mind the part about taking your yoke and joining your journey... We thought you will help all OTHERS to see the truth and give us a clean start again. It seemed to work at first Lord, but soon our human needs and the needs of those around us began to choke us again. The major problem is that neither we nor they see the problems as YOU see them but through our own desires and self-interest.

Let me ask you something Lord, why is it you have been with these people from the beginning, but the people call on the missionaries of past and present for their needs? Did you send your children in the name of missionaries as payment windows and the phone line to ask for more funds? If we did such a good job, as all our friends say, why do people ask the missionaries for everything? How have we failed to instill in them the self-respect, sacrifice of the present for the future of their children, and the desire to be independent and self-sufficient? Did our need to be wanted and needed hinder their growth and development? Why is the only question for any problem is "who will ask?" our friends for help? Are we wrong to insist on their own efforts to search for a permanent solution? Is it better to give them what they want today? It certainly is gratifying to share and solve problems instantly, but in the process, we create another class of "haves" who happened to be connected to missionaries and other donor agencies. We are confused, tired, angry and accused from all directions.

Enlighten us O Lord, we pray. We admit that we've been here before. Our own children accused us of being selfish, judgmental and stingy with money. Perhaps all true, but we tried to teach them with love. Because we loved them, we did not let them have their own ways, we insisted on the fear of God and obedience. We insisted on responsibility, not blaming others for our own mistakes and solving problems with prayers and hard

Simon's father left this as a scripture verse to live by. Are we being true to the Word or just a means to a selfish end?
A friend gave us this banner and it became very useful as a daily reminder and also as a privacy curtain.

work. Of course, we did not succeed at every turn, but we continue with the trust that you will give us love, wisdom and courage when necessary.

Can we do anything less in our current position? Are we to expect any less from the people of Congo, at least the people we work with? Are we to make excuses for them and blame government, colonial masters and all other mistakes of the past? Then what? We are lost we admit. We are accused of being selfish, jealous, lack of love and dogmatic.

May be true, but Lord what can we do? We fear we block your ways with our eagerness to be loved, to do some good and to be praised by people. We do not know what tomorrow holds, but we know you are faithful and remain the eternal truth.

This morning, we vow to take up your yoke upon us and walk with you step by step. Though we walk in the valley of darkness, a walk with you is a walk of life and resurrection. Grant us the time away from the crowd and a time of fellowship and conversation with you. We know you were asked the same questions many times before, but we need the answer. Grant us the confidence that you will answer when we are ready to understand and obey.

Thanks for listening Lord.

Haejung & Simon Park

Dear Friends and Family,

We just got back from our visit home to the States. It was so good to visit with children, family, and friends during the month of June. We truly enjoyed the familiar surroundings, creature comforts, security, and the abundance of everything. The life of meetings, appointments, and deadlines seemed so strange at first, but soon we were in our element again. Too bad.

We were often told that our work here is a "ministry of presence." Being first-term missionaries, we did not quite understand what that meant —we thought those words were mainly to ease our anxiety over not being very useful here at Tshikaji. Many friends told us that our "presence" in Congo provides to them a tangible and real context to being one in Christ. They said they are infinitely more aware of happenings in this region and got to remember us and the people here in their prayers. We put faces to the strange places and news stories. God can use us in any way He wishes.

Many friends also asked whether we believe our work here makes a difference. Our honest answer is that we don't know if it makes a difference in the lives of Congolese friends, but it certainly makes a big difference in our own lives. We entered into mission work wanting to "give back" part of the blessings we received. We were arrogant enough to think that by applying some of our professional knowledge, mixed with Christ's love, we could help move forward this society that has stood still for hundreds of years. It did not happen as we had hoped. Instead, God gave us an uninterrupted period of time to kneel before Him and cry out to Him for understanding and strength to carry on.

He answered! One day in May, as we were preparing to go up to Kinshasa for our journey home, God told us very clearly. "Do not be afraid and do not lose heart. When I ask you to be my servants and carry out my commands, I am not asking you two; rather the command is directed to the life of my son Jesus who abides in you." We knew that!

We had just forgotten the life-giving truth for a moment because we were so busy trying to do something for Him and seek His approval. There will be difficult times, but with this answer we know we can continue to live and work here for another year.

We must not fail to mention our medical exams, the primary excuse for going home. It was a tight schedule, but we got our teeth cleaned, got fitted with new glasses (Haejung with bifocals) and had physical exams. Simon needs to improve on his blood glucose control, but it was much better than when the diabetes was first diagnosed. Simon has to control those snacks taken behind Haejung's back. All other tests came out in the normal range, although the real big tests for Haejung were left for next year.

We got on the plane back to Congo on the July 4 red-eye flight from Chicago to Brussels. We checked four action packers full of food items, videotapes and the letters to Congo. We knew enough to pack only enough clothing for one carry-on bag. We did another red-eye from Brussels and landed in Kinshasa at 7:50 a.m., and we were able to continue to Kananga early the next morning. When we got to the airport at 6:30 a.m. we learned that the cargo aircraft that was to take us to Kananga was drafted to take a group of soldiers to an unknown destination. We just had to wait until the plane came back. After a few hours, the craft came back and we were quickly processed for boarding. There were many more passengers than seats, so small children went two to a seat, and toddlers were on the laps of adults. There is always a room for one more! O, Congo!

Our house was the same as we left it and the village children still remembered our names. We disappointed many by not bringing back many things they wanted. There is a big change in our life here at IMCK though: The Board of the institute accepted Simon's request that he be relieved of his daily responsibilities as business manager and spend his final year as a consultant, developing systems and training Congolese staff to take over the administration of the hospital. As with any change, there were some concerns over the transition period, but they accepted the goal of the hospital being run by the Congolese and the necessity of developing the management capacity to do so. The hospital has yet to find a Congolese business manager, but Simon is staying out of the business office and helping on the sidelines whenever asked.

John and Gwenda Fletcher returned to the States for family matters, and Simon has to take over some of John's duties. He was not only a surgeon, but an excellent general mechanic and a computer technician. Simon is reasonably competent with the use of computers, but mostly in applications. With the departure of John, Simon became the "Renaissance man," unfortunately, in name only. The first week back was spent in the computer lab (correctly placed in the surgery wing) trying to breathe new life into several donated (discarded) computers from the PC(USA). Thus far the success rate would not qualify Simon as a surgeon. Good thing dead computers do not sue for malpractice.

Life is pretty much back to normal. Needy people found out that we came back, so they are at the doorsteps again. But, seriously, Congolese people see our presence as a proof that Christians in the United States have not abandoned them. Some even say that it is the evidence that God keeps

We are packed for another year! It seems meager for an entire year but is more than many Congolese's entire possession.
The plastic boxes, Action Packer, are christened "missionary Samsonite".

His promise to be with them always. Us? Proof of God's promise? Humbling! God can use us any way He wishes— we are only providing the presence. During the coming year we shall concentrate on "being" rather than "doing." Also being with Jesus rather than doing things for Him.

We had three wonderful days with our children, John and Kevin, in Louisville. We do not remember ever simply enjoying the time together as much as we did this trip. Kevin and John both seem healthy and happy. During our separation from each other we all grew in maturity and in faith, it seems.

From the other side of the Big Drink!

Dear Friends

Nice cool and clear weather should begin to visit most of the Congo about now. Friends from Denver have been writing about the extremely hot weather, although Denver should have the season's first snow before the month is over. We have heard nothing about the Olympics in Sydney (?) nor the elections in the United States, not even the big U.N. event in New York. While we miss being in touch, we also enjoy the calm.

Our gardener's wife just gave a birth to their seventh child, a 3.5 kilogram (7.7 pounds) healthy baby girl. Luse Lua Nzambi Bilolo. The given name means "Grace of God," in Tshiluba, and in Korean—Haejung. For a while we thought they were going to call her "Haejung" but they settled on "Luse." We pray for her health and future. We had encouraged and paid

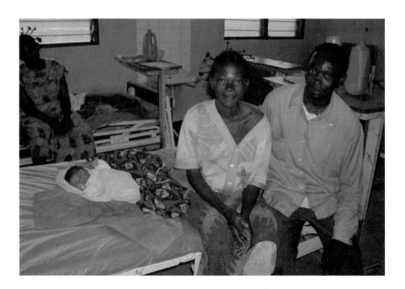

for a pre-natal care program and the hospital gave a 50 percent subsidy for the delivery, as it does for all who follow a prenatal program. Total bill for the normal delivery? Less than $14, including the two-night hospital stay, and yes, that includes the prenatal program, too. At these prices, we should be able to offer a good start to all babies. We do not believe that the low cost of birth encourages them to have more babies, currently averaging around nine…

When Simon returned from Cameroon, he was invited to a special interview at the airport immigration office. The relationship between our two governments are not very warm at this time. We pray Dr. and Mrs. Sager coming to IMCK as new missionaries at the end of this month will have an uneventful entry. Bill is an internist and Sue is a teacher of English as a second language. We look forward to their service to the Lord and personal friendship.

Simon really enjoyed participating in a seminar held for the principals and business managers of the schools in the Cameroon Presbyterian Church. The theme of the seminar was "transparent management." Simon's preaching theme was "open and transparent communication," but with his French it is doubtful that his presentation was "open and transparent." It was difficult, but enjoyable and rewarding. At least one participant—one of the seminar leaders—got the message clearly enough to volunteer for the follow-up work. It is quite humbling to find someone who is so enthusiastic about our ideas and suggestions. Someone told us that good poetry is so powerful because readers read more in the poem than what the poet wrote. Perhaps Simon's presentation had a poetic quality.

Simon is encouraged enough to launch a series of training courses at IMCK. Of course, his status as the office machine repairman continues.

We have not found the replacement windshield for a vehicle from a mishap last month and the chauffeur is sporting a pair of good-looking goggles.

We also heard from our Louisville office that it is already time to start preparing for our six-month "interpretation assignment," which is to start in July 2001. Our appointment includes a period of sharing our experience with people back home. We do not have exciting success stories to tell, but we can share the loneliness, the struggle, and the love of God that gives us new beginning each time we stumble. We will have a few short videos and many photos to share as well.

Should your church like to have us come and share some time with you —minutes, hours or days—please let us know. We will communicate your wishes to Louisville for scheduling. No, our time is not oversubscribed, it is just a way to plan ahead so that we can work in some personal time and possibly some continuing education as well. We pray that we will be able to see many of you during our interpretation assignment period.

We thought God would use the time in Congo to prepare us for an important task elsewhere. We are learning that God is patient and cleanses our slate over and over and waits as we take many false starts. While He prepares us, He does not seem to take active part in building our spiritual holiness. He waits and waits and again waits for us to identify with His son and become one with Him. We have been too busy talking, too busy to listen—professors and consultants tend to be that way. As we enter into a discernment period for our next assignment, we shall listen and listen and let His voice guide us.

Life in the village continues. The return of the rainy season coincides with the start of school, abundant clear water, and the planting of corn. We hear the children singing every morning at school. Secondary school students left for their schools in town, where they live with their relatives. Because there is no secondary school in the village yet and we lack public transportation between Kananga and Tshikaji, it's a 30-minute journey by car.

Nursing school students are back and are seen everywhere in the hospital. Church services will be different with the students back in the pews. Each and every children of the village are responsible to keep the goats out of the corn field. Some children are struggling with goats bigger than they are. Daily thunder and lightning requires Haejung and Simon to listen and unplug the antennas for the e-mail system before the lightning strikes. Haejung baked a Krazy Cake using sugar substitute (Equal). The crazy thing is there is no sweetness in the cake, all must have evaporated. Anyone know the reason?

Hoping and praying the ke
points are communicated,
delivered and understood.

Varying levels of educatio
my ability to explain
effectively, (French
language and
understanding of local
circumstances) as well as
the gaps between the
organization's and
personal goals are many
challenges to overcome.

Frank and open
discussions and
coordination with loc
leaders is a necessar
step.

One sad note is that the economy continues to deteriorate at an increasing rate. Only two weeks ago, we were dismayed to learn that the exchange rate reached 73 Congolese francs to one U.S. dollar; today it is 95, with no end is in sight. Earlier this week some stores in town closed their doors, choosing to keep the merchandise rather than receive the unstable currency. We fear the economic system might collapse completely and give way to another pillage. As the peace process continue to mis-fire, pray for the people of Congo and the children whose future is being taken away by hunger, disease, and lack of education.

Also remember to pray for us, that we find serenity in the faithfulness of our Lord and to become like Him and able to wait for others. Simon's glucose level is another item of concern, and as always, our children are on top of our daily prayer list. Talk to you next month.

Haejung & Simon

Dear Friends

It is only by the grace of God, we are able to write this month. As many of you know, the only means of communication with the outside world—beyond (say) 20 miles—is the miracle of email.

A scary experience:

Let us back up and share the excitement with you. At one of the buildings in the hospital we keep a computer that serves as the local post office covering the Kananga region. This computer is on 24 hours a day, ready to receive incoming messages from numerous email users in Kananga and Tshikaji. When the main office in Kinshasa calls on the high frequency radio, it sends the messages collected from users and receives incoming messages and stores them on a hard disk. On Monday morning, October 9, we found the hard disk in the computer suffered a stroke and was not able to function.

Simon knew what to do when the machine was functioning properly but knew nothing about the hardware and the software to make the post office function. The usual panic reaction of restarting and tire-kicking went on for a while, until he finally had to admit the hard disk was not going to revive itself. Real panic and utter despair set in, only to be heightened when other users started to ask what was wrong with the email.

He couldn't ask anyone for help because it is the only such system in the province, and we have no other communication method with the experts in Kinshasa or in the States. Later, he learned that we could communicate over radio, but he had to go to Kinshasa to learn that! Simon put in 18-hour days for two days just to arrive at the same point via different routes. It reminded him of the days of writing his doctoral thesis 25 years ago.

In the midst of the chaos, we were learning. Two days of communication black-out, and we felt so lost and disconnected; yet we go days and weeks without really communicating with Him. We're really lost, but we don't even know it. The amazing thing is that by arriving at the same broken point several times, Simon started to have some ideas about putting back different links, still groping in the dark.

Wednesday morning at four, the links between the local mailboxes and between the email computer and the computer where all the data are kept were restored. The only one still broken was the radio link between Kinshasa and Tshikaji. The only thing we could do was to wait until 11:30 when the first call from Kinshasa would come—then we would find out whether the link was restored. Not being confident that he could get it going again, Simon had made plans to make a quick trip to Kinshasa. A government travel-permit was obtained by paying three times the normal fee for urgent processing, tickets on both the cargo and the passenger planes were purchased. It turned out the passenger plane was canceled for want of fuel, even though the governor of the province was to travel to Kinshasa on that day.

We all got on the plane and were sitting on the broken seats when we saw a mass of people lining up on the runway: the governor is traveling with us on the same cargo plane! We had to sit in the hot plane while a throne was built on the forward cargo deck and the departure ceremony was held. At 1:30 p.m. we took off for Kinshasa. Meanwhile at the station, at 11:30 Haejung was jumping with joy because messages from Kinshasa started to come in through the radio link. She ran to the hospital to send a message to Simon to cancel the trip to Kinshasa and come home, but the message never made the six-mile trip to the airport in the two hours Simon was still on the ground. C'est la vie au Congo!

As we mused on the experience, we were reminded of a few simple truths. Haejung confessed that while the link was broken, she was concerned that John and Kevin would not be able to reach us should they have problems. As soon as the messages came, she was relieved that there were no messages from them. No news is indeed good news. We wondered about our complaints about the silence of the loved ones, including God. Our anxiousness must be due to our uncertainty whether our communication link with them is solid. We worry less these days when God answers our prayers with silence, for we know we are in touch and He has no urgent corrections to make in our lives.

As Simon was working through the night without proper training, up-to-date documentation, or someone to guide him, he got to understand a bit more about the difficulties the Congolese have in general. In the past, many aid agencies came with good intentions and ample resources and they simply provided for the people. They gave what the people needed rather than helping the people build their productive capacity. When the agencies left, the vision, funds and the knowledge-base left with them, and the Congolese were left with sophisticated systems they cannot manage. A few Congolese who were able to learn the techniques helped a lot, but when their motivation is mostly self-centered, they exploit the situation and set themselves apart for personal gains.

We are also trying to "get some results" before we return to the United

States next year. Quite often we are tempted to take shortcuts in our work to get to results. "Temptation" is simply the desire to get to the results quickly. We used to think temptation was tied to unholy objectives or some selfish gains. Now we know that our goals can be totally honorable and according to His will, yet as our desire to get there pulls us away from the people we serve, and God, we need to pray "lead us not into temptation." Ten days ago, we purchased a tortoise about eight inches long for fifty cents, just wanted to keep him from becoming soup that night. It is a perfect match with our energy level. Oh if we could just match his patience! God has broken His silence and responded to our prayers, His way.

Our short-wave radio is broken, so we get absolutely no news from outside. It really is not too bad once you get used to it. We know the elections are not too far off and conflicts continue all over the world. It does not seem to have any effect on the daily village life. The most urgent problems in Congo today are the fuel shortage and the transportation problem. Each morning, airline operators are given their daily allocations and have to decide on their flight schedule for the day. Each gas station in Kinshasa has at least two hundred cars waiting to buy a few gallons of fuel. They tell me that drivers stay with their car in the waiting line two to three days. I wish I could take some pictures, but it is not allowed. On the streets they sell gasoline in one-gallon bottles and most of them buy just one.

Every available piece of land, private and public, is planted with maize, beans and manioc. Our garden has some pineapple plants and it was a joy for us to watch one grow from the flower to a good-sized pineapple. One morning it disappeared, and we were very saddened. We were saying, "It's not about money, it only costs 30 cents, but we were really attached to it!" But, for the child who took it—we assume it was a child—thirty cents is a

A very hi-tech office at home. All electronic communication starts from here. Written messages coded and de-coded several times over radio waves before entering internet sphere.
We did not realize the value of the system until it broke.

lot of money and it is all about money. When our economic condition is so different, it is so easy to accuse others of lacking honesty and integrity. Had it been a $300 pineapple growing in our garden, we wonder how long it would have lasted in the United States.

Dr. Bill and Sue Sager arrived safely in Kinshasa three weeks ago, but that is as far as they have come thus far. Many people are working on the formalities for their permit to travel to Tshikaji. Simon took advantage of the "unnecessary trip" to visit with them. We pray that they will be able to come and come soon. We need their friendship.

One of the first messages after the link was restored was from Kevin telling us that he finally got the job he was looking for. We are so happy we wanted to share the news with all our friends.

We want to send this message before we have another breakdown.

God bless,

Haejung and Simon

(The 2000 Mission Yearbook for Prayer & Study, 29)

November 2000

Dear Friends

We are spending our second Thanksgiving in Tshikaji. We are truly thankful to God for insisting that we grow to be more dependent on Him each day. We are grateful for your support and choosing us to be a part of your ministry. We are truly thankful for John and Kevin staying physically healthy and maturing in faith. Of course, we do not all grow in a patterned and understandable way, but we trust that all is necessary and has purpose to grow as His children.

Dr. and Mrs. Sager finally arrived in Tshikaji to start their service— Bill as a doctor, Sue as a teacher, both as servants. As you may know, they had to wait in Kinshasa for seven weeks to get the necessary permits to come to Tshikaji. We are delighted to have them here for the people of Kasai, and for us personally.

Towards the end of October, Simon visited two of the Congo Presbyterian Church hospitals in Kasai. The visit to Bulape and Luebo gave us yet a new view of the country and our mission work. Although we were going to visit other hospitals, the preparation was similar to that of backpacking—drinking water, food, insect spray and so on. Armed with all the documents for domestic travel, we set off on the 200-mile journey in a four-wheel drive Toyota Land Cruiser (African version). Somehow, people found out we would be traveling by car, and the car was filled to the brim with hitchhikers and their goods.

Soon after we left town we were stopped at the first of many roadblocks. At each stop we had to produce our documents, register our name, address, and the purpose of travel, and get our documents stamped and signed by the police. We quickly learned that all our official documents without the accompanying "national document" were not sufficient. In the States you will see the portraits of Washington and Lincoln on those documents. We saw many who passed through the checkpoints with nothing other than a folded national document.

All of the 200 miles were dirt road, most of it just wide enough for one car. Often, when the road became impassable, we had to cut our own road through the grass fields of savannah. Many people were walking on the road with goods on their heads. They disappeared into the forest or the grass fields whenever heavily loaded bicycles came along. The bicycles, in turn, had to yield to our car charging at them at a speed of 15 miles per hour with horns blaring. I felt guilty for being the road bully until we faced a truck coming from the other direction. Then it was our turn to go in reverse until we found a space to get out of the way. It's a jungle out there!

Fortunately, the road was mostly dry, and we struggled with sand rather than mud. By the end of the first day, we logged 210 km (130 miles) and reached Luebo. We passed the night at a Catholic mission and continued for Bulape the next morning. We made good time and covered the 80 mile leg in slightly over nine hours, including one long stop at a checkpoint where Simon's refusal to provide "national documents" was met by the order to inspect all the items in the car.

On the return trip, we were again filled to the brim with corn, cassava roots, and a duck, along with two "relatives" of our host. We were stopped at a checkpoint and asked to provide transportation for a military unit commander who had to report to his duty. We reluctantly agreed and were immediately presented to the soldier, his wife and a child, a few suitcases, and a live chicken in addition to his uniform and the rifle. We once again proved the Congolese proverb: "There is always room for one more!"

Apparently, it rained during our trip and we found the return trip was much more difficult than the first as we ran into numerous puddles (a small pond is more like it) and got stuck in the sand several times. All in all, it took four days for a round trip totaling 400 miles, and we spent all but 24 hours on the road.

Hundreds of men were transporting basic staples weighing 400–500 pounds on bicycles. With that much load, it is not possible for them to ride the bicycle, thus they push it for the entire journey of 200–300 miles. They bring the food items to Kananga and carry manufactured goods on the return trip. Each round trip takes about two weeks, potential profit being twenty dollars per trip. Non-existence of passable road and mode of transport causes the great price difference between the place of production and the place of consumption. Quite often the prices in Kananga are more than

double those of Kinshasa, again doubling when they reach villages in interior parts. This is one reason why sound economic policies of the Western world simply do not work here, although the same market forces are in play.

Luebo is a small town, 130 miles northwest of Kananga, where in 1891 Presbyterian missionaries from the United States started their first station for evangelistic activities. The first hospital building was built in 1914 and has served the people since then. Sadly, at present the hospital exists in name only, as there are no medicines, medical supplies or functioning equipment. Unlike in Kananga or in Kinshasa, the patients cannot buy the prescribed medicines from the town pharmacies. Twenty-five employees of the hospital were caring for about the same number of hospitalized patients, but there was not much they could do with empty hands.

Most of the houses on the station stood empty in a dilapidated state.

The missionary cemetery was almost invisible due to overgrown grasses. Dr. Kasonga, the only doctor at the hospital, was apologetic and at the same time blamed PC(USA) for "abandoning" their first mission station. Later I learned that after a long history of mismanagement and improprieties the supporters had no choice but to sever ties and leave them to survive on their own. By now the Luebo hospital has been erased from the memories of the missionaries and supporters and thus they do not appear on the usual list of hospitals to support.

With financial help from the Korean Church in Champaign-Urbana, Illinois, Simon put together a few boxes of basic supplies and medicines as the seed for another try. Simon emphasized that they should use the gift for generating funds for future purchases, not simply use them up and wait for the next delivery. We pray that they will not squander this opportunity to serve the people and to help themselves.

Bulape is another mission station complete with a seminary, primary and secondary schools, a nursing school, as well as a hospital. The last missionaries left more than ten years ago, and so these are now entirely Congolese institutions. Unlike Luebo, however, they are proud to have continued to function and to maintain a reputation as a good hospital. There is no question that they have had to make adjustments and have had to make do with less, but the hospital is running at more than 90 percent occupancy in the midst of war and economic turmoil. The hospital was using pressure cookers over wood fire for sterilization and relying on solar electricity for essential medical equipment, but carrying out their work nonetheless. Continued support from PC(USA) and other friends are barely enough for their operations, but not enough for badly needed improvements in the structures and equipment.

Challenges of traveling in rural Congo is not only the poor state of roads but the "self-financing" nature of local authorities makes corruption and extortion unavoidable and unbearable. After many years they became new-normal.

Just to go 200 miles!
We also had to provide
"National Document"

Each stamp and signature represent a check point we encountered in one trip. Besides the official documents, we had to provide some national document (money) on the side.

On top of their wish list is a "color" computer with a "hard disk." It may sound strange, but the last computer they received had only a floppy drive and a monochrome display. It was not functioning, so I could not verify the processor type. They also had a long list of requests, but somehow, I felt more comfortable with their requests, as I had more confidence that they had a vision and a plan of utilization. A mission hospital without a missionary presence does not run like a North American institution, but it can find equilibrium and serve the people effectively. Praise God.

It may be strange for a missionary assigned to Christian Medical Institute of the Kasai (IMCK) to ask you to consider a broader pattern of giving, but it is clear that IMCK is receiving more than her fair share of help from overseas donors. No doubt it is better known, perhaps better organized, but is the work of IMCK so much more valuable than others? How do we measure the value of Christian hospitals? It is a well-known economic principle that in order to maximize the value of funds, we should use them such that the last dollar spent on each program will bring about the same magnitude of impact. Whether the dollar that came to IMCK after the first $300,000 has the same value, as the dollar after the $30,000 for Bulape or $1,000 for Luebo hospital is questionable, in my mind at least. This is not a simple pitch to give to others. Perhaps mission committees can demand more information from PC(USA) regarding the needs of various partners, and demand that partner institutions be accountable for use of funds—that funds were used for intended purposes and have not been overly wasteful.

Our apologies for writing a letter loaded with difficult topics. We wanted to share our lives and concerns with you as much as possible, trusting that the Holy Spirit would deliver the real message. While we eagerly wait for the day we return home, we are grateful for this growing experience and also to share part of our life here with you.

Happy Thanksgiving.

Dear Friends

As we pray and meditate during this season of advent, we keep return-ing to the purpose of Jesus' coming in the midst of us. Regardless of His mission, given by God, all of us have our own ideas as to the purpose of His coming, and we value the work based on our own personal needs. As we await the birth of the baby, we reflect on our mission here in Congo. We struggled before God to stay true to His commands, not to our own emotions. After much prayer, we decided to share our struggles with you.

We say to each other that Jesus must have felt like "chucking it all and go home" often, but he stayed true to his mission and obeyed God. In a small way, we have experienced the pain of differing expectations ourselves. When we came here, we came with the idea that the best gift we can bring is ourselves. We came to be with the people and share what God has given us so that they can become better stewards of resources and min-ister to the sick and the weak. We wanted to help them experience the joy of hard work and growing, from care-receivers to care-givers. Now we be-lieve we are sent here to learn the realities of ministry in the trenches and help you back home to share in our experience. We know that we could have learned these lessons in the States without coming all the way here, but it would have been so easy to just "go home" when the going got tough. Here in Congo, we have to wrestle before God and wait patiently.

Shortly after our "tourist" period, the realities of urgent need hit us hard. Perhaps because of the suffering, perhaps because of the past practi-ces, or perhaps due to basic human nature, people asked us for immediate materialistic help. In some ways, we were no different, for we sought to receive positive praise from the people rather than walk by faith and wait for His time. As we heard and saw the difficulties people faced, we felt guilty for having so much material wealth compared to them, and we could also see clearly how much difference a small gift can make for the poor. Many of you generously supported us in our efforts to help the needy. Some Congolese—quite a few in fact—told us that it is our Christian duty to help them since we are all in one family of Christ and family members should share what they have. Who can argue with that? We had to question their motives though, when we saw that higher-paid workers had no compassion for the poorer workers, and the richer IMCK (Christian Medical Institute of Kasai) seldom help other poorer hospitals in the family of Presbyterian Church of Congo. We began to wonder whether our mission was to become a conduit for channeling money to people and the institutions.

Another difference was that we saw the workers, at least the leaders, to be our "partners" in the ministry to care for the sick and the poor. We feel at times that our "partners" see themselves as the primary recipients of care. These differing perceptions created resentment and awkward working relationships. As a sad consequence of this, the patients are not receiving the best quality care made possible by generous gifts of the friends back home. When the goals of two partners differ, at times conflict, we have difficult choices to make. When one's own words are different from one's actions, it is even more difficult.

We came as managers of resources, not our own resources, but those given to our partners for their ministry, in this case the Christian Medical Institute of Kasai. One conflict we saw immediately was that while our primary interest was in minimizing waste and misuse, others were more interested in increasing the flow of resources to the institution. The greater the inflow, however, the greater the leakage and waste (or greater benefits, depending on the point of view). We thought our mission was to help them repair the hole on the bottom through which resources were leaking, but others looked at us as the hose that connects North America to Central Africa.

Must we wait until the tank drains completely before plugging the hole? Must we always learn the lesson the hard way? How do we witness Jesus Christ abiding in us through our daily lives while struggling in tense relationships? We know that hypocrisy, when deeds do not match the talk, is rampant in everyday life in the States as well, but God did not put us in the point position there. Can we remain faithful servants before God while being good friends in their eyes? Are they necessarily incompatible choices?

We do not mean to say that our goals are correct and honorable while the goals of others are not. We can only try to be faithful to the mission as we discern it. The Presbyterian Church (U.S.A.) or its member congregations may look at missionaries as a means of delivering gifts, and perhaps the missionary presence gives a sense of legitimacy to the programs or institutions, thus the high correlation between the number of missionaries and the amount of donations.

Leaders of the PC(USA) told us that the time when American missionaries went to foreign countries and created "small poor America" is over, and that we are to assist our partners in their own journey. We believe it is the right approach, and we are doing our best to stay true to the mission. Discipline is hard, and to lead by action is even more difficult. We hear from our Congolese colleagues that missionary presence is in the administration of the IMCK is necessary, since Congolese nationals are not able to withstand the pressures of their extended families and put the institution ahead of their personal interest. We do not accept that as being correct.

Simon visited an old PC(USA) mission station in Lubondayi, which was established in 1924 but hasn't had U.S. missionaries for several decades. The hospital was closed several times due to financial difficulties (mismanagement, economic status of the country). After being closed for four years, they reopened it in January 1998. The leaders of the church decided that it was their responsibility to keep the hospital open for the people.

Simon was very moved when he learned that at the end of each day, they divide up the day's receipts to replace the medicines (60% of medicine sales), maintenance (5% of total), operations (5% of total) and con-

This very basic but clean maternity ward at the Lubondayi Hospital is a very valuable pride of the community. It is now a common knowledge that maternity care is one of the most important factors in a healthy community.

Lacking electricity, this old mimeograph machine is far more appropriate than a copy machine or a laser printer.

tingencies (5% of total) before adding to the fund for their salaries. Their monthly salary comes after the expenditures to keep the hospital operating, and the amount is very uncertain. But everyone knows the score, and everyone knows that their employment depends on the patient care. The day Simon was there it was a good day, and from the 150 dollars of total receipts they were able to put away about $35 for the 23 workers. Should the idea be so strange? Yes, it does happen in Congo, and it was all a Congolese idea. We came away with deep respect and the confidence that they are capable, if and when they want to be.

So, what is our mission? We believe we are here to tell the truth with love, to our Congolese brothers and to you back home as we see it. We will continue to speak for the weak, insist on responsible resource management, and encourage you to truly help our partners to help others. We urge you to insist on accountability from our partners. Hard-nosed demand for accountability is not demeaning but can help support those who want to do it right. We pray for the courage to tell the truth and the wisdom to know what is helpful and what is not. We pray for His love to sustain us in our journey and to remain faithful to His commands. Jesus came to carry out His mission, and we can do no less as Christians. Now, we await eagerly the birth of Christ in this war-torn country.

Haejung & Simon

Dear Friends

Simon continued his visits to remote health-care centers with the medical director of the Presbyterian Church of the Congo, Dr. Mwala. During the last visit, the Reverend Bope (the church executive responsible for the Kasai Occidental) and Elder Kabibu (personnel manager of IMCK—the Christian Medical Institute of the Kasai) joined us. We left for the 400-mile journey to Kabuabua, Moma, and Mboi in a borrowed car. The visit took us to the south of the province and then west towards Angola and finally circled back to Kananga in five days. As always, we were not carrying money or medical supplies, but went only with good news, as Jesus commanded His disciples to do (Matthew 10:9-15).

We arrived at our first town, Kabuabua, at 6:30 in the evening, nine-and-a-half hours for 130 miles is pretty good. We had sent word of

our visit with a traveler who did not arrive until the day after our arrival. The church leaders and the nurses (all in the family) were very delighted to see us but also were very concerned about our sleeping and eating arrangement. We assured them that we were well prepared—each of us had a sponge mattress, and we didn't have to have dinner. They would not hear of it, and finally produced dinner for us at 11:30 in the evening (bidea, manioc leaves, and small eels). Normally eating late at night is not good for a diabetic patient, but Simon ate in faith.

The following morning, we visited the station buildings. In 1958, when the Belgian tobacco company (Tabac, Congo) withdrew their operations, the village chief offered the facilities to the Presbyterian Church of the Congo, which built a church, a hospital, and a school (primary and secondary) that continue to this day. As you can imagine, a tobacco warehouse does not make an ideal building for a hospital. Nonetheless, the work continues, and like the Lubondayi hospital, all receipts are used for medicines and operations first before the workers are paid. As a health center serving more than 3,000 people, on top of their wish list were: a bicycle (they walk 200 kilometers each way for medicine purchase), a stethoscope for each of the two nurses, a functioning blood pressure cuff, and a small fund to stock basic medicines.

At 9:30 we left for a short journey to Moma where a PC(USA) mission hospital once operated. Suffice it to say that it took six-and-a-half hours to go less than 45 miles. Now that the rainy season has been here a while, the effect of rainwater on unpaved roads was in full force. Early in the afternoon, we came across a gully that has been deepened and widened due to water flow; a few logs across the gully were clearly not enough for the vehicle. A pastor, a doctor, an administrator and a missionary became a

bridge repair crew under the supervision of the chauffeur. We often heard the phrase "building a bridge together" to refer to the idea of mission partnership, but this was the first time that Simon literally built a bridge together with fellow Presbyterians!

Simon became very popular, being the first Asian face for many to see in person. The Moma station was constructed in the 1940s, with grand views of the valley and tree-lined streets, stone-constructed water towers and all. Unfortunately, the hospital buildings, built in 1951, were in a very bad state of repairs, with many of the roof tiles missing and large cracks in the walls. Goats and chickens inhabited two of the three hospital buildings while the third was sparsely occupied. On the day of our visit, there were three hospitalized patients.

During the 1950s and 1960s, Moma was the base from which missionary doctors made visits to outlying clinics. Older folks, who used to work with

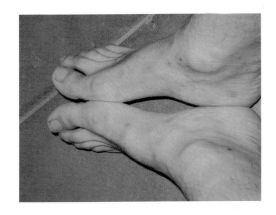

missionaries, grilled Simon as to why the children of the missionaries do not return and carry on the work of their parents. Simon's question as to why the Congolese youth do not return to their birth villages was dismissed as being irrelevant. It seemed that the common belief was that the hollow halls of the buildings built by missionaries can only be revitalized by other missionaries. Even the cry for help was not expressed in terms of what can be done with some help, but rather how much they suffer.

Simon decided two nights of post 10 p.m. meals were not allowed and went to bed early. Unfortunately, Simon himself provided a banquet to numerous bugs during the night, and he is still sporting the scars after almost a month.

Having no material help to offer, we prayed together in the belief that our Lord will provide wisdom, courage, and perseverance for us to serve Him together. We left for Mboi, near the Angolan border, to visit yet another old mission station.

Mboi station was started in 1937 and the last missionary left in 1970. The hospital buildings were also built in 1951, but unlike Moma buildings, they were kept in excellent shape. Even most of the windows were intact. But the cupboards for the medicines and medical supplies were also empty. With hyper-inflation, the receipts from medicines were not enough

to replenish the stock and the nearest town is Kananga, 200 kilometers away. The clinic was non-functioning until July of 2000, when the local church members put together seed money and requested a nurse to reopen the clinic. They were seeing an average of 45 patients per month. We were encouraged to see the active participation of local church leaders in the clinic service to the people. Again, we prayed together and assured them we will do our best to help them find a good source of medicine and encouraged them to serve with Christian love and keep the faith that the Lord will use the clinic in His work.

Before departing Mboi, Simon had the honor of meeting the village chief, who has approximately 100 children from 10 wives. On the way back we all shared how different Mboi and Moma were, not in present conditions, but the hope for the future they have and the desire to be a part of the solution. It took another full day to return to Tshikaji. Just this week (three weeks after the visit), we had a visit from the junior nurse at Mboi.

He came on a bicycle looking for medicines. He was excited to tell us that after our visit, the number of patients at the clinic doubled, so they scraped up all the money available and dispatched him for medicine.

Just the fact that the church leaders and IMCK thought them important

Relatively well-stocked clinic pharmacy at Kabuabua. Pastor's wife is the nurse cum clinic administrator.

If nature calls, a visit to this facility is necessary, but takes some getting used to.

enough to make a visit earned them credibility in the eyes of the village people. Now seen as an extended member of a greater body of Christ, the clinic became the preferred care provider. We at IMCK were able to sell them the medicines and to make them a gift of stethoscopes, blood pressure cuffs, and thermometers, and send him on his way back to Mboi, a two-day journey by bicycle. Although loaded with a carton of medicine and facing a long, dangerous journey, his feet were light with joy.

God is so good. While we bemoan the shortage of missionaries, He raised four other Congolese missionaries to bring the good news to the people of Mboi. Simon is so thankful to be in a partnership with other missionaries, for we have a common mission and a common vision, and most important of all, a common master. Perhaps God's response to Simon's frustration at the institutionalized partnership was the gift of personal partnership with His servants. Dr. Mwala and Simon will complete the visits to Mbujimai, Bibanga, and Mutoto in January.

Meanwhile, back in Tshikaji, Haejung started to let village children borrow our collection of French books. It became very fashionable for everyone to come and borrow the books whether they have any interest or not. Haejung installed a quality-control mechanism and asked each child to bring back a synopsis of the book they read before borrowing another one. Many of them simply copied a sentence or two, but it still served the purpose of weeding out many "fashion borrowers." A more diligent youth came to our door with a troubled look and confessed that he is having a difficult time writing a synopsis. We did not want to drop the requirement just for him, but we made an exception for him when we learned he had borrowed a world atlas.

So, we greet the New Year with joy and thankful hearts. Please pray that our remaining time in Congo will continue to be a time of growth and witness.

                                                        With love,

Dear Friends

This has been the most eventful month, to say the least. As you know, President Kabila was assassinated in January. All was calm in Tshikaji, but we stayed put and did not venture out too far. Simon rescheduled the visit to Mbujimayi and Bibanga until a later date. We received many messages of concern from you and we thank you. We never felt physically threatened, but the ever-present uncertainty and nervousness was somewhat elevated during the week following the assassination.

In retrospect, we should have known something was up. During the week before the assassination, the exchange rate shot up 45 percent (from 150 to 220) and then came down 20 percent by the end of the week. One week after the death, the rate actually dipped below 150. According to conventional wisdom, during a period of turmoil the exchange rate goes up, as people seek the safety of hard currencies. Either the logic does not work in Congo, or it works very well, reflecting the sentiment of the people.

We are sending this note from Delhi, India, this month, and we invite you to consult a world atlas as you follow our journey. Late in January, Simon was asked by the Worldwide Ministries Division of the PC(USA) to visit the church office in India and assist with financial reporting matters. We were told to travel as quickly as possible and were authorized to travel together due to the security situation in Congo.

On February 4, we went to Kinshasa, this time on real passenger flight. We bought tickets for the Kenya Airways flight to Bombay via Nairobi (Kenya) on February 8, which was to arrive in Delhi on the 9th. On the morning of departure, we learned that the flight was canceled due to shortage of jet fuel in Kinshasa, and the next scheduled flight wouldn't leave for four days.

A frantic search of alternative routing yielded Kinshasa—Johannesburg (South Africa)—Bombay—Delhi routing, with an overnight stay in Jo'burg. Our plan to spend an evening watching CNN news in South Africa was scuttled when the Cameroon Air plane landed in Brazzaville, Congo, to take on fuel after a ten-minute flight. By the time we checked in at the airport hotel, it was past midnight. Next morning, we went to the airport early for the flight to India. To our dismay, we were not allowed to board the flight because we lacked valid visas for India. Our plan to purchase the visa once we landed in India, as we were told by Kenya Airways, would not work. We made a mad dash to the Indian Consulate in town, only to be told that for American passport holders only the consulates in the U.S. are authorized to issue the visa. No amount of charm, desperate look, appeal in the name of the Hindi God did any good. They agreed to fax a request for authorization to a consulate on our behalf (costs us $20 for fax transmission). We went back to the airport to rearrange the itinerary and found all the flights were fully booked until the following Friday (one week's wait). We did find seats on the business class for the following Monday and sent an appeal to the PC(USA) office to obtain authorization for us from the Indian consulate office in Chicago. The nine-hour time difference between Jo'burg and Chicago did not permit any direct communication between the two consulates.

During the weekend, we received the discouraging news from Louisville that the consulate in Chicago was not being very cooperative and insisted that we apply directly to the office that covers the region of our permanent address. Not knowing how to do all these from South Africa, we had to make a decision: (1) go back to Congo and reschedule the visit, or (2) wait in South Africa while continuing the efforts for the visa (3) or go to the States and get the visa ourselves. It turned out the additional ticket cost for going back to the States was half of what it would cost to go back to Tshikaji. So, we rebooked the flights and, armed with the fistful of tickets, waited until Monday morning to reclaim the passports from the Indian consulate.

What a shock to learn that the Chicago office had approved our application during the weekend, and we could have traveled that day. Finally, with the visa but no way to travel, we decided to continue on to Louisville. We left Jo'burg at 9:30 p.m., arriving at Heathrow airport in London the next morning, took a bus to Gatwick (the other London airport) for connecting flight to Cincinnati. We should have known that the probability of our bags making the connection was a bit less than a peaceful transition of power in Congo. While telling each other that God has reasons for all these troubles, we went to Louisville in a rental pick-up.

We were able to use the few days in Louisville to meet and discuss with the relevant parties for the India assignment and now we went on the Air India flight to Bombay (via Delhi!) just to return to Delhi later in the day. Simon used to travel several hundred thousand miles per year during his consultant days, but never had to face so many complications in one trip. Through all of these difficulties, we met many people who went way beyond their call to duty to help us make it through the 18 days it took to go from Tshikaji, Congo, to Bombay, India. We are still trying to see what the lesson is in all these detours, but we are certain that we will be able to see it better when our body clock adjusts to the rapid changes. Our work here in New Delhi is to help us become better stewards of the resources given to the Church for worldwide ministries. We pray that the Lord will grant us the wisdom to know the truth and the compassion to share it in a way to further His kingdom.

During the second week in March we will return to Congo to finish the few months left in our term of service. The Rev. Syngman Rhee, the current moderator of PC(USA), invited us to participate in this year's General Assembly in Louisville, and that means we will be going back to the States at the end of May, one month ahead of schedule. Simon will be preaching during the morning worship on June 15. Please pray for us that we will be able to listen to God's voice and share with the 2,000 people attending G.A. the message of reconciliation and peace.

We have been in India for four days by now and have started the work, working through a new set of cultural and working relationships. We pray each day, each moment, that we behave as His children and accompany Jesus Christ as we spend a few days in this vast country of history and culture. Those of you in the States, please accept our apology for not contacting you during our brief stay in Louisville. We will do so properly in June.

Will talk to you in March. Peace.

Haejung and Simon

Yesu wakubika udi ne muoyo! *(Jesus is risen, and he lives)*

The village women ran through the predawn darkness calling all to come out and greet the risen king. Looking towards the northeast, we had a sunrise service. Not knowing the language did not matter, since the message was much louder than the language barrier. After the service the women ran through the village shouting the message for all to hear. Thus, came the second Easter morning in Tshikaji for us.

On Palm Sunday everyone came with their own palm branch, some decorated with various wild flowers, some braided like their hair, some simply harvested just outside the sanctuary door. We took ours from our garden, a very plain one but the largest. There were no Holy Week observations at the congregational level, the pastor's son even got married on Saturday following Good Friday. Nevertheless, the joy of the Lord's resurrection was genuine and complete. Early Tuesday morning after Easter Sunday we even had a minor tremor, which added to the full effect!

The first of the MONUC (United Nations monitors) contingent of 130 Senegalese soldiers came to Kananga to help implement the Lusaka Accord, which was signed by all parties in August 1999, but has yet to be implemented. Is it just us having difficulty seeing these young men in white jeeps and trucks as hopeful signs? For us, they're a painful reminder of a divided country, whose people and resources are being plundered. May the shouting of the resurrection of our Lord also awake the sleeping Christians to speak the truth with love and come before God with true repentance and humbled hearts. Pray for a lasting peace among these suffering people, and may God anoint a humble servant as the leader of His people. People in the village are hopeful that the new president will be more open and caring. Expert commentators in the region are more pessimistic and predict another period of uncertainty, as the neighboring countries try to strengthen their political and economic hold of the Congo.

As we prepare for our return home, we can't help but reflect on the effect of our stay here on the people we live with, on us, and on you back home. At first, we thought we came here to help the people grow in their management skills, then we were convinced that God sent us here to teach us and mold us. Then we heard from many of you how the story of our experience here helped you realize how blessed you were, made you feel guilty, helped you see God in a bigger world. There were various other reactions beyond our imagination.

When we wondered out loud, what God wants to teach us with some of the things we experienced here, a friend sent us a note saying that God does not always intend our experience for us; sometimes He is using us to send a message or teach others. We may be more willing, available, or simply

able to endure the experience, and thus God chooses us for His work. How humbling to be used by God for the benefit of His other children. Any way you wish, Father! As we prepare to leave, our promise to God is that we will once again concentrate on being His children, rather than doing good things. God is alive and present in our sufferings and struggles as much as He is present in our joy. May God be praised in our every breath.

This may be the final note before we return to the States at the end of May. We will be staying in Louisville until the end of this year. Where we will be sent next is unknown. We are in listening mode.

We will participate in the 213th General Assembly of the Presbyterian Church (U.S.A.) during the first half of June. During the last week in July we have a week of sharing with other missionaries in "interpretation assignment," also known as home leave. We have a visit scheduled to Norfolk, Virginia, at the end of September and the mountain states for three weeks starting the last week in October. This is to say that other than these commitments, we will be available to visit you and share our experience in Congo. Should your church wish to have us come and share the story, please let us know. Since we would like to combine visits to the same geographical area, we do need some advance planning.

We thank you and God for the support you have given us as we went through all the growing pains as first-term missionaries.

In God, anything is possible!

Photos from D.R. Congo

Our original letters from Congo did not include any photos as the technologies did not allow. We inserted some in this book hoping the photos will provide better understanding of the letters. We present some additional photos from Congo.

▲ *Traveling choir group. They insisted on wearing the choir hood backwards.*

◀ *After a Sunday service at a rural church in Kasai, DR Congo*

▲ *An old tree fell in the village. It's time to make planks.*

◄ *Who needs a shopping cart when you can carry all on your head?*

▼ *This long and narrow basket used in forest areas so the woman can walk through between the trees. Congolese women do a much better job than Haejung tries to demonstrate here.*

▲ *Not having electricity nor propane, the energy for autoclave had to be supplied manually.*

◄ *Incubator is warmed with hot water in empty pill bottles.*

▼ *One equipment any amount of ingenuity cannot bring to life is an x-ray machine!! They remain as a symbol of good old days and a wish item for a better future.*

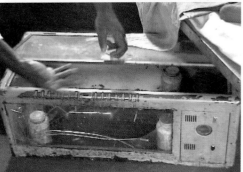

Haejung getting ready to attend a wedding ceremony.

Our gardener Tatu Bilolo's $250 house. They supplied their own labor except for the window framing.

No reason to make the facilities any larger than necessary! Boy's and Girl's outhouse at a primary school.

Musasa Kumi (the Tshikaji village school) is a converted chicken coop left behind by a missionary. Meager in physical attributes, yet a place of learning and hope for many.

Unable to attract trained medical personnel to rural villages, most rural hospitals run their own nursing school.

◀ *Leaking pipe is not an issue in Congo. This solution served us for two years.*

▼ *Village folks helped us cross the gully by building a bridge for $5. When we came back the next day, the bridge was gone and we had to pay $5 again to rebuild the bridge. challenges, challenges !!*

Cargo earns more than passengers for the airline. As honored missionaries, and as frequent flyers, we are given the bulkhead, but after the cargo.

Grains weighing as much as 400 kilos are carried on a bicycle for several hundred kilometers. Everything is more expensive in rural areas.

There is always a room for one more! Overloading is a par for the course in Congo travels.

◄ *It is not that Haejung h*
a tiny head. This mushroo
was not very good in textu
and taste.

▼1 *We know it is a good*
source of protein, but we
passed.

▼2 *We will let you figure*
our yourself. I traveled wi
this delicacy for three day
we had windows open all t
time for breeze.

But it is much cheaper here!

When Simon visited a rural village, folks came out to see an Asian face for the first time in person. This father wanted to make sure that his son does not miss the opportunity that may not come again.

Haejung was able to enjoy a real Belgian waffle during a layover in Brussels. She prefers this to the pure protein.

◀ *Friends from Central Presbyterian Church in Denver at the General Assembly of the Presbyterian Church (USA) in Louisville, June 2001.*

▼ *Finally, a Christmas together.*

Dear Friends and Family

Long time no see, almost a year! We have been back here in Louisville, Kentucky, since June of 2001 and are preparing to start our new assignment as Presbyterian Church (USA) missionaries, this time in Nepal.

We came back in early June to participate in the 213th General Assembly of the Presbyterian Church (USA) where Simon served as a Missionary Advisory Delegate (his vote did not count) and also preached in one of the morning worship services during the assembly. All the worship services were wonderful, and the meetings were, well, informative and interesting.

During the summer months, we concentrated on returning and reconnecting; Kevin and John came to visit us at the furlough home, we visited our home church in Denver (Central), and we tried to get used to the material abundance everywhere. We had our end-of-term physical, and Haejung left for Korea to see her mother in September. While she was on the plane crossing the Pacific, Simon learned that he needed a coronary bypass surgery immediately. All the mission interpretation visits had to be canceled.

Fortunately, John was visiting and he handled most of the communication and driving. Haejung cut her visit short and returned on September 11th. Her plane landed in Minneapolis rather than Chicago, but she was finally able to get to Louisville two days later. Simon's surgery went well and he was able to go home after only three days of hospital stay. He has recovered well and his heart is back to normal, although the recovery from the surgery itself will take a while longer. We thank God for protecting us while we were at a place where these procedures were not available. The doctor thinks our healthy lifestyle in Congo kept the condition in check and prevented any damage to the heart muscles.

After six weeks of recovery, in early November we got back on the mission interpretation circuit and made numerous trips to west and east coasts and places in between. Simon even made a couple of short visits to El Salvador to work with a partner church there in their earthquake recovery ministry. We expect to continue with these visits until we leave for Kathmandu, Nepal. The more visits we make, the more we are convinced that it is all in God's hands, and we are only a small part of the entire Church obeying God's commands. We do not have any accomplishments to report, so we end up sharing what we learned during our preparation and stay in Congo. We know God will teach us what we can handle until the day he calls us home.

We are now called to serve with the United Mission to Nepal (UMN) for the next three years. Set up in 1954 by eight mission organizations, including the PC(USA), UMN has grown to include 51 member bodies and affiliated member bodies from 17 countries. When it was founded it was the first interdenominational, multinational Christian consortium of its kind in the world.

Nepal is located between India and China with a population of 22 million people. Being the only Hindu kingdom in the world, foreign missionaries are not allowed to proselytize directly to the Nepalese people, but we are invited to demonstrate the love of Christ through development, education and health ministries. What a challenge to walk the talk. We even made a short discernment visit to Nepal in January of this year.

Nepal of natural beauty and history, but also with inequality, poverty and violence.

Simon will be working as a consultant for organizational and financial administration, and Haejung will be working with missionary children in their education. We have completed our physical and psychological evaluation and are waiting for the visa. We hope to be in Kathmandu by early August to start our language training, again. When we left Congo, we prayed for three things: no more malaria prophylaxis, telephone availability, and no new language. Two out of three aren't bad, not bad at all!

Seriously, we found that language training is a good lesson in humility and a demonstration of our genuine concern for the people. Just like in

Congo, we know the folks appreciate our effort regardless of our fluency in their language, and it opens the relationship. We expect our five-month orientation and language training period will be difficult and frustrating, but we pray that we can stay up-beat and trust in God.

Until we leave for Nepal, we will continue to visit churches and share our stories. If you would like to invite us to visit your church, we still have a few open dates in May and June. The PC(USA)'s policy is that the inviting church is responsible for our travel costs and lodging, but since we are on the payroll of PC(USA) we do not accept honoraria.

We know we should be preparing for our Nepal assignment, but more prayers and the right attitude is what we need most at this time. It is not our knowledge base or contacts, but the obeying heart God demands of us. We know when we go to Nepal, we are not going alone but with the prayers of all our friends and family. Please pray that we remain faithful and obedient.

We promise to write more often this year.

In Christ,

Haejung & Simon

Dear Friends and Family

"Have you got your bags packed?" It was Susan Ryan of the Presbyterian Disaster Assistance on the phone, asking Simon how quickly he could get ready to go to Malawi to assist in the famine relief efforts. The call came on Maundy Thursday, and at four in the morning of the Monday after Easter, Haejung was driving Simon to Cincinnati to start the 30-hour journey to Blantyre in southern Malawi.

The Presbyterian Church (U.S.A.) and its members have strong relationships with our partners in Malawi. As early as August 2001, the folks in Malawi knew that the country was facing a very bad food shortage. By February of this year people were dying from hunger and malnutrition and it became a national disaster.

In many African countries, churches step up to provide care to the people when the government response is slow and inadequate. Presbyterian Disaster Assistance (PDA) has decided to support the Church of Central Africa-Presbyterian (CCAP) - Blantyre Synod in their relief efforts. Normally, PDA does not implement the relief program itself, but rather relies on the partner in the field of ministry. However, the urgent need combined with the lack of capacity in the partner church motivated PDA to take the lead this time. Mr. Hudson Lugano, a Kenyan Christian with a wealth of experience in relief work in Africa, was hired to set up the initial system and build the human capacity within the church. Simon was called in to assess the situation regarding the need, financial accountability systems, and the training needs. Too often, outside helpers rush in when the disaster strikes only to leave when the real rebuilding process ought to start. Please visit the PDA site on the web (http://pda.pcusa.org) and learn more about the ministry.

It is both a personal privilege and a good learning experience to participate in this ministry in a small way. I just want to share a few items I noticed along the way.

With heightened security, Simon tends to get picked for extra checks. It seems Simon stands out as being peculiar—he is traveling to unusual destinations on very short notice, traveling with little luggage, and is not talking on the mobile phone while boarding. The longest leg in the voyage was the Atlanta-Johannesburg segment. On the way over it was a non-stop 14-and-a-half-hour flight. On the way back we had to stop at the island of Sal in Cape Verde, West Africa (see if you can find this on the map) for a fuel stop, making it an 18-hour flight. All in all, it took over thirty hours each way.

We, the relief team from CCAP, arrived at a village in southern Malawi to distribute relief food items and were met with joyful singing of young mothers with babies in their arms. Pretty soon, the singing turned into angry shouting. It turns out that GTZ, a German Aid agency, was in the village distributing high protein porridge for children under five. When our truck showed up, they stopped the distribution and prepared to leave. The young aid-worker told us that he could not collaborate with us due to the European Union's regulation that they will not distribute food in any village where others are helping. It was not as bad a regulation as it seemed at first. The EU was concerned that the help not be concentrated in small areas with good contacts, such as the hometowns of government officials. Sometimes, church partnerships can also have the effect of distributing help according to the connections rather than need. We made special efforts to provide help based on the need rather than tribe, religion, or family ties. Once again, I learned firsthand the value of working together and coordinating the efforts. While the EU policy was a reasonable one in Brussels, it was a difficult one to explain to the mothers with starving children in their arms, and it put the staff on the ground in danger.

When we are doing relief work, the checks and balances, the system of accountability, and other bureaucratic processes seem so cold-hearted in the face of immediate need. Proper planning and coordination are necessary, especially in the chaotic situation of emergency work. One day spent in proper planning seems to save days later. Dr. Terry Hatch in Illinois told us that giving too much nutrition at once to a malnourished child actually hurts, even kills, the child by overloading the child's ability to handle the energy. Simon believes the same is true when financial resources are rushed into relief efforts. Without the organizational capacity to properly administer the resources, good-hearted gifts can be wasted and abused. We are very glad that PDA sent the management capacity along with the funds for food items. Perhaps a better solution is to enhance our partners' capacities before the disaster strikes again. Perhaps we can even prevent some disasters due to mismanagement and incompetence.

Simon was fortunate enough to meet with Dr. Ellard Malindi, who is heading up the Food Security Commission for the government of Malawi. Dr. Malindi spent nine years at the University of Illinois earning his graduate degrees in agriculture. He and his wife were active members of the First Presbyterian Church of Urbana. We were briefed on the national plans and discussed the ways PC(USA) can coordinate our relief and redevelopment efforts to complement the government programs. It was more than a business meeting; it was a time to reaffirm our respective responsibilities in

God's ministry and to encourage one another. Remember Dr. Malindi and his team in your prayers, for wisdom, courage, and health, as they seek to lead the country to a permanent solution of food security. It was a very tiring trip, but a rewarding one. We thank God for the opportunities to assist in the church's efforts to accompany partners in long-lasting relationships.

Meanwhile, in Nepal the United Missions to Nepal (UMN) has accepted us and has begun our visa process. We hope to arrive in Nepal by the end of July. Maoist guerrillas are continuing on their destructive path. Many lives on both sides have been lost and already minimal infrastructure is being destroyed. Many hydroelectric plants, roads, and airport control towers have been put out of commission, keeping much of the rural population isolated. Please pray for a peaceful resolution to this conflict and for the missionaries at UMN and their ministries. Also pray that the $20 million in military aid from the United States furthers the peace process and doesn't fuel the hatred among the belligerents towards America and its people.

We continue to be on the road visiting churches and sharing the stories of God's ministry. We are privileged to have these opportunities until we leave for our next assignment.

And so went another month in home (?) assignment.

Talk to you again next month.

May the coming Spirit descend upon you and minister among you.

chapter II

Letters
from Nepal

Dear Friends and Family

When we were leaving Congo, we made three requests to God: (1) no more malaria prophylaxis, (2) good telephone service, and (3) no new language. On July 29 we will be leaving for Kathmandu to start on our 20-week language training in Nepali and orientation for our work in Nepal. We learned that the value of language learning, especially in the country of service, is not only in the functionality we gain, but the relationship it opens up with the people we serve. It seems the more difficulty we have with the language the more appreciative they are. God's sufficiency is proven in our weakness.

We will be serving through the United Mission to Nepal. Founded by eight mission organizations, including the PC(USA), in 1954, the United Mission to Nepal (UMN) has grown to include 51 member bodies and affiliated member bodies from 17 countries. It was the first inter-denominational, multinational Christian consortium of its kind in the world. Our orientation group includes eight families from five countries. The UMN exists to serve the poor and marginalized in the name and spirit of Christ in the areas of education, engineering and industrial development, health services, and rural development work. You can find more detailed information about UMN and Nepal at www.umn.org.np. We consider a large part of our mission is to share with you the experience of developing new relationships in Nepal, seeing God's hand in unexpected places, and expanding our worldview to see the love of Jesus in suffering as well as in rejoicing.

Simon will be working with UMN project units to evaluate financial situations and help develop Nepali management personnel to enable orderly transfers of the projects to Nepali people. Haejung will be working with missionary children in their schooling, especially for adjustment of the children from non-English speaking countries. We thought we would be doing something different and unique when we are in mission service, but we are learning once again that God uses the talents that he has already given us and challenges us to use them in ways to witness his goodness.

During the past year we have visited many congregations and made many new friends. Some of them have been supporting us in prayers and in financial support of the church's international ministries. The visits were at times quite tiring, but always uplifting and affirming. We were always received with love and we were able to share our stories in an open and honest manner. We are especially grateful for the opportunity to make new relationships with many Korean Presbyterian congregations and invite them into full partnership with the mission efforts of the denomination.

Many say the General Assembly is a once-in-a-lifetime experience, but we were fortunate (?) to participate in two General Assemblies, 2001 and 2002. Simon preached one year and served as a translator in the other. Our love and respect for the ministry of the church grew and we were overwhelmed by the level of support for mission work demonstrated by all the participants. Should you wish to financially support our mission work, we have some suggestions for projects and how the funds can be properly received at the church. Simply drop us a line and we will send you the information via e-mail. We do not want to lengthen this note unnecessarily.

We will be leaving Louisville very early on July 29 to drive to Boston to leave the car for John and Kevin's use. We will catch a red-eye flight to Paris on the evening of July 30, with a quick connection to Delhi, India. We'll stay overnight in Delhi for the Kathmandu flight on August 1. All together, about 70 hours! We look forward to seeing Jeff Anthony, a duty manager for Air France who personally helped us to sort out the baggage problem during our trip in January. One never knows when and where a Christian brother will lend a helping hand. We will write as soon as we get settled in Kathmandu, but here is some information for continued communication.

Our current address <Parks@ParkSquare.net> will continue to function in Nepal, we pray. We will have fully functioning Internet service in Nepal. Unlike when we were in Congo, you can send long messages, pho-

On our way back from the interview trip to Nepal, we stopped at Agra, India to visit the Taj Mahal. Due to much diminished tourist travel after 9/11, we almost had the entire place to ourselves.

tos, and everything else you want to share with us. We will also be able to send and receive messages in Korean. If you wish to receive the Korean version of our newsletters, drop us a line.

Our mailing address is c/o Mission Co-worker Office 100 Witherspoon Street Louisville, KY 40202-1396. First-class mail that will be mailed to us monthly. We will be talking to you from Nepal.

Grace and peace,

Haejung & Simon

Namaste!

We arrived safely here in Kathmandu, Nepal, and started to get ourselves into the sights, sounds, and smells of the city. Today is the first day of the Language and Orientation Program (LOP). We had hoped to have settled most of the "settling in" issues before we start the program. We are getting another lesson in patience and letting go.

We wanted to limit the things we brought from the United States to the four checked bags allowed on our tickets. In the post 9/11 climate, traveling with excess baggage is very difficult, and we also wanted to discipline ourselves to live on the bare necessities and what is locally available. This would also be a better lifestyle for missionaries. So, we packed our memories, Korean spices, minimum clothing, a year's supply of diabetic and heart medications, and the equipment for our technical work. We were proud and thankful when we managed to put all these in four footlockers. Our plan was to arrive one week before the start of the LOP and settle in with four bags and willing hearts.

Well, friends, plans do not always work out as intended. When we were leaving Delhi for the final segment of the journey to Kathmandu, we noticed that only one of our four bags was transferred from Air France to Indian Air. We continued our journey with one solitary bag (the clothing) and assurances that the other three would arrive soon.

Today is the seventh day with no information on the whereabouts of the missing bags, and the assurances are getting weaker each day. Talk about insurance and compensation is not what we want to hear. We have done and will do everything we can to locate the bags but are also planning for the possibility of never seeing them again. Airline compensation will be less than 20% of the replacement cost, and there are many irreplaceable items. Travel guidelines say to keep all irreplaceable items with you on carry-on bags. But when one travels three days to get to the destination, the carry-on space gets filled with essential travel items such as travel documents, money, minimum change of clothing, medications, and toiletries. When you pack for three years into four bags, each and every item is an essential one.

We are not ready to give up on the bags yet but are thinking about the lessons to learn from this experience. We believe the generic versions of medications can be found locally, but we want to get the consent of the doctors. We will have to learn to work with less equipment and find acceptable local food items more quickly than we had planned, but we have faith in our God, each other, and you. We know we will come through this and come out wiser and closer to God.

This morning's devotion material was on Corinthians 12:12-25, about teamwork. How appropriate for today, as eight families from five countries gather to start the journey of service together! This assignment in Nepal is going to be much easier than our assignment in Congo was in terms of living conditions, but the work itself will be more complicated, since people from many different cultures, faith and worship styles have to harmonize to witness in this Hindu kingdom. We will need to accept and adjust to different ideas about mission, values, and the concept of partnership with the people of Nepal.

Just during these few days we have been here, there have been moments when we wished the body of our mission organization had four left feet rather than two hands and two feet. Although uniformity makes it simpler than the search of harmony and unity in diversity, we need to struggle harder to find Christian unity. We remember well the advice given to us during the first week of our orientation five years ago. "You need to sort out what the few 'non-negotiables' are for which you should give your life. All others are mere preferences and learn to treat them as such." We referred to this advice at least daily for the past five years and will continue to do so.

We need to live this principle today—in our common journey with other United Mission to Nepal members and also in search of our bags. We will write soon about our new life here in Nepal and the continuing saga of our bags. We do not have a permanent house or internet connection, but we will be keeping this e-mail address. We may be slow in responding to your messages, but we will get to them eventually. For the moment, not all messages get into the "non-negotiables' category. We ask your prayer for our obedience, and we pray that you find your 'non-negotiables' and keep them on top of your priorities.

Danyebhat for listening.

Dear Family and Friends

It is already first of November, three months since we arrived in Nepal and two more months to go in our language and culture training program. We have not started on any of the tasks on our "job description," but the prerequisite task of relating to the people of Nepal has begun. When we arrived here in August, we focused, like tourists, on the differences in people, culture, and practices. Everything was exciting and exotic. As we began to settle in, we experienced the annoyances and yearned for familiar surroundings so we could function as competent adults. Relying on others' help to survive at a minimal level affected our self-esteem and mental health.

We are just beginning to relate to local people as unique individuals with whom we can share our feelings, expectations, and hopes. Compared to our experience in the Congo, the peaks and valleys this time seem less extreme. The well-organized orientation program at UMN has helped us to cope with the emotional and physical oscillation. Perhaps it is the presence of many others with whom we can share the experience, or we may simply be learning to better handle the challenges by trusting that God is in control and his love for us never fails. We are very grateful to God for his care.

Our apartment is finally finished, except the bathroom mirror, only two months after we moved in. As the mornings and nights begin to get nippy, it is nice not having to leave the front door open all the time for the workers. Houses here do not have any central heating system, but we just purchased two space heaters that should help us stave off morning chills. Four couples started to meet for weekly Bible study at our home. All of us attend different churches and came to Nepal with different mission organizations, but the time to pray for one another and to study Scripture is the most valued time of the week. We decided to worship in a expatriate congregation until we become more functional in Nepali language.

As we mentioned in our September letter, the Desain holiday season is over and we are entering the Tihar season. We will take the holiday season to take a break from daily language studies and travel to the mountain and lake region for a few days. As we observe the activities during the festivals, we feel as though the Nepali folks believe their gods have limited blessings to give and they must act promptly and properly to get their share of the blessings. Worse yet, if they do not get the blessings, they may face the wrath of the gods. Many have told us that they do not believe in the rituals, but they dare not take the risk of receiving punishments for not following

the rituals. They readily admit that at the root of their religious and cultural activities lies the fear of uncontrollable and negative forces. Undoubtedly, this is an over simplification. Nevertheless, we are grateful for our God with abounding love and justice. How great is thy faithfulness!

Another benefit (?) of living in Nepal at this time is

the ability to view world events from more than one perspective. Nepal is not immune to violence. In fact, we get our share of daily bombings, although they do not kill as many people as the more publicized events. President Bush's position on Iraq comes up often in discussions with Nepalese and friends from other countries. They find it difficult to accept the logic and morality of attacking Iraq in order to protect the innocent lives in the United States and its allies. Can one justifiably risk innocent lives in one country in order to protect them in another? Would ordinary people in America sustain their support of attack if they were able to get to know the ordinary people of Iraq and the region? We feel at times very hypocritical: our church sends missionaries to serve the people all around the world, yet our country is ready to justify killing others "in proactive self-defense." These days our daily prayers are longer as we seek God's forgiveness, love, and wisdom for all.

Three days ago, we were invited to a Nepali church. This village church is located on top of a hill a few miles outside of Kathmandu. Most of the elderly members of this village could not come to the main church in town (Baktapur) on Saturdays. Each Tuesday, the pastor and some members of the church go up the hill for worship service. It was only two kilometers, but straight up the hill. After an hour and a half of hard climbing, we arrived at the church. The church was founded by the family of a leprosy patient who was cured at a mission hospital. We met the old lady with missing digits but a glowing happy face, giving thanks and witnessing to others.

It certainly was a service many Presbyterians would find unorderly and undignified in form. Although we understood only a few words, we felt the presence of the Holy Spirit amongst us. We could not help but to wish that

*In the same village where the church is, we saw a face of poverty.
This lady earns one dollar a day for crushing rocks into gravels for
construction.
We later learned that this work is very common among the poor
throughout the country.*

those of us who continue in Book of Order battles could worship together in this church with these illiterate Nepali Christians. Simon was especially grateful for the healthy heart that handled the three-hour walk to experience this Christian community.

Our computer system had a terrible virus attack and we had to reformat the hard disk. We managed to reconstruct most of the email addresses, but not the mailing addresses. Would you be kind enough to drop us a line with your mailing address and phone number?

Please continue to pray for us that we remain spiritually and physically healthy as we enter the last third of the language study. We are also beginning to discuss the details of our assignments beginning next January after the language study. Now is the time to learn and listen and we are trying to be patient and open.

Grace and peace,

Haejung & Simon

Dear Friends

Thanksgiving dinner on Friday with Tandoori (heavily seasoned with Indian spices and oven-baked) chicken is not exactly a traditional Thanksgiving feast, but quite like our lives these days.

December is our fifth and the last month of language and culture training period. Officially this is the time to increase our knowledge base, but in truth we are learning to survive with limited language, limited familiarity, and limited ability to satisfy our needs in the usual ways. We are learning that for every item we cannot find, we can find two or three passable substitutes, and heretofore necessary items are often just an item on the wish list. The more we substitute and make adjustments, the more we come to appreciate what we have. Compared to our life in Congo, we are basking in the lap of luxury. While our lifestyle is very luxurious compared to the Nepali nationals, there are truly luxurious enclaves for foreign missions and the ruling class which we only hear about. Their list of wants seems to be much longer than ours, just as ours is longer than Nepali folks'.

While struggling to express our ideas and needs with our very limited language skills, we experience a small dose of the frustrations of the voiceless and powerless people. Trying to cope with the frequent strikes and imposed restrictions, we taste a bit of life out of our hands. Watching Hindu festivals as outsiders, we appreciate the bewilderment of ordinary people having to simply watch incompressible destruction taking place in their homeland. Beginning today, December 9, all the educational institutions in Nepal are closed due to threats of the Maoist Student Union. No one knows how long this imposed strike will continue. In order to avoid the damaging effects of frequent disruptions, rich folks send their children to India or other countries for education, further depleting energy and financial resources from the country.

This Christmas season we hope to see and hear our surroundings with the eyes and ears of the coming King. What did Jesus see, hear and feel during his thirty years of preparation? How would what we see today help us serve as faithful and good servants in the next two and a half years of our time in Nepal? We do not know specifically what but feeling their pain as our own pain must be the beginning of our service. Otherwise, we tend to become able "problem solvers" intoxicated only by the feelings of accomplishment. We will be receiving our assignment letter from the United Mission to Nepal next week, and we pray that we receive and tackle each assignment with the attitude of serving the people and our Lord. No matter how much we tell ourselves to be faithful and humble, we fail again and again. We ask for your prayers that we serve with humility, but with knowledge built on the truth that God will free these people in His time. Most of the time we are the ones on the move, but in Nepal we will welcome newcomers and send off those returning home. Next year, we hope to become helpful "welcomers" and dependable "stayers" serving other missionaries as well.

A few Nepali folks have been asking us about Christmas, trying to understand it based on numerous Hindu festivals. In general, the Hindu religion instructs its followers on how to earn enough credits to overcome suffering. No one can earn all the needed credit in one life, thus they keep returning in different forms and try and try they must. Our loving and holy God coming to free us from our sins is incomprehensible without changing their view of the world. But those who are able to overcome receive the good news with a childlike heart and pure joy.

Tihar is one of the two major festivals in Nepal, and it fell in early November this year. People decorate their houses and store-fronts with flower laces and light strings. Our landlord had strung several colorful blinking lights on a tree next to our entrance. We were hearing very poor-sounding Christmas carols when the lights came on. It turned out the Chinese made lights were siphoned from the shipment to European countries for Christmas, complete with a tiny speaker for Christmas carols. So, this year we had Christmas before Thanksgiving and enjoyed God's sense of humor once again.

Looking back, it has been another year of change and another period of training for being flexible for God. We shall listen to His voice.

May you all have a wonderful Christmas and listen well.

Simon & Haejung

Dear Friends and Family

Already a full week passed since we welcomed in the year 2003. Here in Nepal, we use the Hindu calendar, and New Year's Day was an ordinary working day, as was Christmas. We did have a full Christmas: a carol service on Christmas Eve, a Christmas dinner at our home with close missionary families. Instead of having John and Kevin with us, we had surrogate children, young volunteers from Korea, and we played surrogate parents to them. We even enjoyed being surrogate grandparents by giving a two-year-old, battery-operated guitar. By the end of the evening we were so glad that he was taking it home and we no longer had to endure his "music." Ah, the joy of spoiling a child without paying the price.

As many of you had written to us, we were saddened and in prayer over the killings of Christians and missionaries in Pakistan and Yemen. Here in Nepal, we are not targeted specifically because we are Christians or missionaries. Generally, the Maoist rebels leave foreigners alone because either they see us as helpers or they figure any harm to foreigners would be counterproductive. We pray daily for the wisdom and courage to live and work as Jesus commanded us. We completed the formal orientation program at the end of December and began to poke around in search of the right opening for entry into our assigned work areas. Simon's work is to provide consultation in resource management areas, starting with Patan Hospital in Kathmandu. Although Simon left full-time teaching many years ago, his call and gift seem to be in educating those who have never had an opportunity to learn management techniques yet are called to manage resources.

A friend sent us a message noting a National Public Radio program on missionaries. Our view of mission these days is one of living out our Christian faith, not necessarily inducing conversion and measuring our "success" based on the number of souls converted. In Nepal, one finds the entire spectrum of missiology—from pure relief or development work where one's Christian faith is kept entirely personal, to directing every effort to conversion including coercion and bribery.

We not only have to learn tolerance and mutual respect between religions and cultures, but between different views of Christian service. At times, this difference within the family is more painful than the difference we find with Hindu colleagues.

Simon's primary contact at the hospital is the Hindu administrator. Should Simon provide less assistance because he is not a Christian? We pray that the assistance Simon provides be so genuine and useful the administrator would ask about the source of energy and motivation when he himself cannot give any reward. We hope to be ready with an answer (1 Peter 3:15-16). For those missionaries who deliver care and service directly to the people, the context in which they share the love of Christ can be secondary to the service itself. However, for those of us whose mission is to support others on the front line to care and serve more effectively, we rely on the expressed and demonstrated core values of the organization through which we serve.

We are grateful for the Presbyterian Church (U.S.A.) and the United Mission to Nepal for giving us the structure within which to serve. Thank you for the Christmas cards and messages during the holiday season. Your notes made us feel close to you and again reminded us that we are in God's

family. Many of you wondered how we are coping with the cold, snow and all. In the Kathmandu valley it does not get below freezing. During December and January, the daily lows are between 0-5C (32-41F) and during the day it gets to 15C (60F). While the absolute temperature is not very cold, the inside of the house does not have a chance to warm up, as the houses here do not have any central heating system. After a while, the cold inhibits activities and penetrates to the core of the body.

We do have propane heaters and blankets, and manage to stay

comfortable. During our French language study we spent a winter in northern Quebec in Canada where it reached 40 degrees below zero before the wind chill factor. (In case you didn't know -40 is -40 in Celsius or in Fahrenheit.) The body made sure to let us know that it was extremely cold and to take protective measures. Here, the chill is gradual, and we are lulled into thinking the body adjusts to the change, until we are shivering and become inactive; perhaps "boiling frogs" in reverse.

We wonder whether our faith can suffer a similar chilling effect. When we are faced with direct challenges and difficulties, we spend time with God and put up the guard. But when we continue on the ordinary journey, our spiritual health gradually comes to a dormant state and no longer energizes our daily lives. Many of you noted that living as missionaries, our sacrifices in material wealth are well compensated by rich spiritual overflow. Well, we find the exact opposite. When we lived in Denver, we were "rich" but "poorer" than most around us in the neighborhood and in the church to which we belonged. As missionaries, we have more material resources than most we live with. Also, working as missionaries, we think that we are close to God and feel less urgency to cry out to the Lord for our own spiritual needs, although we spend time to pray for the people around us. As we "do" God's work our personal relationship can enter the dormant state. We ask for your prayers for our spiritual challenge and health. When we think about leaving the field often, at least daily, it is a healthy sign that we are struggling and seeking the truth from above. Did not mean to preach, but to confess.

When we were leaving the States, several friends asked how they could help financially. We had a plan to purchase a vehicle and some of you contributed generously to the vehicle maintenance and operating fund. After spending several months here, we have come to a decision that owning a personal vehicle is not a necessity for our mission, in fact it can create a gap between the folks here and us. We will be asking the donors for their permission to re-channel the funds towards teaching and presentation equipment for Simon's teaching ministry.

Just today we received a care package from a couple in Illinois, whom we probably have never met (our apologies if we had). We felt the care and love in the selection of food items, and in the careful packaging. In addition to the hefty postage, it must have cost quite a bit. We accept the gift and love with gratitude as your kind act reminded us that we are representing all of Jesus' disciples in the land and many are praying for us. It was a jolt for us to reexamine our spiritual life and kneel before God.

Thank you friends, thank you God.

Dear Friends in Christ

We live in confusing times. Just in Nepal alone, on Sunday, January 26, the Chief of the Armed Police, a force that was especially set up to counter the armed insurgence of the Maoists, was assassinated, along with his wife and a bodyguard, about two miles from where we live. Along with other residents of the country, we were bracing for an escalation of the violence that has already killed more than 5,500 people in the past fourteen months. Four days later, the government and the Maoists declared a cease-fire. We are hoping against hope that this time a lasting peace would hold, and everybody will come to the table and work out their differences through dialog.

Then on February 4, a Reuters news article quoted Assistant Secretary of State Christina Rocca commenting on the cease-fire "Maybe this is a reason for hope but the fact of the matter is it's a deteriorating situation." She went on to say that the United States is giving $12 million to "help the government of Nepal have enough force to bring the Maoists to the table." Maoists came to the table, but "the situation in Nepal is really not looking very good," she added. These are confusing times.

Add Iraq, North Korea, Palestine, the loss of Columbia, and an assortment of local and personal difficulties to these happenings and we know we live in confusing times.

Many friends have written to ask if we are finding a foothold here in Nepal. According to experts, unless we are able to settle in within six months of arriving, we may have a difficult time throughout the period. We have been here exactly six months. We are pretty much settled in terms of physical things: we know the main roads, shopkeepers know us, and so on. We still need to be more certain of our roles, relationships, and work priorities. This is not unique to those of us living outside the homeland. It is only heightened when we are here for a defined time period and under the pressure to accomplish some worthy goals.

It is at times like this we need to get back to the basic reasons why we are here. During our morning devotions, we came across the message to the church in Ephesus (Revelations 2:1-7). Busy doing good works, they lost their love for Christ. We wonder whether we are making the same mistake, trying to carry out our mission and in the struggle to stay true to the theology, we may have distanced ourselves from the love we have for our God and the source of all good in us.

We have been praying to get back to the basics and find a firm foundation for our mission service. We have settled on the idea that mission service is a form of worship. We do not have the idea well developed yet but wanted to share what "mission as worship" means to us and how it can guide our attitudes towards mission activities in these confusing times. More important than that, we want to hear your ideas and comments and to ask you to pray for us. We are not asking or planning to apply this idea to anyone other than ourselves.

Our mission service starts when we respond to the call to worship. As in worship, we never bring God to our mission field, but join God where He has been already working. We join in the worship where people with different traditions are brought together in the common worship of God. No one is more worthy than another to participate in worship, yet each is called to worship God according to the measures given to us. All of us must repent our sins to approach God and hear the words and see the glory of

God. As in worship where the Word of God is preached, God's truth must be proclaimed in every mission field.

We also must accept that God's word can and does get pronounced in many creative ways. Just as the preachers have to struggle with the Word, we must struggle with the way the gospel comes to life through our relationships and lifestyle. What we actually do in the field is our response to the Word, as forgiven sinners and as Spirit-led servants. You get the idea. What we would like from you are your own reflections on this metaphor and other Biblical foundations that will help us keep our eyes firmly fixed on Jesus and his commands to guide us through these confusing times.

As many of you already know, our church, the PC(USA), is going through another cycle of budget cutbacks and the efforts to deploy missionaries to bring salt and light around this confusing world is severely affected. May we humbly ask you to pray individually and as congregations and consider increasing your support for the church to respond to the partners' requests for missionaries? The staff at the Worldwide Ministries Division is doing their best to prayerfully carry out the stewardship responsibilities well in order to earn the praise of the master and His will to trust the Church with more.

The 2002 General Assembly urged all congregations to make special contributions in order to build back the number of long-term mission personnel, which had been reduced during the budget cuts of April 2002. This "Faith Factor" ECO account ("ECO" stands for "Extra Commitment Opportunity") has been established to receive these contributions. Funds donated to this account will be used to recruit, place, train, and support new mission personnel in 2003 and beyond. Through this support, the PC(USA) intends to increase the number of people serving in PC(USA) international mission as rapidly as possible.

PC(USA) congregations can pledge and send contributions through the normal channels. Individual gifts are accepted at: Central Receiving Service, Section 300, Louisville, Kentucky 40289.

Haejung is spending two hours a day at a United Mission to Nepal hospital, the Patan Hospital, "playing" with God's little children. Some are patients at the new pediatric wing built with the donations from the Montview Presbyterian Church in Denver, Colorado. Others are the siblings and children of patients who have to stay at the hospital because their parents are patients there. She is well on her way to reclaim her name in Congo, "Mama Haejung," but here she is simply known as "auntie."

Simon is continuing to search for opportunities to share his skills and compassion, but also learning to be patient until the timing is right. At the moment, he is responding to any request for help, big and small, knowing that God speaks in mysterious ways. This Sunday, he is going to visit a rural hospital in Okhaldhunga district, approximately 100 miles east of Kathmandu. It's a 20-minute flight in a light plane followed by a three-and-half-hour hike. What a luxury compared to the 12-hour road trips Simon used to make in Congo for the same distance! Pray for Simon's health and that the four-day visit be an occasion of service to our Lord.

Keep your eyes fixed on the truth in these confusing times.

Love, death, and mission

Dear Friends,

War seems to be imminent and we are in the third week of Lent. "What would Jesus do?" is not a rhetorical question, but a life and death question today for us. Last month, we shared with you that mission for us is a part, a large part, of worship. A friend wrote to us that in Hebrew, the word for work, service, and worship is the same word. Now that we know the theory, we only need to live it. This month Haejung and I decided to write separate letters, Haejung in Korean and I in English.

When my father was terminally ill with cancer, I heard my grandmother cry out to God, "Grant however many days I have left to my son and take me home now. He can serve you better than I can." I do not know whether God granted her wish, but I do know that she meant every word and she believed it to be according to God's will. Her prayer of almost thirty years ago resonates today and become one with Jesus's prayer in my heart. First is the love of a mother for her son, and the second is the clear sense of priority she had in making the request.

During the several years I have spent in the mission field, I have faced difficult decisions where none of the alternatives seemed desirable, but we had to choose one. Most of the time it is the search of a clear sense of priority rather than more calculation. In the hospitals, I saw young children going through limb amputations, truly a sad event, but something that had to be done to save their lives. As radical an action as it was, considering the alternative, it was a non-decision.

But what is more important than one's life? Jesus and my grandmother showed me that a loved one's life can be more important that one's own. How do we put others before ourselves as Jesus did? Personally, what are my priorities in the mission field? Is it the "rewarding experience" that many mission volunteers so excitedly talk about? Is it the number of "converts" some churches advertise on their web pages? Is it my personal growth? Should I be spending time worrying about this rather than "doing whatever needs to be done at this time"?

Jesus had the clear priority of obeying the Father's will, and he had the love to place our lives in him above his own life. Do I have the vision and the love? Is our opposition or support of the war grounded in clear vision and love? I have been trying to understand what motivates the passionate debates and what assures them of the correctness of their positions. Here in Nepal, we do not hear the arguments as much as in the Western world, but it is so difficult to believe that the world leaders got on their knees seeking answers to this question. I pray that the willingness for all the sacrifice is based on love, and the path we take is based on God's priorities.

Last month, I made a visit to the Okhaldhunga Health Project in the remote eastern hills of Nepal. A 30-minute flight on a 17-seat plane took us to the dirt landing strip of the town of Rumjatar. Seeing the numerous bullet holes on the control tower and the surrounding buildings and seeing the military patrols in flak jackets reminded us of how real the Maoist conflicts are.

A family of porters came from Okhaldhunga to carry our luggage. A lady barely five feet tall who must have weighed less than hundred pounds took my bag and another one as our group of eight started our four-hour journey. My pride did not allow giving up the small backpack I was carrying, so I kept it. I had not seen a single vehicle, not even a bicycle, during

all the time we were there. In fact, once we left the town of Rumjatar, I could not find even one acre of flat land. It was either going up or down, resulting in a gain in altitude of half a mile. Within the first hour I was regretting my decision to keep the bag and was having a good test of the bypass surgery of sixteen months ago.

My admiration of the majestic hills and layers of ridges quickly changed to turning to the sky asking for journey mercies, and the prayer that I may finish. Layers of clothing came off, but still drenched with sweat and resting every ten steps, we finally arrived at the hospital and community health complex, which was started forty years ago serving the people of this remote district. Next came the search of a stool-style toilet, only to learn that none existed in the station. My respect for the missionaries who served years in this station went up manifolds.

I did find a school for missionary children that stands empty today, and

many houses for expatriate doctors and missionaries being used for occasional visitors. There are ample examples of how important the hospital is to the people of the district, who may walk as many as five days to reach the hospital. But due to lack of doctors who can perform surgeries, conflict between the government and the Maoist guerrillas, and the lack of funds, the number of people seeking care at the hospital is much reduced from a few years ago. Our discussion of the situation quickly turned into finger pointing. Some point to the lack of dedicated missionaries of years past. Some say that nothing has changed in 40 years and point to the absence of local ownership and the futility of continuing expensive operations that don't build the capacity of indigenous to care for themselves. These arguments are happening all over the world in almost all mission hospitals. No one answer is the right one, and I certainly do not have a good one.

Can we apply the love and priority standards to this question as well? At the risk of sounding like a "know it all," let me share questions on mission giving. When you give to help those in need, you are partnering in God's work rather than being God yourself. There are people in place who have the hearts and skills to care for the God's children in need. They ask less about whose fault it is but ask what we can do to help them. God has given us the gift of compassion and the resources to share. Do we clearly see the promised future for others and love them, or God, enough to share what we are given? Is it necessary that we support only Christian workers, or is it more important that our actions start with the love of Christ? For practical suggestions, I recommend that you support the activities in partnership and demand accountability. When we support the activities, we are affirming the common worship of our God, and what God does to the people rather than organizations. At the same time, we have stewardship responsibilities to be generous, yet to guard against waste and misuse.

It is very common to give donations to a mission hospital to care for the destitute. Usually the money is given in return for the promise of caring for the needy. The hard-nosed demand to hear about the activities is not demeaning but actually encouraging to the field workers. This way the hospital has the incentive to actually provide the care, control the cost, and show that they are the worthy partners. I understand it is almost impossible for an individual or a congregation to have sufficient leverage. My recommendation is to work through the organizations that practice this system already. A little bit of homework will give you the confidence that your love is well grounded in God's priorities. Consider this an invitation for discussion.

I will be visiting Korea and the States for four weeks starting in mid-May. Haejung will stay here in Nepal and continue her work and witnessing during my trip to see family and friends as well as get my annual physical and have some meetings with church leaders. My plan is to visit Korea (May 17-24), then to go Denver during the General Assembly of the PC(USA) (May 24-31) and finally to Louisville (June 1-14). I look forward to seeing many friends and sharing stories from Nepal.

May this Lenten season find you getting closer to God and journeying together with Christ.

Simon

A father and son team of porters taking a rest before the hard climb. They each earn two dollars for the round trip which takes six hours.

Telling the truth about Jesus

Dear Friends,

It's been a while. I saw many of you during my visits to Seoul and the Stateside. The return trip from Louisville to Kathmandu was a character builder. Saturday morning 6:30 local time I left Louisville for Chicago, then on to Los Angeles, Seoul, Bangkok and finally to Kathmandu, arriving at 5:30 p.m. local time on Monday. Total duration was 54 hours with 28 hours of flying time. I thank God for arriving safely, and the luggage also made it through all those connections.

It was mainly a trip to check on my health and to discuss our work with the folks at the Presbyterian Church Center. All the test results came back normal and I returned with another year's supply of medications and doctor's permission to do fieldwork for another year.

Kathmandu is very hot and humid these days, reminding us of our days in Singapore. We are well into the monsoon season, which gives reprieve, albeit temporary, to the heat and the dust. The rains bring other problems, such as muddy runways at rural airports and side streets that become muddy, impassable paths. Also, the snow-capped mountains are all hidden by the clouds until early September.

During the trip, I had several opportunities to share our story of mission and missionary life. I also met several "missionaries" who do not carry the label of missionaries but are living the life of Christ's disciples. Some are caring for aging parents with love and dedication; some are raising birth and adopted children in God's bosom, and others are supporting field workers like us with prayers and financial contributions.

Haejung and I have been reflecting quite a bit on what Christian mission is, in general, and on our mission in particular. Six years in the field brings up more questions than answers. We have come to believe our mission is "to tell (live) the truth" about God and Jesus. In fact, the mission of every Christian is to tell the truth about Jesus in words and deeds.

How does an accountant "tell the truth" about Jesus? This was my question six years ago as we offered ourselves in mission service. As I gained experience in the mission field, I became acutely aware that not everyone has the privilege (or the burden) of seeing the financial consequences of our mission work. The gift of the Spirit given to me through my training and work experience is to "tell the truth" about the stewardship of the resources entrusted to us.

Many, even some of us in the mission field, think that stewardship is limited to the technical aspects of funds management and accounting for funds. In reality, management of mission funds also includes fundraising, disbursement, and reporting policies that reflect the key values held by the organization. Can we justify anything less than total transparency, especially when we are trying to "tell the truth" about the holy and compassionate God and the Jesus, God incarnate?

Information regarding the sources and uses of funds in the mission field often brings out different approaches to mission. Since 9/11 this topic has been discussed even in secular presses, especially as it relates to mission work in environments hostile to Christianity.

I am asked often to design financial control systems to maintain transparency and accountability. Transparency refers to clear and open ways of disclosing the source and use of funds, while accountability deals with questions such as whether the funds were expended for intended purposes, and whether they were used as efficiently as possible. Thus, a good accounting system necessarily reflects the goals of mission, the way we do mission, and the truth of Jesus that we want to live.

Whether it is the compassion of God, justice of God, or sovereignty of God all shown through Jesus, the truth must not be compromised. Organizations pursuing their own self-interest, such as governments, can justify "secrets" for greater good. Can those of us working to reveal the hidden secret, the "truth about Jesus," ever justify secrecy about what we do and how we spend resources, before God and people?

I mean neither to preach nor to lecture, but to share the spiritual and moral struggle some of us have to face and pray about during the course of our days in the field. We ask for your prayers and hope you can share your wisdom and experience with us. I also hope this letter reveals the uniqueness and additional requirements of Christian mission—that we must reveal the "truth of Jesus" not only in the ends but also in the means of our work.

Sometimes it is easier to do some of the work myself, rather than working with and through Nepali colleagues, but we need to reveal the truth that Jesus valued human beings rather than accounting systems. My priority is to work with Nepali colleagues to share technical knowledge while demonstrating that they, not the work, are the primary reason for our presence in Nepal. At the same time, I insist upon the "accountability" Jesus demanded of us rather than accepting opaqueness or less than honorable behaviors based on "cultural sensitivity."

I am also aware that our society is not free of these struggles; American corporations and political entities hardly come out clean but are saved by individuals who struggle to tell the truth. Some of my colleagues, mis-

sionaries and nationals, tell me that I am too idealistic, but I do not apologize for maintaining some idealism in our mission work, as it keeps me closer to the "truth of Jesus." Confessing our sins and enjoying the grace of forgiveness starts with the struggle, so we find joy in the struggle. I hope to periodically share some concrete examples of telling "the truth about Jesus" and how others see the truth and come to accept Jesus.

Our second son Kevin is coming next Saturday, July 19, to visit us for three weeks. This is the first opportunity for us to see any of our children in the mission field. We look forward to sharing the time together. Our invitation to all of you remains open. Also, John will be on his mission trip to Paraguay from July 19 for two weeks. Please remember all of us in your prayers. See you in cyberspace next month.

Economy of Sufficiency

My grace is sufficient for you, for my power is made perfect in weakness.
2 Corinthians 12:9

We have had a period of very hot days, reminding us of the hot and humid Singapore weather. Kevin's visit with us is in its third and final week. We are glad to see how much he has matured and become wiser during the time we spent apart since we entered mission service. Kevin feels the same about us.

The process of changing our mission strategy at United Mission to Nepal has begun in earnest. Instead of implementing projects ourselves, we now work through Nepali partners and UMN. We assist and consult. UMN's goal is to relinquish direct implementation responsibilities in two years. Until then, the organization will have to function under a dual system, gradually shedding its role as implementer.

Simon's primary responsibility is to prepare a team of in-house consultants to guide the mostly Nepali management personnel to take over the stewardship functions of the newly organized implementing partners as well as for the new decentralized management structure of UMN. Naturally, much of Simon's time is spent on "transparent and accountable" use of mission funds and proper reporting systems. When UMN leadership wrote to its overseas partners to inform them of the upcoming changes and to request their continuing support even after the work is transferred to Nepali organizations, most of the partners asked two questions. First, how will the

Nepali organizations manage the funds and communicate the "transparent and accountable" management? And second, what is UMN doing to ensure the integrity and effectiveness of the ministry?

Whenever we visit churches and attend church gatherings back home we are moved by the unquestioning and overwhelming support for missionaries. Yet at the same time people can ask pointed questions about the overall mission of the church. We thought we would use the next several letters to share our thoughts on the use of financial resources in Christian mission, including our personal use of resources as well. Our motivation for telling this story is to share some information on one important area not often discussed publicly: financial support of missionaries. The opinions we share in this letter are strictly our personal opinions and may not reflect official positions of UMN or the PC(USA).

We are very fortunate to be two of three hundred long-term compensated (salaried) mission personnel. Being employed by the Worldwide Ministries Division of the Presbyterian Church (U.S.A.)'s General Assembly Council means we have steady income and we are not personally responsible for raising funds for our use. We are called to take part in the mission of the entire church, as every member is expected to do. We are, however, asked to devote full-time effort to the ministry in places geographically afar, culturally distinct, and where the societies are in conflict. Although the official work hours are similar to those in the States, most of us are in effect on call 24 hours a day. Why do it then?

During Simon's student days and the 22 years he spent teaching and consulting, the driving concept was "maximizing." Maximum income, maximum pleasure, maximum recognition, maximum everything. Then we entered mission service. All PC(USA) missionaries are paid the same salary, adjusted for family size, children's education, and a cost of living adjustment for different locations. If one serves more than ten years, a 10 percent service increment is given, 20 percent for 20 years of service. No attempt is made to reflect earnings potentials in the secular world, nor is any consideration of the responsibility levels given. The call for mission service includes a call for the "economy of sufficiency" in place of "maximizing economy." The salary in effect is not a compensation for the value of services, rather a provision from God for full-time service.

Is the salary sufficient for us? We cannot speak for everyone, but for us, it is more than sufficient.

Our monthly gross salary is $1,461 for each of us. This amount is reduced by a small sum since Nepal is a low cost of living area, and taxes such as Social Security and Medicare are deducted also. In addition, we receive housing allowance, approximately $140 for both of us, and health insurance coverage. This salary in Nepal would put us in the top 5 percent of families for sure. It is sufficient for comfortable living in Nepal, but not too much to completely insulate us from the inconveniences and discomforts of daily life in Nepal. For example, we do not have to watch the price when we buy groceries in the local market, but are not able to afford all the imported frozen food items. We are learning that the fresh good quality vegetables in season are the least expensive ones in the market. Price does not correlate to quality, as long as we decide to live among the local folks and consume what is grown locally. One can pay very high prices for frozen salmon or fancy European cheese costing upwards of twenty dollars per pound. Our salary is not enough to keep a personal vehicle complete with air-conditioning, or to pay for electricity to run air-conditioning at home or central heating during the winter. Those are luxuries available only to the diplomats, UN personnel or some freelancing missionaries. For PC(USA) missionaries, such a lifestyle would negate the very purpose of living and working among the people in Nepal. Simon's rule is to walk for less than four miles, and take taxi for longer distances, and simply put up with dusts and loud horns.

We do not mean to say that we live exactly like the Nepali folks. We have to take extra care for hygiene and other health issues. Getting a cardiovascular bypass surgery like Simon did, would be an unimagined luxury, but we do not apologize for getting the care. Nor do we consider saving from our monthly salary for an annual check-up in Louisville an unsavory excess. We simply do not want to build a wall around our lives to sever contact with the people we came to work with. The support from the church is sufficient for all our financial needs. We must remember to thank all the congregations and friends who send gifts to PC(USA) in support of our ministry. While the "designated" support amount does not affect our salary levels, the church will not be able to maintain the mission force without these gifts.

We occasionally receive gifts directly from personal friends who want to support our ministry. Unless it is specifically designated as a personal gift for us to splurge on something we cannot normally afford, we consider it as an expression of their desire to partner with us in Christian service. We keep a record of these gifts and try to report back as to how their specific gifts have been used. We provided some needed school supplies, gave scholarship money for a Bible school, purchased some equipment for mission organizations among other uses. We do not consider it a burden but a privilege to become conduits of sharing. We thank you all, and thank God for His children, givers and receivers alike.

Her material possessions are meager, but who dare call her POOR?

Some of you have mentioned the "great sacrifices" we have made to serve the Lord. We do what we do for our self-interest, though we hope it is not selfish interests. There is no need to feel sorry about us or feel guilty for not doing what we do. There are many ways to serve in God's garden, none more important than another, but all should be accountable.

The Worldwide Ministries Division of PCUSA spends approximately $12 million per year, 26 percent of its total budget, to support approximately 300 full-time, long-term missionaries. The remaining $35 million represent support given to other partners, money spent on programs and training global church leaders. Next month, we'll discuss a bit about the programs and how they are supported.

Remember, God's grace is sufficient for us all.

Haejung & Simon

Dear Friends and Family

Long time no see. Several friends started to ask whether everything is alright with us. They were concerned since we have not written for a while. Well, no news is good news! While we were quite busy with many things, we did not forget you or forget to write you. We just could not find one unifying theme that would tie together everything other than the fact God has his hands in all things we do.

The end of September to early November was a period of traveling for us, especially for Simon. Simon traveled to the countryside in Nepal for his mentoring duties. This was followed by a two-week visit to Japan for the PC(USA): Tokyo, Kobe and many other cities. After conducting a three-day management seminar for United Mission to Nepal (UMN) staff, we joined a group tour to Tibet. Now that we've been back for a week, on November 24 Simon is off for another week to work with UMN projects that are preparing to operate as independent entities. Imagine preparing to send off eleven children to college within two years, all with different ideals and abilities.

During the first week in December, Simon will be in India for another PC(USA) assignment, followed by a short visit to the Woodstock School, which was run by PC(USA) in the past and is now running as an independent school of excellent reputation. Confucius once said that a wise person learns from others' experiences while an average person learns only from his or her own errors. Simon is trying to become wise and learn from Woodstock's experience.

We shared with you earlier that Simon's major responsibility these days is to assist current UMN projects in their efforts to have an active and productive life after they leave the bosom of UMN and won't benefit from UMN's management expertise, its good reputation in the Christian community, and extensive personal contacts of missionaries from overseas. As is often the case in mission work, this phase of growing up, when the responsibility for survival is handed over to the national staff, is a period of uncertainty, anxiety, and, sometimes, resentment. The tremendous opportunity it presents for a more mature relationship and the possibility for the local leadership to step up is often forgotten due to the concern over the uncertain future. Simon's challenge is to help Nepali staff see the inherent uncertainty as a necessary part of growing up. Current political, economic, and security uncertainties in the country contribute to the heavy sense of insecurity overall. Please pray that we may find permanence in God and be able to share the strength with all around us.

Going to Japan from Nepal was quite an experience. These two countries were more different than any two we could imagine. In Japan, the crowded sidewalk flowed smoothly since everyone stayed to their left. In Nepal, even the vehicles do not stay to one side of the road; sometimes cars drive on the left side of the sidewalk. In Tokyo, school children were scraping off chewing gums from the sidewalk, while in Kathmandu heaps of garbage line the streets. However, Christians are extreme minorities in both countries. While the two societies were not reconcilable in Simon's mind, realizing that our God accepts these different situations and shows his grace and love in all circumstances made this year's World Communion Sunday a special one. Incidentally, the Christian population in Japan is approximately 1 percent, the same proportion as PC(USA) membership to the U.S. population. The influence in the society is much greater than the membership count. Christian hospitals and Christian schools represent quality, in their programs, people, and their ideals. God grants power and strength to small number of humble and obedient servants. Simon came away with great respect and gratitude for fellow Christian servants in Japan.

During the month of October, we had a rendezvous with friends from the States. Pete and Gingy Heyler from Missoula, Montana, came to Kathmandu on their way to Tibet, and Milo and Susan Tedstrom from Denver stopped by for a visit on their way back from Tibet. Joyful experiences they were. Our own trip to Tibet was an eight-day affair. We left Kathmandu early in the morning to reach the border by early afternoon. After crossing over into Tibet, the eight-kilometer journey to the immigration checkpoint took more than one hour. Only on reaching the checkpoint did we learn that immigration was closed for the day. Tibet is in the same time zone as Beijing, which is two hours and fifteen minutes ahead of Nepal. We had to spend the night in the border town, which did not get light until eight in the morning.

Going through the immigration checkpoint again, waiting for the broken bus to be repaired, giving up on the bus and looking for alternative transportation were all part of the tour. Once we got going, however, twice-a-day flat tires and no showers for three days were quickly forgotten. Crossing the

◀ At the Portala Palace where Dalai Lama resides, at least used to.

◀ Monks in training for debating fine points of Buddhist scripture.

▼ They are not praying to Haejung. She is simply in a wrong place at a wrong time.

Himalaya Mountains at a pass that was 5,220 meters (17,200 feet) above sea level was an awe-inspiring experience. The Tibet side of the mountain was so different from the Nepal side. Narrow terraced fields of Nepal gave way to vast plateaus and flat fields in Tibet. After a two-day drive towards Lasha, we came upon a large lake at 4,000 meters (13,000 feet), a view only God could have given us.

Now that the harvest is over and animals are herded, all the Buddhist monasteries are filled with Tibetans on their three-month pilgrimage. The strength of their faith was unquestionable. Nepalis and Tibetans must be among the most religious people in the world.

As we spent time in daily prayers during the trip, we became ever more grateful for the fact that what counts is not the strength of our faith, but the strength and truthfulness of the object of our faith. Some may believe in the flags and stone statues with all their hearts and minds, yet the true effect is no more than the power of positive thinking. Our God and our Lord know our weaknesses and through the Spirit leads us into fellowship with Him. As missionaries, we depend on God's love and power that we proclaim in Jesus' name; our faith is not any stronger than yours. We came back feeling closer to God and ever more dependent on Him.

Our surroundings are no less certain than before, but we can continue to rely on the faithful God. Please pray for us that we may not lose sight when the storm comes. We shall pray the same for you.

Will write more often, we promise.

Simon & Haejung

Dear Friends and Family

This is already the sixth Christmas we have spent away from home; in Quebec, Canada, in the Democratic Republic of Congo, and now in Kathmandu, Nepal. We know that our faithful God is present in all these places, but not everyone experiences the comfort and joy during this season of Advent and a new hope for the New Year. At first we thought it was due to the harsh life dealt to them, but we know that is not true. We sang and danced in celebration with the poorest of the poor and praised God for his gift of eternal life with the dying. We also sat in anguish with people who have much material and other tangible wealth and yet are deprived of peace and filled with bitterness and anxiety. It seems the critical difference is whether we have been freed by the truth of Jesus Christ.

We are now living in the only Hindu kingdom in the world, where the king is considered a god incarnate. As most gods in the Hindu religion, the king is also an object of power and fear rather than one of love and hope. While we are not allowed to proselytize directly, we try to share the hope and trust we have in our Lord. Haejung spends her time with the sick children and their family members at one of UMN's hospitals, sharing the "reason" for the hope that we have (I Peter 3:15).

Simon also tries to share his faith and joy while working with Nepali staff of the UMN projects, as they prepare for their future as independent institutions. Management and accountability are often misunderstood as very calculating and cold-hearted. When our management and stewardship practices are grounded on mutual respect, compassion for the needy and humility before the Lord and the disciples, we have a system demanding good performance and responsibility, yet caring and building-up relationship with each other.

This is not to lecture, but to share that, after questioning the purpose of our lives here in Nepal during the early months of the year, we are now at peace. We came to realize and accept that God allows us enough struggles and challenges as we grow in Him, and we are at the right place where He wants us to serve and grow closer to Him. We try to walk with Christ in our daily lives and we hope and pray that we become a little bit more kind to those dear to us, far and near.

When we were traveling through Tibet under quite primitive conditions, Simon was concerned about his glucose levels, as the choice of diet was quite limited and his routine was interrupted. But what a surprise! Throughout the week the glucose level was about thirty points lower than the previous week, comfortably in the normal range. Perhaps the moral of the story was that as long as we stay on vacation mode, Simon is OK.

The playroom a the Patan Hospital, funde by a PC(USA) congregation, i frequently the first occasion fc some children t meet purpose made toys.

Haejung corrected Simon by saying that the vacation was beneficial precisely because we had work responsibilities in other weeks. There went the early retirement idea, and we thanked God once again for using us in His ministries.

John and Kevin are busy with their own lives in Boston, and we remember the joy of having Kevin in Nepal during the year. We hope to see each other during 2004 wherever it may be. Although we do not have a permanent house, wherever we are together is our home. When we gave up a house, we gained homes around the world.

May you also have a wonderful Christmas complete with the joy of receiving the King into your lives once again, and knowing that our God is the truth! Let us also pray for peace on earth and in the hearts of all who suffer physically and spiritually.

In His peace,

Haejung & Simon

Dear Friends

During the Advent and the Christmas season we have had a period of quiet meditation. Living in a Hindu country and away from family and friends, we experienced a period of prayer and reflection. Hiking to visit a village hospital, freezing through a Kathmandu winter, being filled by the spiritual richness of a Congolese children's choir are only a few examples of things that can never be explained fully, must be experienced firsthand. We wanted to share with you on this day of New Year one comforting conversation with God we've had that we hope will nurture us and help us keep going in our work.

We have written often how we pray that Christ be revealed through our lives to those with whom we come in contact. We have admitted how we frequently feel discouraged by our inability to follow through our words with acts of love, and even when we do act, not with complete joy as the Lord commanded. We felt like the very hypocrites Jesus rebuked. Other times, we were also dismayed by the responses of others towards us. They seemed duplicitous, self-centered, and uninformed. People were simply not responding in a manner we hoped they would. Our cry to God was always the same: Lord, we can't do this and we want to go home. Of course, we phrased it differently every time but the grumbles were always the same.

During Simon's corporate consulting days, he used to get upset when the clients failed to act on his undoubtedly good recommendations. Simon often questioned their motives and integrity, but continued on the assignments, since the money was good, very good. In our letters, we shared similar frustrations in the mission field while at the same time shouting the need for more patience, understanding, and compassion. Here at the United Mission to Nepal, we have worked exactly one year since our orientation period, and we've experienced very few "eureka moments." The frustration was not just with the Nepali staff but with other missionaries as well as the offices in the Worldwide Ministries Division of the Presbyterian Church (U.S.A.), not to mention with John and Kevin.

Simon has been working with one of the UMN projects that will become independent, ready or not, in July of 2004. The Rural Development Center (RDC) is a skills-training institute focusing on equipping poor and marginalized farmers with practical skills in farming, forest management, animal husbandry, and basic hygiene. For 20 years, the field staff members were on a good salary, carrying out the training work and leaving the fundraising, planning, and evaluation to senior management at UMN.

Their initial plan was simply to find another overseas donor who would continue to give them money with few questions asked. Simon rightly pointed out that we cannot go on a new direction by going harder on the same direction, and they must take ownership of the services and prepare their own vision and plan. These suggestions fell on deaf ears and when shouted loudly enough they complained about the noise. Nine months after the initial discussions, a very interested but also demanding financial partner from Finland wanted to know how the RDC is going to account for the value and cost effectiveness of their work. After two additional months of work, the new leadership (all Nepali and none from the headquarters) came up with a plan Simon would have been proud to call his own. Why did it take almost one year to get to the "obvious" solution? The RDC folks tell Simon, "You were explaining to us, but we did not understand fully, thus we had neither the confidence nor the commitment to make it our goal. Thank you for sticking with us and not giving up."

Simon has had other similar experiences. Several times, Simon was given a task which he carried out with dedication and made "good" recommendations with the study, which were not followed through and died a natural death. Simon questioned the commitment and integrity of the people and labeled them as political animals. Subsequent reports were always more critical and condemning rather than assisting in the discovery of the truth. For this Simon asks for forgiveness and new opportunities.

Reflecting on this, we found very few instances where we "explained" or "showed" sufficiently well for others to be convinced and commit themselves in the "new way." True change occurs only when it's based on "firsthand knowledge", and the resulting confidence and commitment provides the power. The greatest change to accept Jesus as the Lord and Savior requires true firsthand knowledge, and no amount of good explanations about God and Jesus or the exemplary life of missionaries is sufficient to set others off on the journeys of Jesus's discipleship.

Now we know that our responsibility is neither to convince others with our knowledge of Jesus nor by our model lifestyle of love and compassion. When we are convinced of the truthfulness of Jesus, we can afford to stick around and wait to be used by God to reveal himself to others. God can use our weaknesses and strength with equal effectiveness. We experienced effortless days with the indwelling Jesus, and we also experienced very tiring and energy-consuming days with little true joy while trying to live a Spirit-filled life by our will and efforts. While we yearn for the Spirit-filled life, we are no longer in anguish over our failures. We can never explain

Our hopes for the people of Nepal is as high as the Machhapuchhre, 23,000 feet tall in the Himalayan mountain range.

Jesus fully or be an adequate model of Jesus even for one moment, but we know God can and does use us to reveal himself, and our only duty is to be a faithful presence.

As we start another year in Nepal, we begin our new journey wanting to be used by God so that His other children can gain "firsthand knowledge" of Jesus through our strength and weakness. But in God's ministry it is just another day waiting for Simon and Haejung to live in the joy of "firsthand knowledge" of God and Jesus. May you also be blessed with the firsthand knowledge and be used by God to pass on this knowledge of Jesus.

Simon & Haejung
on the first day of 2004.

Dear friends

February was a short month, not only in number of days but also in terms of time to carry out our duties. But during February, the bone-chilling winter has passed, and flowers are blooming and walking in the midday sun feels hot these days. Unfortunately, street demonstrations and frequent bundah (forced closings) are also back. Among many meetings and trips, we are happy to be able to sit down and write our March letter, all matter of priorities.

First of all, we would like to correct the impression we gave in our January letter that we are struggling in the frustration over the state of our work here in Nepal. We meant to say that after a period of struggle we now accept our role and find peace in the Lord who struggles with us and the people we are to serve. We do struggle daily against the tide of poverty, injustice, and the enormity of suffering as well as the futility of our efforts. But, when we reflect on our frustrations, God always leads us to see one child we can help, one person who wants to learn, and one small work we have done that was Spirit-led.

Without the struggles we probably could not see the small patches of sunshine in our lives. Without the struggles we probably could not see the enabling power of our Lord and the enabling capacity of the people we work and live with. We need them and they need us. We are OK now. It took a long time but now we are at peace and can see how we should spend the rest of our time here in Nepal. We would have blamed you for misreading our January letter, but when the response of sympathy for our frustrations came from the head of a linguistics department at a major American university, we knew our writing was flawed, not your reading.

While we are on the subject of correcting misinformation, we just learned that we will be returning to the States for interpretation assignment at the end of December 2004, not in March 2005. We will be in the States for six months sharing our experiences and reporting on the work God is doing through you and us. We will write more about this part of our work in the coming months. We have already begun to pray and seek His guidance in discerning where He wants us to serve and grow after this term. We hope to continue in mission service with the Presbyterian Church (U.S.A.), but we do not yet know where and what. We will share with you as we discern our call over the coming year.

Many of you expressed interest in coming to visit Nepal while we are here. During January a friend from Korea, a medical doctor in training, came to visit us for ten days. She observed and absorbed Nepali people, culture, and nature with eagerness and an open mind. She was also interested in seeing how our lifestyle has changed, since she lived in the same community with us ten years ago. She learned that missionary life is not one of sacrifice and need, but one of joy, challenge, and adaptation. We hope you can come and see the same. At first, she had a difficult time accepting the abject poverty, very basic medical facilities, and the streets where garbage piles, stray dogs, pedestrians and all sorts of wheeled vehicles claiming same space. After a few days, she saw the people, their joys and sorrows, and the wise culture of living in harmony with majestic yet harsh nature. She also saw efforts to put broken lives back together, one at a time: Haejung working with the sick children at the hospital and Simon teaching management class.

When you come for a visit, we hope you can see that our life here has the same worries and joys as back home. We hope you will see God in the mountains, in the poor people, and also in the mission workers who want to obey God's commands. You will see the poverty, but also the poor who are doing an honest day's work to put food on the table and making sacrifices (investments) to educate their children. Sadly, you will also see the defeated and hopeless ones simply waiting for helping hands to come. You will see the helpers from all over the world working in their corner of God's assignments as humble servants. Sadly, you will also see many modern-day Pharisees, whose daily lives are shielded from the realities of Nepal, thanking God for their "blessed" lives (Luke 18:9-14). All in all, it will be a time to meet God as He reveals himself, not as we want Him. We want you to come, as we will grow in your experience as well. The climate is best September through November, but the weather here is never very extreme unless you want to see rhinos in the Chitwan National Park (then avoid April through August).

You will also meet our bahini (little sister) Gita who helps us with household chores. She grew up in a village where few children went to school and most married early. She is now 40 years old (she thinks), a single mother with four children. She worked for a Japanese missionary family for years, during which time she received Jesus Christ as her savior. She learned how to read at the church and is able to read the Scripture but can hardly write. Gita earns approximately $70 per month for helping us with laundry, cleaning, and other chores.

Several months ago, Haejung asked Gita to accompany her to the children's playroom as the volunteers were not very diligent in manning their shifts. Gita came alive in this opportunity to help care for the sick children.

Not just helping helpless children but to share hopes and concerns with their parents and to stress upon the importance of discipline and being responsible.

Then, Gita met Ambika, a 5-year-old paraplegic who was abandoned by her mother at the hospital. Gita has become the primary caregiver, bringing clothes from her home, knitting caps and socks and exercising her legs for blood circulation etc. We are blessed to be a part of Gita's joy, Gita is blessed to be able to give, Ambika is blessed by the loving care, and we know God is blessed by the love we share. Come and meet our bahini (younger sister) Gita.

Tomorrow, Thursday March 4, is another bundah, with yet another scheduled for Monday. In addition to the hardship for everyone, bundah days are usually marked with a bombing, usually homemade, and other violence. Please pray for the safety of all, dialogue among the people, and the replication of the relationship between Gita and Ambika all over Nepal.

During this Lenten season, we hope to take determined steps towards the command given to us. Pray for us that we may be obedient and walk humbly with God and his children.

Haejung & Simon

Dear Family and Friends

We are in the middle of a three-day bundah (forced closing) called by the Maoist guerrillas. Most businesses along the main roads are closed and the vehicular traffic is prohibited. Many government (white plates), diplomatic (blue), and tourist (green) vehicles ply the road; and also some taxis (black) which have their license plates covered up. Those most affected by the bundah are the ordinary folks who work for a living, the very people Maoists claim that they are fighting for. Personally, I am grateful that I am back in Kathmandu tending to my work responsibilities and writing this letter.

Early in March I was having chest pains hauntingly similar to the discomfort I had before the bypass surgery in 2001. Haejung and I did not think that the pains were caused by cardiovascular problems, but were very alarming, nonetheless. Following discussions with PC(USA) and the UMN in Nepal, I decided to travel to the States for medical examinations. Since I was scheduled to travel to Pakistan and Africa, the positive knowledge of a well-functioning heart became a priority item. With medical advice and prayers of all, I took on a very long trip, 23 hours of flying time plus 20 hours of layover. The doctors are confident that the discomfort is not heart-related and with this knowledge I can live with the minor irritation. It was the uncertainty that did not allow me to concentrate on ordinary daily tasks.

Now I am back in Kathmandu, getting back into the routine. Routine in a mission field is never a routine. The people I work with for the moment are struggling to deal with the effects of uncertainty. The political environment is very uncertain except for the fact that it will undoubtedly remain volatile for the foreseeable future. Their own economic situation is uncertain as they are "forced" to leave the job-secure environment of UMN and venture out on their own. Even those who are continuing with UMN are uncertain as to their duty stations, which brings uncertainty to their family situations. We can all find enough uncertainty in our personal lives to unsettle us, such as my chest pains.

For the past several years, I have been hearing and saying a lot about vision. When I was a business teacher, I used to emphasize the importance of a clear vision, as it defines our destination. Lacking vision, we end up concentrating on the activities that keep us busy, which helps us "forget" the fact we do not have a destination. I find this phenomenon in mission work, perhaps even more pronounced than in the commercial world, where bottom line profit is universally accepted as an important goal.

On the way back from the States, I was able to break the trip at Bangkok and make a quick visit to Lahore, Pakistan, to attend a meeting between the PC(USA) and our mission partners in Pakistan. I was very glad to be at the meeting, not that I was contributing much, just glad to be there! The meeting was to discuss the uses and management of PC(USA)-owned properties in Pakistan in God's ministry.

When I listen to the concerns of partners who have a clear vision of how they are to demonstrate the love of God to His children in the world, we can generally overcome procedural difficulties and find a way to serve the people and God. However, those who lack vision tend to bicker over minor issues and are not able to see the big picture. Based on my training, my hypothesis is that when the future is uncertain or the goal is not clear, the future is discounted heavily, risk-adjusted discount rate, and we tend to concentrate on preserving the present, no matter how meager the present might be. Making a commitment of time and resources at the present for the future is not seen as a prudent investment, but as a sacrifice.

It was heartwarming to see and listen to the ministry plans of educational and medical institutions in Pakistan, which are infused with hope and the vision of serving the people in the name and Spirit of Jesus Christ. Especially in the case of Christian schools in Pakistan, where the schools were nationalized 30 years ago and were only recently returned to the Church in dilapidated conditions, both in facilities and in educational activities. The challenges that remain are monumental, but the staff and alumni are committing themselves to restoring the places of education where they grew in knowledge and spirit many years ago. I know God will be blessed by their efforts and God will bless their service.

PC(USA) mission worker Dr. Carol Brees and the hospital director, Dr. David Sohail, at the Christian Mission Hospital in Sialkot, affectionately known as "the Mission" by the locals, were recently recognized by the Islamic government for their love and care of the women and children in the region. Together with 300 other Christian and Muslim staff members, they serve God by educating and providing health care to a mostly Muslim population, because they know what God calls them to do so. I believe God is blessed and honored when our services in obedience to God are received by this world with joy. Sharing in their vision is our mission, and I was grateful to be a part of the discussions.

Sadly, there are other partners who do not seem to have a clear vision, thus they end up blaming others for their failures. Cooperation and shared responsibilities demand too much "sacrifice" in the absence of a shared vision. I am certain this difficulty is not limited to worldwide missions of PC(USA), and you don't need us to tell you more examples.

Another behavioral difference I notice is the patience. When one is confident that the vision is one that builds up others and is correct before God, one can wait for others to share the vision, rather than to force a solution that usually does not work. Looking back on our limited mission experience, I can see many situations where I forced a solution or discipline to obtain desired results. I still believe many of them were correct solutions, but forced solutions never took root or bore fruit. I do not know why I was not more patient and surer of my own vision or did not trust that the partner would eventually come to the truth. Perhaps my lack of faith in God (Heb 11:1) led me to doubt my own vision or I did not have enough trust in the partner. I know now that I have no solution other than to be patient and share the vision.

As we prepare to meet the risen Lord in a few days, I pray for my firm trust in Him and to be sufficiently convinced of God's plan to patiently share with His other children and wait. Problem-solving activities can wait until we experience the risen Lord together and partake in His vision. May this Easter finds you walking with the risen Lord, and showing the world that He lives.

Simon

Dear Friends and Family

It is already the last day of April. This is Simon writing from Kinshasa, in the Democratic Republic of the Congo. I have been on the road since April 16 and plan to return to Kathmandu on the May 20. I am on an assignment from the International Health Ministries office of the PC(USA) to assess our programs from the field perspective. Haejung is in Kathmandu continuing her work, and we exchange email messages whenever possible. We do not want to miss the monthly letter for April and decided to send a short version from the road.

Some of you will remember the story of Gita and Ambika. Haejung and Gita found a daycare center for Ambika, and she spends a few hours each day with other children with developmental challenges. Haejung "drives" her to the center in a stroller, and has to ignore many cars and motorcycles honking

at her. (The sidewalks have many steps, and so she can't push a stroller there.) We pray for a permanent home for Ambika, but also appreciate the experience of sharing love while she stays in the hospital. Gita remains the principal caregiver for Ambika.

This is my first return to Congo since we left in June 2001, and I was apprehensive about working in French after three years of not practicing at all. As I struggle to recall the French phrases, Nepali words and expressions creep in. And yet the folks are kind and patient. With their encouragement I was able to participate in the meetings and share stories of our lives.

Things have changed a lot where we used to live in the Kananga/ Tshikaji area. There are cellular telephone systems, and internet is also available. Almost everyone is carrying one or two phones, for different companies. Availability of internet brings in the news of the outside world. For hospitals and churches, the communication system cuts down long delays in deliveries and waiting times. Quiet meetings with no disruptions are also a thing of the past, as the practice of shutting off cell phones has not yet arrived. Things remain the same in other areas, with sad but comical results.

Perhaps through the telephone system, the news of my visit preceded my arrival, and old friends and colleagues all came out to greet me. I do not doubt the genuine joy they had to see me again, but many greetings were also accompanied by the usual "requests." They are in dire need. Many said, "We don't have anything to eat, please help us." When I said that I would consider their requests, several of them asked me to call them on their mobile phone! In the past they asked "When shall I come back?" Perhaps they had nothing to eat for spending the money on the mobile phone. The fact that I do not have a phone to make the call did not register in their minds. Also, I sensed that with the arrival of instant communication, their patience for a solution is also reduced. The good old American virtue of instant gratification is taking hold in central Africa as well. On balance, however, it was good to see that average people have means to communicate. With the increased communication capability, we hope to see increased accountability as well.

Our team made many visits to outlying areas, taking advantage of much more relaxed travel controls in the country since the ceasefire. The road conditions were the same as before but most of the security check-points are gone, having moved to Nepal (just a joke, folks) and light air-planes are allowed to fly. Three years ago, I wanted to visit two hospitals in the neighboring province, Kasai Oriental, but had to cancel due to on-going war and the trouble within the Congolese Presbyterian Church leadership in that area.

This time, we left early in the morning with the Congolese church leaders to make the 50-mile journey to Bibanga from Mbuji Mayi. After 20 miles we left the paved road and started on some of the worst roads I have traveled in Congo, or for that matter, anywhere. At one point, a broken down jeep completely blocked the road requiring massive manpower to push it out of the way. The trip took three and one half hours. When we got near the village, we were met by the women dancing with palm fronds around their waist and palm leaves waving in their hands. They were so glad to be in the proper care of the church, after being torn and suffering

No horse power but human power can also move the car out of the way. The power of working together for a common goal!!

under the destructive behaviors of the rogue leaders.

We walked the last half mile to the church together with the village folks. I could almost imagine Jesus' entry into Jerusalem; there were more palms than on any Palm Sunday that I experienced, and the pure joy of the people was moving. After the emotional service of thanksgiving, "evaluation of programs" had to be shelved-it just wasn't the time. When God moves, our human efforts are inconsequential! It was good to put our work in proper perspective. We will return another day to do evaluation. Many difficulties remain, but on this day the joy of God's affirmation and the hope for a better future overshadowed any practical concerns. It was a very humbling but joyful lesson I learned. I pray that the joy and hope become infectious and spread throughout this land, and in America.

We will write a more detailed report next month. Please also remember Nepal in your prayers, as Nepal's condition is actually getting worse. A small bomb exploded very near our house two days ago, thankfully no one was hurt, but it brought our vulnerability home. We especially ask for your prayer during the time Haejung and I are in different countries.

May we all find the joy in risen Christ and have hope!

Simon & Haejung

Dear Family and Friends

It has been already two months since we sent you our last letter from Kinshasa, in the Democratic Republic of Congo. Simon managed to complete his assignments in Malawi and returned to Kathmandu safely.

Due to the pressure of catching up on the work at the United Mission to Nepal and writing the report of the visit to Africa, we failed to write for the month of June.

Those of us working in the development side of mission, not in direct evangelization efforts, often ask how our Christian ministry differs from secular aid efforts. That is, are there differences between engineering, surgery, or management done by Christians and the same work being done in a secular setting? Should there be differences, and if so, what are the differences?

Based on our limited exposure to fellow Christian missionaries and others who serve through secular organizations, we see no discernable differences in terms of professional competency and the commitment. We all have heard about the Christian mission workers risking their lives to serve the people, but we met Red Cross, World Health Organization staff, and Peace Corp volunteers among many truly dedicated folks. We have heard that secular organizations have more professionally qualified people since they have more resources for programs and the staff compensation is better. We have found that the professionalism and competency among Christian workers are no less solid in technical areas and that their professionalism matches up well against any group. Is it just like working in different industries then, much like working in universities, government or in the world of commerce?

During my trip to Malawi, I got a partial answer to this question. Malawi is situated just north of South Africa and is said to have third-highest HIV infection rate in Africa. The Church of Central Africa Presbyterian (CCAP) Synod of Livingstonia serves the northern third of the country. In 1994, the Church recognized the need to address the devastating impact the HIV/AIDS pandemic has brought on church members and the population in general.

While health care institutions were mainly concerned with the physical concerns of the patients, the Church experienced the pains of broken hope, broken relationships, and despair wrecking the mental and spiritual health of the families and the communities. The Synod organized LISAP (Livingstonia Synod AIDS Program) to provide holistic care for people living with AIDS (PLWA) and to demonstrate the healing power of Jesus.

LISAP provides care at the homes of the "infected" through a network of volunteers from the local congregations. Volunteers receive two weeks of training on home care of the patient, nutrition basics, and the counseling of family members. The program aims to mobilize the community to provide the care for the "infected" and "affected" rather than giving help to the communities. The volunteers visit the patients at home and bathe them, put on ointments, and give them medications to help ease the physical pain. They share the hope in Christ with the patients and their family members. The PC(USA) provides funds for training and the medical and care supplies for the home-based care visiting team.

LISAP quickly learned that the nutritional needs of PLWA are a critical component of the care program. In a creative effort to involve the community, the program provides seeds and fertilizers while the community members provide the land and the labor for farming. Food items from these

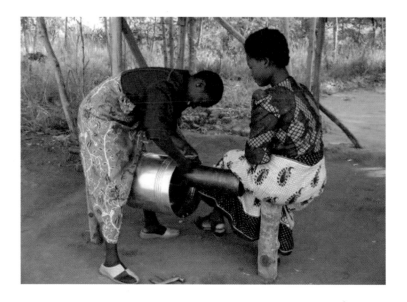

efforts are given to the affected family and a portion is saved as seed for the following season.

LISAP also provides job skills training for the teenagers who will become heads of households responsible for the younger siblings. The Church looked beyond just the disease to the whole family and the welfare of the family in the long run. One such example is the job skills program for the teens who lost their parents to AIDS.

Dr. Andy Gaston, coordinator of the program, shares a story of true healing. When the volunteer care-givers visited the patients and cared for them without fear or judgment, the family and community members began to overcome the stigma and accept the patients again as their fathers, mothers, and neighbors. The affected ones began to care for the infected ones. In fact, many of the volunteers are the ones who lost loved ones to AIDS, and they get comforted by sharing their love. More important than the temporary relief of physical suffering, the broken relationships are restored. We believe that would have been Jesus' priority and our God is blessed by this healing in Christ's love.

We also believe this program demonstrates the basic difference between Christian work and other aid programs: we address the people in a holistic way rather than the "problems," and our motivation comes from "obedience to God" rather than personal desire to do good. Others fight the disease, but Jesus heals the people, not only the "infected" but also the "affected" and the relationships between them.

We will be returning to the United States in late December for six months of interpretation assignment. Although our plans are not firm yet, we want to share our preliminary plans hoping that would also help you plan for our interpretation visits.

We plan to stop in Seoul for a week (December 16-21) and arrive in Louisville, Kentucky, in time for Christmas. We plan to be in Louisville during the month of January getting our physical examination, renewing driver's licenses, and finishing other urgent "getting back" activities. We hope to spend February and March in Denver, making mission interpretation visits in that part of the country while sharing love and stories with our friends. We also look forward to tasting the joy of being a part of the life at our home church, Central Presbyterian Church, in downtown Denver. We will return to the Louisville area, perhaps to central Indiana, for the rest of our time in the States. If our next assignment gets finalized in time, we will leave at the end of June, otherwise we will continue our discernment while sharing the story of mission with you. At the moment, we are free to visit with you any time except for our commitment in Iowa City on the first Sunday in May 2005.

LISAP team, Livingstonia, Malawi. LISAP cares for People Living with AIDS (PLWA) by caring for the patients and families as community members and addresses their disease, economic needs as well as their dignity.

Several of you asked when we plan to be in your area, and you would like to fix a date close to our other visits in your area. Why don't you be the first one to suggest a date in your area, then we will ask others to schedule accordingly. Though many of you already know, please allow us to repeat: we do not accept honoraria for our visit, although your church is responsible for a share of the transportation cost and lodging. We will come whenever you ask, but if you could take advantage of our time in Denver and in Indiana we can perhaps minimize travel expenses. If you are interested in our visit, please write to us and we can work out the arrangements. We are very excited about renewing friendships and making new friends in God's garden.

Kevin moved to New York City in June and started working for Beethoven Piano near Central Park as a piano technician. We thank God for the talent God has given him and the opportunity to grow in new experience. John continues his work in Boston. Please remember them in your prayers.

On this Independence Day we wish you a dependence on God.

Simon & Haejung

Dear Friends and Family

Simon just returned from a trip to Pokhara (Nepal), where he was working with one of many United Mission to Nepal projects that went independent on July 16 this year. Although on paper the transition from a UMN "project" into an independent Nepali organization has been completed, the real "transition" has just begun.

When Simon got back to Kathmandu, we learned that a long time PC(USA) missionary, Charles McKee, went home to the Lord on July 24. We got acquainted with Charles and Anne a few days before we left for Congo in our first assignment for the Presbyterian Church (U.S.A.). The McKee family's service in Congo started several generations ago and continues to this day. There is a special place in our heart for Charles.

Through Charles and Anne, we met many Congolese pastors and professors at the seminary in West Kasai province where we served. Being first-term missionaries "rushing" to help Congolese leaders to become accountable and effective managers of church programs, we were discouraged and frustrated, and we shared those times in our letters to our friends like you.

Charles wrote to us more often than anyone, encouraging us and gently correcting us while pointing to the faithful God who will accept our obedient service even when it comes with our short-tempered diatribe. The McKees left Congo more than 20 years before our arrival there, yet Charles was still a generous friend and a stern but encouraging mentor to the Congolese in "present tense." We were finally able to spend two days with Charles and Anne in Greensboro, North Carolina, in the spring of 2001, before we came to Nepal. We pray and hope that our interpretation journey takes us back to Greensboro to share fond memories with Anne. This letter is not only for remembering Charles. Charles, in his gentle way, tried to explain to Simon the difficulties of transitioning from a missionary-led organization to an indigenous organization. We understood in general terms, but not enough to develop specific plans. During our stay here in Nepal, Simon's work was almost exclusively in helping institutions through this transition. We want to share some insights gained through this experience, and we want to thank God for using Charles to write to us even when his eyesight was failing him.

Simon often tells the Nepali leaders of UMN "projects" that working for UMN is comparable to living the life of a Nepali child adopted into a foreign family. Although they have Nepali faces and live in Nepal, they do not grow up with Nepali values, customs, and relationships. Going from church-supported institution to independent organization (mostly non-governmental organizations, or NGOs) is like leaving home and starting a Nepali family of their own. It is no surprise that they find it hard to adjust to the society they lived in all their lives because suddenly there's a whole new set of rules. It's a frightening experience for them.

When missionaries hand over control of a program to Nepali leaders, or any indigenous people group, three distinct changes occur:

Credibility loss – Whether deserved or not, missionaries enjoy the deep trust of the supporters and the people we serve. Supporters like you are always ready to give us the benefit of the doubt when our accounting or reporting is not clear. Services provided to the poor and marginalized are always perceived as being proper and of high quality. When missionaries are not on the scene, the perception of quality and integrity is reduced, at best. Supporters and beneficiaries and governments demand a higher standard of accountability and demonstrated quality. Demand for accountability and quality is not a bad thing; the problem is that the level demanded is higher than what was asked for before.

Capability loss – Nepali leaders do not always possess the technical and administrative capabilities of the professional missionaries. Most of the governments insist that the doctors, engineers, and administrators entering their country bring a level of competence not readily available in their population. Most missionaries try to transfer their technical knowledge and professionalism to their colleagues. It is rare for the national (indigenous) leaders to have acquired these qualities fully by the time they assume responsibility for the institution. While we are not advocating a delay in transfer until the national leaders are fully developed, we should recognize and plan for this loss. The mission and the complexity of the programs should be adjusted to take into account the technical and managerial capabilities of the new directors.

Visibility loss – Another inevitable result is that the locally managed programs do not enjoy the same level of visibility among overseas supporters than they did when they were managed by missionaries. Overseas contributors no longer receive regular reports from folks they admire and support. While most missionaries do not want to be seen as a source or channel for funding, it is a fact that the correlation between the presence of missionaries and the amount of financial support from overseas is extremely high, even when the missionaries do not actively raise funds for the programs. Contributors from overseas find it easier to identify with programs to which their family members or friends are devoting their lives; it is natural for them to direct funds to these projects, which may not reflect relative needs. Furthermore, communications with overseas supporters were traditionally left to the missionaries, and this remains one of the most difficult areas for the national leaders.

We describe these effects in detail to share our concern with our mission work. The PC(USA)'s method of ministry is one of partnership. Our goal is to assist our partners to establish their vision and ability to own and manage programs to serve God's children with love. In the case of development programs, we need to provide more human and financial resources during the first stages, with a goal of turning over the project to national leaders as they develop. This transition process is a long and difficult one, and thus the process must start right from the beginning. That is, our primary goal in administration and health care should be to help build the capacities in national leadership. Secondly, we must design and develop programs suitable for management by the national leadership, not by missionaries. Otherwise, these programs are not sustainable as growing institutions; they can only survive by permanent life-support systems, overseas funding, and monitoring. We will revisit this issue in greater detail next month.

We are not discouraged by past results, as we see the people of God have unlimited sources of determination and dedication in their faith in God. Jesus also showed us creative ways to overcome difficulties by relying on God's wisdom and love. Our experience with Nepali and African

We gathered to study together the lives of UMN mission hospitals after the departure of missionaries. Strong local leadership and vision are necessary though not sufficient. Development of local leadership must begin at the beginning of the institutions, not near the time of handover. To the remining folks it feels like an abandonment rather than a handover, but we continue to try.

leaders is that when they understand some of the reasons for their difficulties and uncertainties, they are resilient and make proper adjustments in their objectives and ways of doing things. What they still need is the assurance that we will be with them as they work through the challenges. Is it not what our Lord asks of us? Charles was patient with us as Jesus was with him, probably. Thank you Charles, thank you Jesus. Pray that we would be patient with others and continue our journey alongside the people who need us.

We are beginning to hear from some of you regarding our interpretation plans. We plan to be in Hollywood, California, during the first weekend in March; We'll be in Hastings, Nebraska, from 29 March through 4 April, and in Iowa City, Iowa, on May 1. We hope to update you with more plans next month.

In His grace,

Haejung and Simon

October 2004

Dear Friends and Family,

October is almost over, and we will be returning home before Christmas. As is always the case, when we get near the end of our term everything seems to happen all at once. Since the beginning of September we have experienced a mini-riot, subsequent curfew, and are following the surreal presidential race from afar.

On September 1, United Mission to Nepal's security officer wrote:

Today, a sudden Bandh (closing) is observed in Kathmandu against the killing of 12 Nepali hostages in Iraq by a militant group Ansal al- Aunna. The streets are deserted, and the tires are burned in every junction of the roads. People across the country have expressed shock and sorrow over the killing of innocent Nepalese. They were accused of helping the Americans in Iraq against Muslim and were abducted on August 19.

In Kathmandu, these acts led to several days of general curfew, which had been lifted for a couple of hours in the mornings and evenings for grocery shopping. This incident helped (forced) us to reflect on the lives of the people who have little control over their own. Allow us to share a bit more on those who were executed in Iraq.

During the recent past, hundreds, if not thousands, of manpower agencies sprang up to supply Nepali workers to industrialized countries in East Asia (Japan, Korea, Taiwan and Malaysia) as factory workers and seamen. Many Nepalese also went to Middle East countries, mostly as construction and domestic workers. Most recently Iraq has become the favorite destination, offering good pay for unskilled workers because of extreme danger. Remittance from the diaspora is the number one source of hard currency for Nepal, especially since the tourist traffic plummeted due to the Maoist insurgence, which started in 1996 and continues to this day. Since most Nepalese are Hindus and Buddhists they seem to be acceptable in Muslim countries as well as in Christian societies. The job seekers must pay thousands of dollars to the manpower agencies for the opportunity of foreign employment, transportation, and formalities. Each one of the 12 who illegally crossed the border from Jordan is rumored to have paid $3,000. Quite often, the extended family network is mobilized to secure loans necessary for this journey. When the 12 men were killed in Iraq, the tragedy fell upon at least twelve villages that are in debt they may never recover from. Imagine the anger and dismay to hundreds of thousands who have family members in Iraq and how their hopes hang in the safety and earnings of the people they have invested in.

The cycle of poverty, indenture, and the ever-shrinking opportunities for the people of Nepal weighs heavily on our minds, as we are supposed to be sharing hope and opportunity with the voiceless, powerless, and the moneyless. If we are making a difference, why are more people leaving the country in search of opportunities? We continue because we believe that in God anything is possible. We pray always that we may be the instruments of Christ's love rather than stumbling blocks.

This brings us back to the topic we introduced in our last letter. We said that when missionaries hand over projects to local people the Nepalese face three major losses: credibility, technical ability, and visibility. We want to share a bit more on this topic.

First of all, these difficulties should never be used as justification for delaying handover. A better way is to hand over the projects as quickly as possible and stand ready to assist when the need arises. However, we believe there are ways to design and manage the projects that will enhance the prospect of success after the transition.

First, and the most important in the long run, is shared vision. Quite often missionaries arrive with a vision for the people and hire the locals to help with the work. Sharing the vision with the local partners is crucial because during this process we can make sure that the projects fit with the local priorities, culture, and environment. In fact, probably a better method is to learn what the hopes of the people are rather than bringing our own. As long as the vision remains the missionary's, all others are never "partners" in mission; they are but hired hands.

Projects should be designed to nurture the grounds for others to value the services and want to provide more effective, efficient, and local-market-friendly alternatives. That is, we should design projects in such a way that the local people will see the value of our services and products and will want to duplicate them, having seen their value and that they are sustainable within local technology, management, and economy.

We should never, almost never, start a project that will eliminate honest local industries. Consider the following well intentioned effort by missionaries to help secure health care for the poor. Burdened by the poor quality of health care in a community of "poor and marginalized" people, a group of missionaries established a "free" clinic with donated medicines and regular short-term visiting medical teams. They wanted to set an example of Christian love in a poor and neglected Hindu community. As long as the "mission clinic" was running the community benefited, but when the missionaries went to the next village, the clinic could not function on its own and the very people were left with no health care of any kind, since all the others were put out of business by the "free" clinic.

The third leg of preparing for handover is to develop a "business model" that will survive and thrive with local resources. In developing economies, it is very difficult to finance the capital investments (buildings and equipment) locally but the costs to run an institution should be met with local revenues in order for the project to continue when the outside funding is interrupted. Medicines donated from developed countries may be higher in quality, but the locally produced ones are generally cheaper and readily available. A salary scale that can only be sustained by overseas subsidies only creates another economic caste while we are trying to level the field.

A shared vision, a proper business plan, and mutual trust between partners can overcome many difficulties and equip our partners with hope, confidence, and dedication. All this is to say that we should learn to look at the world from the perspectives of the people we are trying to assist. We hope to have opportunities to share and discuss these ideas in depth during our interpretation visits. We still have some time in February, during the second half of March, the second half of May, and the entire month of June available. If you are interested at all in our visit, please let us know. Also, please remember not to send any snail mail to our postal address here after November 30, use our email address instead.

May you be with the Peace of our Lord in these uncertain days.

December 2004

Dear Friends and Family,

As the time to return home gets near, our life seems to be closely tied to the calendar: November 2 (the world held its breath), December 7 (Haejung leaves Nepal), December 22 (Simon leaves Nepal) and December 24 (John and Kevin join us in Louisville). We look forward to all four of us celebrating Christmas together for the first time in eight years! Here in Nepal the Hindus rushed to clean and decorate their houses and businesses by the second day of Tihar (Festival of lights) when the goddess of wealth (Laxmi) came to bless (November 13). We start our days by checking on the appointment calendar.

Yet, on our lectionary for the first Sunday in Advent (November 28), we find Jesus telling us not to count the days of His second coming (Matthew 24:36-44):

> *But about that day and hour no one knows, neither the angels of heaven, nor the Son, but only the Father.(v36) [···] Therefore, you also must be ready, for the Son of Man is coming at an unexpected hour (v44).*

What does it mean to be "ready?" Does it mean that we need to complete the tasks given to us before his coming? And since we do not know the exact hour, we better hurry up? As we look back on the past seven years and ask what we accomplished in mission, we can only say "not much." Though we accomplished little, God has deepened His relationship with us and we are less anxious about our life in general.

We learned to appreciate "sufficiency" over "maximum," an "assist-ing" role over a "controlling" one, and to appreciate the growth from "un-expected and strange" rather than the comfort of "predictable and familiar." Most of all, we believe God worked on us to value "harmony" over "victory" and to think in terms of "we" rather than "us and them," es-pecially with the people we have little in common. Perhaps the command for us is to appreciate "peace" and to become "peace-makers."

Here in Nepal, as was the case in Congo, we follow in the footsteps of missionaries who gave their lives to love and nurture God's children. Our task, as late-comers, is to encourage and assist the people here to stand on their own feet, rather than continuing to rely on missionary leadership and resources from overseas. Certainly, venturing out on their own is an en-deavor on the order of an Abrahamic journey. Simon used to question their motivation for wanting to maintain the status quo, until we realized that our Nepali colleagues feel the same anxiety and insecurity we felt seven years ago when we left the familiar lifestyle of the United States and ventured in-to the life of a missionary couple. Once we began to use this set of eyes, we see that so much of the world's population is on a forced march. At least we started on the journey based on our trust in God's assurance that he is with us to the end of this earth. Is Simon's assurance that it is the right path enough for the project staff and their families to take steps into the wilder-ness? How do we share the assurance so that Jesus' words and promises come alive in their lives? How does Simon carry this out as an accountant?

We pray to be "ready" at all times to be peacemakers, speaking the truth with love, and to point to Jesus Christ as the proof of God's love for and commitment to us. We also pray that we will be less concerned about the calendar days but remain focused on the destination to which God calls us. As we rejoice in the birth of our Lord, may we be "ready" to receive Him amongst us and share Him with those who are not "like us." We pray that we would not try to fit Christmas into our schedule, but to live for sharing Christmas.

We do not know what plans God has for us for our next term. We believe we are called to serve through the Presbyterian Church (U.S.A.), thus we are listening carefully where and in what capacity God wants us to serve. We will have at least the first half of 2005 to listen and respond. A large part of listening is to share our stories with Presbyterian family members through visits during our interpretation assignment. Should you want us to come visit your congregations and groups, please let us know. The best way to contact us through the mail is c/o Presbyterian Church (U.S.A.), 100 Witherspoon Street, Louisville, KY 40202. We will communicate with you again when we get phone numbers and mailing addresses in the United States. The email address will remain the same: Parks@ParkSquare.Net.

May you rejoice in the birth of our King.

Haejung & Simon

chapter III

Life In-between

May 2005

Dear Friends and Family

Christ is risen! We came back from Nepal the day before the birth of Christ, celebrated the resurrection, and now we are waiting for the Holy Spirit to come upon us. The past four months has been a joyful period of seeing old friends and making new ones, including fellow diabetics. In Hastings, Nebraska, we even met a canine diabetic needing two insulin shots per day.

We also miss several old friends who went to the Father's house while we were in Nepal. We miss them, but we rejoice for their rich lives and the eternal peace they found. We have to admit our life in "itineration" is more hectic than it was in the "field." Almost every week we are in different towns sharing our story. Though physically tiring as the travels are, it is truly a joy and privilege to share the stories and to learn that so many have been praying for us and others. We are humbled to be an object of such a support.

We will not be returning to Nepal for a long-term assignment. Instead, Simon will probably visit Nepal for consulting assignments in support of many UMN projects we assisted during the past term. Simon is asked to be a consultant for partner churches and institutions in wider geographical regions to help enhance their administrative capacities. Haejung will concentrate on communication with more than 300 Korean congregations within the PC(USA).

Simon's first assignment is to assist in efforts to "update" Presbyterian Women's health ministry projects in Africa. While the needs of the people and the institutions that care for them remain, we need to study ways to benefit from the communications revolution of the past decade. It promises to be a wonderful opportunity to learn together. Similarly, Haejung's work is to help improve the quality of information going from the General Assembly Council's offices in Louisville to the Korean congregations in order to enhance the impact of partnership in mission.

As we look back on the short seven years since we began our mission journey, two things stand out as "lessons learned." We often think of mission as doing things for less fortunate people. We learned it really is not about "doing" but "being." Being "creative" to find ways to overcome difficulties and see God's love in all circumstances. Being "open" to different flavors of God's love. Being "humble" to leave room for Jesus to work through us.

We learned that one doesn't discover God's love by changing the circumstances but by realizing that God has been loving people everywhere since the beginning.

The second component of being in God's mission is not to insist on our own vision and hope. Certainly, being able to envision possibilities is important, but one must take care not to be fixated on our vision over that of our local partners. After all, our mission is to assist our brothers and sisters to be in God's household and enjoy Him forever. Most of us "missionaries" entered this profession with strong conviction that God calls us to be His workers. This conviction can contribute to the misunderstanding that our ideas and vision are the same as God's vision for the people. We learned to appreciate that God can and does give dreams and hopes to His poor, uneducated, and suffering children as often as to missionaries. It took us a long time to realize that the proper question isn't which of the missionaries has the correct vision, but how we can help the poor and oppressed to articulate their hopes and to discover and realize God's plan in their lives. This posture requires patience, humility, and complete trust in God.

These days we are visiting churches and sharing our stories. The visits help us relate our field experiences to faith life in the pews. We learned that creativity, openness, and humility are not only the necessary characteristics for being missionaries, but also for being Christians. We learned that to be near the center of God's mission often makes us struggle against divisive forces among us and against our natural selfish tendencies. As we reflect and grow from these missionary experiences, we thank God for His forgiving and abundant grace.

Until we decide on a good location to base ourselves as regional consultants, we are working from our log cabin in beautiful Brown County, Indiana. We picked this location for several reasons besides its beauty.

Being 100 miles from the Presbyterian Center in Louisville, it is not too far yet not too near. Consultation with the staff at the Center is only a day trip.

Also, it is quite near Indiana University for our continuing education and new opportunities to work with young servants. We hope you will consider visiting us when you are in central Indiana.

As always, the joy of coming home is the opportunity to be together with John and Kevin. We spent Christmas all four of us together for the first time in eight years. And last week they drove for 14 hours each way to spend two days with us at our new cabin. It is obvious that God was with them while we were overseas, and we all grew to appreciate our blessings all the more.

We promise to write more often as our interpretation visits slow down and we gain more field experiences to share. In the meantime, stay creative, open, and humble before God.

Grace and peace,

Haejung & Simon

July 2005

Dear Friends

Since we wrote to you in May we have begun to settle in our log cabin near Bloomington, Indiana, while continuing to be "missionaries." Simon traveled to Malawi and the Democratic Republic of Congo to confer with the partners on ways to improve their mission projects and to provide some management consulting to the administrative team of the Good Shepherd Hospital in Tshikaji, where we served from 1999 to 2002.

This year's vacation Bible school curriculum features Nepal in which we contributed a letter to the children from the field. Haejung delighted the children in Terre Haute, Indiana, by showing up in person on the day they read the letter.

It is very hot and humid here in central Indiana. We are learning that living in the woods in Indiana has much in common with our lives in central Africa. Living in harmony with God's nature requires a balance of finding beauty in the wilderness while avoiding unnecessary risks, such as dead trees falling on the roof.

One newly found joy these days is to harvest the abundant blackberries growing wild all around us. We are learning to wait for the fruits to ripen before picking. It reminds Simon of the necessity of patience when working with partners. We often get dismayed by the lack of good stewardship and transparent reporting on the part of our partners. During his visit to Africa this year, Simon became convinced that the lack of good steward-ship is not necessarily due to the lack of will. When one does not know how to carry out certain tasks, the will to do it right does not last long. It was a joy and celebration as Simon sat with the Congolese and Malawian partners to develop ways for better and direct communication, better stewardship and management, and open and honest dialog in a "safe setting"-all the necessary ingredients of a good partnership.

During the trip to Africa Simon read *The World is Flat* by Thomas Friedman. Mr. Friedman advances many valid points, among which is that the revolutionary development in communication during the past decade gave power to "small players" to act big. During the visit to Tshikaji, truly a remote village in central Africa, Simon was able to call Haejung in the woods in central Indiana on a cell phone, for about forty cents per minute!

The main impact of this development is that our partners in Africa do not have to depend on us, the missionaries or the church hierarchy, to speak for them any longer. The same is true for members of the community who support the ministries. The communication technologies are finally available to most of the partners with whom we share ministries. But in many cases, the technical capabilities of communication outpace their ability to manage projects effectively and to communicate the results; such things are new and foreign tasks to them.

Another major development in Africa is that large international programs are starting up with financial resources measuring in millions if not billions.

More aid is advocated and promised as seen in the Live 8 and G8 summit meetings recently. At the same time, respected economists and development experts voice their concern whether African societies have the capacity-both the will and the ability-to manage the funds to help the population rather than simply lining the pockets of a few dictators. This article is an example of an economist concerned about this. Simon hopes to study these issues from "Christian economist" perspective.

Our immediate and narrower interests are to assist our partners to find more opportunities to further their own ministries. The specific questions are: How can our partners find a seat at the table where national-level planning is done? How can they gain access to funds for national programs? And how can they improve their management and communications capacities?

PC(USA) has been a major innovator, developing pioneer programs in comprehensive HIV/AIDS prevention and care, malaria prevention, and rural health issues. How can our partners effectively bring the knowledge and experience to help design large-scale programs in all aspects-management and accountability, field operations as well as key values and priorities? On our side, how do we reshape the mission partnerships to continue to be relevant and effective in this time of change?

We are grateful that the church calls us to concentrate in this area of ministry. We are to assist the partners in their own management capacity and development efforts regardless of the geographical boundaries. For the first two years of our assignment, we will work from our charming log cabin in Bloomington, Indiana, and respond to training and consulting requests from our partners around the world.

Due to our language and cultural understanding, we expect most of the requests will come from Asian and African partners. Since this pattern of service is quite new, in fact we are the only "global" missionaries at the moment, we hope to use the next two years to learn the nature and the frequency of demands to decide where to base ourselves after the discernment period.

We hope to use this period to retool ourselves for the type of expertise necessary to assist our church-based partners in their internal management and communications efforts. During my trip to Africa, several partners requested help in starting their own Web sites, which I know nothing about. We plan to set up our own home page on the Internet as an opportunity to learn about the technical aspects of Web presence and to use the site to better communicate with friends and family. We hope to share the details of the site in our next letter. If you have experience in Web administration or know someone who does and is willing to help us get started, we would be most grateful to hear from you.

We will be continuing our mission interpretation work in between our overseas assignments. We have plans to visit Denver (mid-September), Minneapolis-St. Paul (early October), and Detroit (late October). Should you need "real live missionaries" to share stories, please let us know.

Grace and peace,

Simon & Haejung

Dear Friends

This morning I (Simon) hiked for an hour in the Yellowwood State Forest adjacent to our house. The comforting sights and sounds of nature are so different from the fields and villages in Niger where I was working during the last three weeks. I was privileged to assist in the efforts of ACT (Actions by Churches Together) to intervene in the food crisis in Niger. This project is led by the Lutheran World Relief (LWR) and supported by many partner churches, including our own Presbyterian Church (U.S.A.).

LWR has been supporting local community development projects for many years in Niger, but had no experience in crisis intervention. The local partners working in the communities had seen the suffering firsthand and requested emergency help. Presbyterian Disaster Assistance (PDA) asked me to go to Niger and help the local team set up financial and food distribution management systems.

Nine days after the initial call I was on the plane to Niamey. Obtaining the visa took the longest. I kept a journal during the trip and would like to share a few of the entries with you in this letter.

September 1

Amadou (a Nigerian staff person) was able to record food distributions for 300 families on to the database and promises to continue. While I stay back for the ride to Maradi, Amadou and Sani go back to the field. I start on a message to send back to LWR in Baltimore in anticipation of finding Internet access in Maradi. The vehicle does not arrive until 3:30 in the afternoon. We start out towards Dakoro with the idea of stopping in Maradi, a larger town for a quick stop at an internet café. By the time we arrive in Maradi it is already past seven and dark. Driving on a dirt road for another three hours in the dark is not a good idea, even for foolish people. Trying to find a suitable hotel to spend the night, we learn that most of the rooms are taken by the many aid workers in the region. Finally, we find a $35 room with noisy air-conditioner, toilet with seat missing, and a thin sponge mattress that forces me to feel all the skeletons of the bed frame. Worst $35 room I've had, but it's mine for the night. With the air-conditioner, at least I can keep the mosquitoes out, but not the bed bugs. I donate my share to the hungry bugs. The saving grace is that I will get up early for the six o'clock departure.

September 2

It is six o'clock and still dark, but it will get lighter by the time we get out of town and hit the dirt road. A quick stop to get some baguettes for breakfast. I hand over a dollar and get five of them. The dirt road starts fine, just like the gravel road at home, but soon turns into potholes and gullies making the ride uncomfortable. Not quite as bad but reminds me of Congo roads I used to travel. After three hours to cover 70 miles, we arrive at

Dakoro. The distribution team for today and visiting dignitaries are waiting for our arrival. We leave for the village of Farin-Baki as a convoy of five vehicles with four-wheel drive. When we arrive, the village leaders have arranged to display the most malnourished babies. I do not feel good. It is true the photos will be difficult to see, but is this a way to get more aid? Even the people here in the remotest corner of the world understand the power of the images.

Simon threatening a home delivery on a camel's back.

The distribution takes on a circus effect, as there are many people in the small area designated for distribution, and the logistics have not been well thought through. I wait until the dignitaries leave before suggesting some changes. After the noon pause, we try a new system of putting people in queues, which seem strange to the people. But the system increases the throughput by at least 50 percent. Finally, the team is happy; less time spent under the hot sun is always appreciated.

At the end of today's distribution, a group of people came forward and demanded food rations for them. It turns out that they are nomadic people who do not have roots in any particular village where food distribution takes place. We promise to convey their needs for future distribution.

One man is brought to me as a special case. He is from another village where food distribution is not planned. His wife just delivered a baby boy and the family has no food. Why he was brought to me, I have no idea. I suspect because I have different skin color and therefore, I can break the rules. I have three choices: ask the village committee to release some food from tomorrow's distribution, give some money out of my pocket, or just

Villagers in Niger are thankful for the newly gotten millet.

say sorry. None of the three options are good, it certainly is not community building. I ask what they would have done had food been available in the community. They said they would have shared. I reminded them that each family in the village has received enough millet for 10 days. A young man took the sack from the man and asked him to wait. He came back in about fifteen minutes with enough food to sustain the new mother for four to five days. Our food distribution also helped restore the community tradition of caring for one another, even those from other villages.

We return to spend the night in Dakoro. At the guesthouse for CARE International I find a television with a French movie. After a while I realize that it is not a videotape but a satellite dish. Searching for a news channel, I come across CNN with images of people in desperation and confusion. For a moment, I think that CNN is showing the sufferings in Niger until the images of New Orleans streets fill the tube. How surreal to be in Niger helping the people to deal with a crisis and watch another crisis unfolding back home. I am glued to the television until the power goes out.

Getting used to the traditional squat toilet is not as much of a problem as it is to fight a swarm of mosquitoes at the same time. It rains very hard for a couple of hours and it will help me sleep tonight.

During the assignment in Niger, the difference between development and disaster relief became very clear. In development we hold on to the vision of brighter tomorrow and strive to overcome current constraints for a better tomorrow. But in disaster relief, we have to operate within the current limitations for immediate survival, thus having to choose among unsatisfactory choices to minimize the negative effects.

I came away convinced that the disaster relief must be linked to long-term development programs. Otherwise, it is simply delaying the eventual demise. I came home on September 8 and am on a standby for another deployment in Mississippi to help set up camps for volunteer workers from the Presbyterian Church (U.S.A.). Before Mississippi, we will make a quick trip to Denver to share the stories of God's people helping each other at the Central Presbyterian Church's mission fair.

We will be on the road for most of October participating in mission fairs and to work with our partners in Pakistan. Who says the heavy travel season is over at Labor Day weekend? We thank God for giving us these opportunities to serve and the health to endure.

À la prochaine nos amis!

Simon & Haejung

I could tell it was a Presbyterian Church right away. Two minutes before the hour the worshipers were in the pews, and most of them sat in the back three rows. First Presbyterian Church of Bay St. Louis in Mississippi was the place, and I was really surprised to see so many in attendance, almost thirty of them! Exactly one month after the Hurricane Katrina completely destroyed the community, I was privileged to be a part of this worshiping community on this World Communion Sunday, worth every minute of the two-hour drive.

Let me back up a bit. I told you in my last letter that I learned of Katrina while assisting famine relief efforts in Niger. Shortly thereafter, Haejung and I drove to Denver for a mission fair. On September 19, Haejung drove back to Indiana alone and I went to Mobile, Alabama, to assist in the relief efforts of the Presbyterian Disaster Assistance on the Mississippi Gulf Coast. Initially there were no lodging facilities available for the relief workers and our church decided to build tent villages to accommodate volunteers from all across the region. In times like these, it is not just the labor they provide, but the sense of community struggling together to work through the difficult times. This is very similar to our purpose in overseas missions.

All the furniture, clothing, and other personal goods had to be discarded as they were under water for a few days, then spent weeks in 95-degree weather. The houses had to be gutted to the studs before an assessment could be made about whether the house can be saved.

Bay St Louis is one of the most severely damaged towns in Mississippi.

Although New Orleans got more press coverage, I doubt whether they had it any worse than Bay St Louis. One full month after the hurricane, two gas stations are the only stores open for business. Miraculously, the church, which sits less than fifty yards from the ocean, is largely intact. A few floor tiles had to be removed and one window pane and a few roof shingles blew away, but the church itself does not need much repair.

The houses of the members are a different story. The Reverend Ted Hanawalt lost his house, along with most of the members. This is a church with 71 members, out of which only three families remain in town, all others are staying with their children or friends in other towns.

The first time I met Ted we went on pastoral calls together. The first call was at a member's house where volunteers were doing the back-breaking work of cleaning out the water-logged house. All the furniture, clothing and other personal goods had to be discarded, as they had been underwater for a few days followed by a few weeks of 95-degree weather. The house had to be gutted to the studs before an assessment could be made whether the house can be saved. I asked one of the volunteers, a pastor from Huntsville, Alabama, whether, in his opinion, the house could be saved. He replied, "Probably not, but as long as the owners want to try, we

have to support them." This is a labor of love. There is something more important than efficiency of labor in this ministry.

We may not be able to save the house, but the owners want to try. Ministry is to support people, even if the efforts do not save the structure!!

Ted led me to another house, actually a site of a completely demolished house with a sign that said the owners are OK. We prayed together for their physical and spiritual well-being, then moved onto another site.

We met a man there who had lost all his possessions, but his spirit was high and he did not dwell on the difficulties. When I asked him whether he will buy a house and stay in the area, he replied that he would, but "now, I don't need a house with big closets." I was moved and honored to be with a man of faith.

I had to be a part of the service at this church on World Communion Sunday. I found most of the church members were elderly folks, yet held onto their faith firmly, like Ted, and were excited to talk about the opportunities to reach out. PDA's decision to establish a work camp on the church grounds and operate as one body together with the volunteer efforts

already active in the church was well received, and I believe it was an encouragement. I saw the church at its best, I am so privileged.

Now there are four tent villages serving as bases for volunteers to reach out to the local communities and provide a variety of kinds of support. Each village operates in close cooperation with the local church or municipal authorities. We are not occupying forces but are a part of support force for the people to get their lives together again.

These efforts will continue as long as the needs are there. The PDA team remaining on site is working diligently to match the groups wanting to help with those who are in need. They are also educating volunteers about the need to be sensitive to the emotional state of the people who have lost all their possessions. We have also learned that the work villages need volunteers without a strong need to be pulling down sheet rock and cutting up fallen trees. We also need volunteers who stay at the camp and do housekeeping chores, answer phone calls, orient arriving volunteer teams, able to be good listeners to those who are struggling to control their emotions in the face of devastation, which is almost every one of us.

We have committed many errors during the start-up period, but it is amazing how far we have come in five weeks: People are being served.

There is much to learn, but we are very encouraged by the expertise and the energy that exist in our church. One good example is the Westminster Presbyterian Church in Durham, North Carol-

Unfathomable destructions are overcome with unlimited hope, compassion and love.
PCUSA relief efforts at Mississippi Gulf Coast.

ina. They arrived on the scene with all the skills, experience, and materials to set up a functioning camp very quickly. Yet, they were humble, flexible, and caring as a group. I personally learned a lot from them and adopted their procedures for all the camps, and I was supported in every step of the way. Thank you Paul, Dorene, and all the angels. My heartfelt thanks go out to everyone. I have to mention a few homeless persons from California and Indiana who volunteered to come and help, and the church groups who invited them to join their groups. I do not know enough to judge whether our efforts are technically sound, but I am blessed to experience the goodness that exists in our church and the people.

I know our God is blessed. Visit the Presbyterian Disaster Assistance Web site for further information.

I got home at 8:00 p.m. on October 6 and left for the mission fair at the Twin Cities Presbytery in Minneapolis-St Paul the next day. We enjoyed the hospitality of all, especially the love of Walter and Susan. Our personal highlight was Haejung making the debut as a preacher on Sunday morning! We returned home safely on the October 10, yesterday afternoon. In three hours, I will be leaving for Lahore, Pakistan. No, I am not directly engaged in the relief efforts for the earthquake victims, but we continue to pray for them and should the opportunity arise for me to help the children of God I will be ready. Niger, Gulf Coast, now Pakistan. I hope these are correlations not causation.

I hope to see beautiful autumn colors when I return from Pakistan and walk in the woods again.

Haejung & Simon

November 2005

If your enemy is hungry, feed him; if he is thirsty, give him something to drink. In doing this, you will heap burning coals on his head. Do not be overcome by evil, but overcome evil with good. Romans 12:20-22

Dear Friends

Many of us know Taxila Christian Hospital from the tragic terrorist event in August 2002 when four nurses died as they were leaving the morning chapel service from a bomb thrown by Islamic extremists. Now Taxila CH is providing medical and other care to the earthquake victims in northern Pakistan. Taxila CH and the Memorial Hospital in Sialkot are the two hospitals the Presbyterian Church (U.S.A.) supports through the International Health Ministries office. Both hospitals are actively helping the population directly through their medical care and through other efforts of the government.

During my recent visit to Pakistan to work with the Presbyterian Church of Pakistan, I had an opportunity to visit the earthquake sites and see the relief efforts of fellow Presbyterians.

We nearly succeeded in getting to the epicenter of the earthquake until we came to another road blockage due to a fresh landslide only four kilometers from our destination, the town of Balakot. But I saw plenty. Although the damage to structures is similar to what I saw after Hurricane Katrina, the loss of lives and the effects afterwards are much more severe. The earthquake came without warning, it came at a time when the children were in school, the country does not have the abundance of resources as we do, and many of the most affected places are unreachable. With winter coming, the relief efforts and survival will become even more difficult. But the true disaster is the damage it does to people, not only physically but to their soul.

But in Christ, some turn these events as an opportunity to live out the teaching of Jesus. Taxila CH staff each gave one day's wages to the relief

effort and the hospital is offering to set aside 100 beds for care free of charge to the earthquake victims. An additional challenge facing the hospital is that the victims have no place to go after their discharge from the hospital. The Presbyterian Church of Pakistan is making plans to receive the discharged patients and care for them until a permanent place is found for them. This truly is the way to "overcome evil with good."

Many more Pakistani Presbyterians are contributing to the relief efforts. Students at the Gujranwala Seminary are working as translators for the foreign relief workers, and the Presbyterian Church in Abbotabaad, the nearest large city to the epicenter and the site of the northernmost Presbyterian church, is serving as the base camp for many Christian relief efforts, providing coordination and logistics support. The manse for this congregation was so severely damaged that the pastor's family had to find shelter elsewhere, but the pastor is leading the efforts. Members of the church opened their homes for lodging for the relief workers and also serve them meals. I was a recipient of this hospitality during the visit.

Being a small minority, Christians have been persecuted and discriminated against for many years, and we often wondered whether the oppressive environment forces the church to have a victim's mentality and not be able to reach out with the love of Christ. I saw the Spirit at work and the proof that we can all answer the call of service regardless of the challenges we face. It was a personal honor to be a part of this community even for a few days.

I have been involved with disaster assistance for the past several months, starting with the food distribution efforts in Niger, followed by the work camp in Mississippi Gulf Coast and the earthquake in Pakistan. In between these efforts, we have had many opportunities to share the story

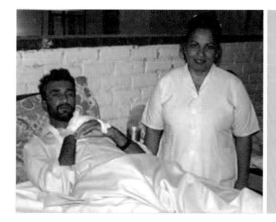

An earthquake victim and a Christian nurse at Taxila Christian Hospital.

of how God's people responded to the enormous challenges. One amazing and encouraging fact is that people of faith are able to rise up and serve the people in distress while they themselves are suffering from the crisis. I have never seen Presbyterians so united in service and able to put aside all the issues that keep us apart.

Personally, it was a period of humility before my Creator, time to grieve with the suffering people, and to be filled with hope as I assisted people of faith to share the love of God with others, some of them traditional enemies. Haejung and I will be traveling to Pakistan on Thanksgiving Day to work with the Presbyterian Church of Pakistan as they develop their denominational office, in part to help the church in outreach ministry and to assist Forman Christian College, which was returned to the church after 30 years of nationalization. We will return a few days before Christmas.

We now have an Extra Commitment Opportunity account which supports the expenses of our mission work. We are very appreciative of your continuing prayer and financial support. The details are as follows:

The project number for "Management/Financial Consultant-Partner Capacity Building" is E051786. Individuals make checks payable to PC(USA), put the project number on the memo line of the check, and mail to:

PCUSA

Individual Remittance Processing PO Box 643700 Pittsburgh PA 15264-3700.

Happy Thanksgiving!

Haejung and Simon

... whoever wishes to become great among you must be your servant, and whoever wishes to be first among you must be slave of all. For the Son of Man came not to be served but to serve, and to give his life a ransom for many. Mark 10:43-45

Christmas greetings from Lahore Pakistan! We have been in Pakistan since Thanksgiving and will be returning home on December 21, just in time for Christmas. We heard that some churches are canceling Sunday service since Christmas falls on Sunday this year. We are determined to find a church and worship God on Christmas Sunday.

We are here in Pakistan to work with the leadership of the Presbyterian Church of Pakistan to help develop their administrative capacity. When a church reaches beyond its traditional "sanctuary" ministries, administrative ability and communication (as well as transparency and accountability) become very important. We are grateful for the opportunity to walk with the Pakistani brothers and sisters in this journey of faith.

Last Thursday we came to Lahore from Gujranwala to visit Forman Christian College, where Simon serves on the board of governors. FCC was established by Presbyterian missionaries in 1864 but it was nationalized by the Pakistani government about 30 ago, and then finally returned to the Presbyterian Church (USA) in 2003. Rector Peter Armacost is eager to receive help from experienced academics to restore the college to its place as the leading institution of learning in Pakistan and in the region. We will share more about the opportunities in future letters.

This month we want to share some observations we find humorous and biting. On Friday morning, after a meeting with professors at FCC, we returned to the Presbyterian Church's guesthouse stopping at a store to buy food stuff, a pot, and a hot-water bottle. As we went through the checkout counter at the grocery store, one young man put our purchases through the scanner, which sounded out each item, while another person sat at a computer monitor observing each item being registered and a third worker counted the number of items while bagging. What customer service to ensure that the computer system and workers are not making mistakes! A more realistic explanation might be that it is a system to prevent improper behavior by the employees.

We went to the next floor to buy a water bottle and a pot. At the counter a man wrote out the slip in duplicate and gave us the original. We took that to the cashier to make the payment and were then told to go to the delivery counter to pick up the items. After a few minutes, another young man brought the items, the very same ones that we had taken to the counter in the first place. Then our receipt and the products were carefully compared before we finally took possession of the items. This may sound very cumbersome to you, who are used to scanning and bagging your own purchases, but it had much more significance for us.

When Simon stressed the importance of internal control systems and the "segregation of duties," he was often heavily criticized for imposing a "Western" system upon a society built upon relationships and trust. Simon was told repeatedly that Pakistanis (insert Indians, Nepalese, Congolese, and others, as appropriate) will never accept such a system. We hope they never have to work in a department store or a grocery store. Come to think of it, Indian-run stores in Congo and the Nepalese post office both had similar systems. Perhaps I'm not saying it right, but I am encouraged to find a system that is being followed in this culture and shall continue to try telling the truth with love.

Then, on our way home, we saw one illegally parked car being picked up by a forklift and carried away. The small Maruti was traveling slowly through the traffic seven feet off the ground. Almost at the same instant, a flashy new BMW 740 passed us sporting a California license plate. It went by too quickly for us to jot down the number. It could not have been purchased and used in California, as it had the steering wheel on the right-hand side. We asked the driver why the policeman hitching a ride on the forklift didn't stop the car. Our driver said that the police dare not stop someone who can drive a BMW 740, especially one with a California plate. I hope we never understand the logic and never accept the necessity of such a truth.

When we neared our destination, the traffic came to a complete standstill. Three lanes became four or five lanes, and motorcycles filled in all the space between the cars. A few donkey carts in the midst added to the chaotic situation. The intersection ahead of us was in total gridlock as cars turning after the traffic light changed got tangled up with other cars not yielding. After a good twenty minutes a policeman showed up and directed traffic, he himself ignoring the traffic light. Finally, we were able to move. When we recounted this experience and expressed our belief that the incident demonstrated the value of a system and the need for everyone to follow for the benefit of all. We were certain that everyone would have gone through much quicker had everyone waited for their turn. But many disagreed with us on the moral of the story: they insisted that the situation demonstrated the need for and value of a forceful authority figure, a good policeman.

We experienced the above in the short span of two hours. We tried to sort through these and reconcile differing opinions on the cause and solutions to these happenings. Based on empirical evidence alone, there is no way to choose one over the other assertion; the choice must be one of values-either you want the systems to be respected by all, the powerful and the powerless alike, or you call for powerful authority and obedience to it.

For now, we prefer to stick to our understanding, which is based on Jesus's saying that he came to serve not to be served. Before we talk about others, we pray that we celebrate this Christmas by serving others. We are convinced all three of the situations described above can be answered by "serving others." May God bestow upon the powers of this world the secret of "serving others" in humility, wisdom, and compassion. Christ our Lord is born.

Haejung and Simon

... speaking the truth in love, we must grow up in every way into him who

is the head, into Christ.(Ephesians 4:15)

It was a two-day journey-a car ride and four flights-and I am here in Niamey, Niger. It is six hours ahead of Bloomington, Indiana, and sixty to seventy degrees warmer. Hot!

I am back in Niger for a week to assist Lutheran World Relief and their partners as they review their famine relief efforts and to prepare for another cycle of crop failures and suffering. Unlike last year, the local partners are trying to focus their famine relief efforts to support their long-term community development projects. While the focus of world attention has moved on to other disasters such as Katrina and Pakistan earthquake, the devastating impact of crop failures continues.

Even in normal years, the price of millet rises throughout the year, from the low at harvest time to the high of growing season. When commercial interests buy up the crops during the harvest, this forces poor farmers to pay a much higher price later. During bad yield years, the price variation is especially pronounced. The presence of funds from overseas raises the price ceiling and the opportunity for quick profits. I am not here because I have a solution, but to struggle together as we seek ways to break out of this cycle, at least for some people.

Government's denial of the crisis, shameful exploitation of the food shortage for financial gains, and cultural acceptance of discrimination against poor, women, and children all contribute to the miserable existence for have-nots. As we shared in our December letter, it all seems to be caused by the spiritual poverty resulting in a chronic disease called "status quo."

As a diabetic, I know how difficult it is to properly control my blood glucose level, even when I am aware of the disease and the consequences. It is easy to find excuses for not exercising and to allow for occasional lapses in proper diet for short-term pleasure and laziness. Sometimes I justify my lapses by insisting that it is my life and I am the one who will pay for the consequences. And sometimes I concede to an elevated glucose level as an "acceptable compromise." But my well-being affects more than just myself, but my family, friends, employer, and the larger community who will bear the burden of my illness.

At times, unhealthy lifestyles have good reasons. Since August of 2005, I have been running from one disaster to another; famine in Niger, Katrina on the Gulf Coast, the earthquake in Pakistan. I was in a situation where regular exercise and careful diet were luxuries beyond reach, and the demands of the work seemed so urgent. But at the start of this year I received the warning sign-my three-month glucose level average was clearly above normal, according to the test called HbA1C.

Whether I was preoccupied with other urgent matters or simply lazy did not make any difference, neither to the test result nor the consequences. It was a wake-up call, and I became more diligent to living a proper lifestyle. If we define "poor" as "inability to enjoy the richness of life that God planned for us," then the cause of my poverty is not material or intellectual or even caused by the social system, but a failure of the spirit and faith that guide my actions. Continuing trips to disaster sites pose enough challenges to a proper lifestyle. But at least now I am more careful and plan better, and I try to remember my limitations, because justifications do not mitigate the consequences.

What kind of test will reveal an objective measure of our spiritual health? The problems I see in Pakistan and Niger I see all over, including our own society. How do you find the debates raging in our political arena, at work, and at home? Is it only me who failed to find in the words and actions of our leaders the humility and compassion with commitment to justice and God-given responsibilities? Did Jesus always side with the powerful and rich? Did he always take the path of least resistance?

I am especially troubled when I see the same type of behavior in our own community of faith, where we are called to speak the truth in the spirit of Christ. Sometimes, a misguided notion of compassion allows us to let unhealthy situations continue at the expense of Jesus, I dare say. Rather than speaking the truth in love we become apologists for others in the name of culture and compassion, often to avoid the pain and awkwardness of doing the right thing. Oh, how often have I heard "Let's wait until he retires," as if it were ever an adequate response! Most of the time the retirement simply provides an opportunity to lay all the blame on the person who is no longer around. Wouldn't the compassionate thing be either to help him retire after putting his affairs in order or to help him find another path?

What are the responsibilities for us missionaries who are called to be in company with the people who are oppressed and to shed light in darkness and pour salt on infections? How do I speak the truth in love, without being cynical or sanctimoniously self-righteous? How do I know that my take on the situations is the correct one? There certainly is no test as objective as the one for glucose levels. Perhaps this is the way God makes me pray

The reason why the woman is asked to carry the 100 kilo (220 pounds) sack of grain is that it is only sure way to get it home. Giving it to men risks the gift leaking to a bar or to a market.

more and search for his will in the Scriptures. I am blessed to be here in Niger this week, assisting with technical issues for our Muslim partners to be accountable, transparent, and to grow in their ability to serve others. Being demanding is an expression of respect, provided we are willing to help in their efforts. I find this relationship much healthier than the ones we see in the media these days.

To work in the mission field is always a learning opportunity. I do not know why God allows disasters to happen, but we can and should always learn appropriate lessons. During the past six months, the clearest lesson for me has been to assess my spiritual health and to speak the truth in love. May the peace of our Lord be with you always.

Simon

Niamey, Niger

Dear Friends and Family

We have just returned from a wonderful family vacation in Korea. John and Kevin were able to join us for a week in Seoul. It was their first visit to the ancestral land in more than ten years. We were able to meet many old friends, quite a bit older, and even met some distant relatives we have not met before. Simon and Haejung also visited Hannam University, founded by a Presbyterian missionary in 1956. During the two-day visit, Simon spoke at six chapel services. By the fifth or sixth time the delivery was reasonably well polished.

The economic and technological growth during the past ten years or so in Korea is truly impressive, especially after the financial crisis in East Asian countries in 1998. Most of our old friends are far ahead of us in professional standing and in economic measures. Many admired us for "giving up" so much to pursue the missionary career. We do not feel we gave up anything but gained much abundance in life.

How do we explain that? We certainly do not know the answer but allow us to share a bit of our understanding. Korean society, like many developed societies, seems to be very linear in their concept of success. It is linear in that people are measured based on uniform criteria and often ranked on their scores. Individuals, universities, and even churches are routinely compared on "accomplishments." This competitive environment helps produce impressive results, but at large costs, we fear.

Reflecting on the past eight and half years in mission service we described our mission as "being in community with the people who are poor,

Simon and Haejung with Hannam leaders in front of a mission house built in the 1950s on the campus of Hannam University in Daejeon, Korea.

in obedience to God with the Spirit of Christ." Anyone who is not able to enjoy the abundant life God intended for us is "poor." Lack of economic resources is certainly a very important factor for being poor. But there are many other factors; poor physical and mental health, voiceless and power-less in the society, lack of education and often-ignored spiritual poverty. We learned that maximizing any one factor does not bring about an abun-dant life, but balanced sufficiency in many factors do. The optimum meas-ure of balance seems to be specific to individual needs, not wants, and changes over the life cycle. I confess that I don't always know the right bal-ance, nor do I find it easy to put the knowledge into practice. I am certain that there is a way to explain this truth in a tightly argued in economic theo-ry but is beyond my ability at this time.

Our work as "global missionaries" continues. Based in our home in the woods of Brown County, Indiana, we respond to calls for assistance from our partners. While the requests are all in the area of management, the circumstances range from disaster recovery to long-term organizational development. In fact, we spent much of last year in assisting partners as they try to minister to people suffering from large scale devastations: famine, earthquake, and hurricane. Simon's work is to set up administrative systems and train the local staff in competent stewardship and clear communications. While these systems do not directly save lives, they are necessary for long-term sustainability of the ministries.

We do not know why God allows these disasters to happen, but we do know that God is revealed in our interactions. In an earlier letter we shared Simon's experience in Niger, assisting in famine relief efforts. At the end of a grueling work schedule Simon was breaking bread with the local team, all Muslims. One Nigérienne staff asked, "Simon, we are all Muslims here, the beneficiaries and the staff, we are all Muslims. Why are Christians working so hard to help us?" Not knowing the proper answer, I replied. "That is a very good question. I hope you pursue the question: you will find the truth in Jesus, my Lord." As lay missionaries, we know we have done our duty when someone asks, "Who is this Jesus?" and we have helped them on the path to a more abundant life.

These blessings do not flow only in one direction. Often, we are blessed by the faith and courage revealed in the lives of victims of disasters. We shared in our past letters the stories of people in the Gulf Coast and the staff at Taxila Hospital in Pakistan. They are but few examples of ordinary people responding heroically and blessed with abundant life. Perhaps the disasters forced them to count the blessings that remain rather than mourn the losses. Picking up pieces after a great loss allows us to see many needs we are able to meet. Unfortunately, many of us are not able to

After a hard day's work in disaster relief, we give thanks for the most abundant table.

enjoy the abundance and instead are fixated on the loss and dwell in their bitterness.

I would be disingenuous to insist that I never miss the creature comforts I used to enjoy. Facing 30-hour flights in economy class, I often think about the trips I used to take in business- and first-class. But when I remember sick ladies yearning for a ride in the back of a pick-up truck on their way to a distant hospital, my discomfort seems very minor. We thank God for the blessings we have and the more abundant life with less. May you all be blessed with more abundant life today.

Grace and peace,

Haejung and Simon

Dear Friends and Family

Christ is risen! He is risen indeed and is actively urging us to share the good news. April was a busy month for us. On April 2, we shared our stories at the Second Presbyterian Church in Norfolk, Virginia, then on to the First United Methodist Church in Champaign, Illinois, on the 4th and completed our visits in Denver at the Central Presbyterian Church (our home church), sharing stories with friends and representatives of Denver Presbytery (April 30). In between these visits, Simon went to Leogane, Haiti (pronounced ah-ee-TEE) to work with the leaders of the L'Hopital Sainte Croix, and participated in the annual meeting of Presbyterian Disaster Assistance's National Disaster Response team meetings.

On the way home from Denver, we learned through email that PC(USA)'s national headquarters has adopted a massive reduction in budget and a large number of staff positions have been eliminated. In addition, the Church will need to reduce the overseas mission force by as many as 55 positions. Forty of these positions are people who are leaving due to "natural causes," such as retirement, and in fact I've learned that 18 of them have already ended their term of service. Worldwide Ministries will work hard to not to cut beyond the 40 who were already leaving, but still, the best-case scenario is that the number of long-term Presbyterian mission workers will stabilize at the end of this year at about 240.

For a denomination of 2.4 million members it represents one missionary for every ten thousand members. I put my accountant hat back on and did some figuring: the budget shortfall of $1.2 million, which necessitated the reduction, represents exactly one cent per week per member (or half of one dollar per year). That means that ten cents per week per member ($5 per year) could double the mission force. Let us all pray together to seek God's priorities. It has been our experience that the members in the pews are very supportive if they just know what the missionaries do and how they can support the ministry of the church. If you'd like to contribute directly towards support for missionaries, please give to the Faith Factor ECO.

We pray that we mission co-workers and the national staff take this financial difficulty as an opportunity to examine and realign our work and to communicate effectively throughout the church. Mission energizes the church and brings the light of hope into darkness. After all, is that not what all Christians are called to do?

Let us not dwell on the difficulties. Simon just returned from Leogane, Haiti, where he was working with the leaders of L'Hopital Sainte Croix, searching for ways to continue their medical services to the poor. Port au Prince can be reached by air from Miami in less time it takes to travel 24 miles from the airport to the hospital by car-an apt description of a country, so near yet so far. The hospital was always on the radar screen receiving much financial support from many churches in the United States. Due to political unrest, the Americans could not visit for almost one full year, and the real situation of the hospital came to surface. After years of bad management, the hospital was in terrible financial health and the future of the hospital is in doubt. Simon was asked to join the first team returning to Haiti after the recent presidential election. His task was to review their financial state and make suggestions for eventual self-sustaining operations.

After a few questions, a few things became very clear:

The hospital did not have funds to pay salary for the workers, diesel fuel for vehicles and generators, nor for medicines and other medical supplies. Our arrival was seen as the opening of the tap to renew the flow of funds."

There is not, never has been, a system of management to serve the patients. Operations and salaries did not depend on the patient income, but on donations.

Reliable historical data allowing an analysis did not exist.

It fell on Simon's shoulders to speak the truth that:

- The hospital might have to close soon.
- He cannot provide any meaningful analysis.
- He cannot recommend that the supporters continue to infuse funds for short-term bail out.

For a consultant working on daily fees, it would have been proper to pack up the bag and leave at this point. But, as a missionary called to be in community with the people who are poor, Simon and the leaders continued on. The part of "love" in "speaking the truth in love" is to find "hope," for in faith hope dies last. Our hope is based on God's faithfulness and the resurrection of Jesus.

We sat down to discuss ways where we can work as partners and not to be anxious about the immediate hurdles we faced. We agreed that the use of donated funds should be tied to the medical care rather than the salary, vehicle, or the fuels. Since the economy of Haiti does not allow for full recovery of costs, a subsidy is necessary, and the outside donations can provide this subsidy. But for now, this is a task beyond L'Hopital St. Croix's capacity. We started with a modest task of recording the number of patients receiving medical care from the hospital, and the number of patients spending the night at the hospital.

The night before Simon's departure, a member of the visiting team shared her joy. "Simon, seeing you working with the staff with such energy encourages me. It is obvious that you believe that this situation will be salvaged." Simon replied that he would be happy to bat .200, maybe even .100. Although he knows that the result will be disappointing 80 to 90 percent of the time, he must approach each encounter with the conviction that this is the event that will be successful. Our Lord deserves no less, and so do God's children! Mission is not solving problems for them but to struggle together in search of durable or sustainable solutions.

The situation we face at Presbyterian Church (U.S.A.) as a body of Christ is just as difficult to admit and the light at the end of the tunnel seems very dim at best. This is especially hard for proud Presbyterians. But let us not lose hope. Let's make it an opportunity to minister to each other. We know many friends who are going through a period of personal disaster. To you all we send our prayer of hope.

Simon is leaving for the Gulf Coast in a continuing effort to tell the complete story of how your gifts at the pews get spent in the hurricane relief efforts and give hope to many people and congregations. More on this next month.

In the meantime, let us continue to pray for ourselves and for each other.

June 2006

Dear Friends and Family

Today is Monday June 19, exactly halfway through the biannual meeting (General Assembly) of the Presbyterian Church (USA) here in Birmingham, Alabama. Simon is assisting the meetings by providing simultaneous translation to Korean-speaking delegates and guests. Not being trained in this special task, Simon's ability does not match his strong desire to provide accurate and complete translation. One benefit of this duty is that Simon is listening more carefully than other participants in this gathering.

On the first day of the meeting, a surprise gift to the Church was made. Mr. Stan Anderson from Central Presbyterian Church in Denver announced that he and his partners are donating $150 million of personal funds to establish the Loaves and Fishes Church Growth Fund to support church growth, mission, and theological education. This generous act is being described as "historic" and "electrifying" and some other seldom used adjectives. Now that a few days have passed, the conversations begin to shift from what he has done (gift) to who he is (faith in Christ and the trust in the Church). Some of you already know that Haejung and Simon are members of the same congregation, and we knew Stan as a generous and faithful elder, but we did not know the extraordinary extent of his commitment and the size of his love for the Lord. We are proud to know him and his family.

Having said that, this letter is not about the "historic" gift. Since our last letter, Simon made visits to Cameroon in West Africa to work with our church partner, the French-speaking Presbyterian Church of Cameroun

(EPC) and to Presbyterian Disaster Assistance's Gulf Coast operations. Over the years, Simon learned that every worthwhile venture requires the desire and resolve for the work (commitment, heart) and the ability to carry out the necessary tasks (capacity, hands). Simon's translation and Stan's gift are the same in these requirements. The work with the EPC was to explore together ways to improve the EPC's financial conditions by engaging poor but faithful believers of the church. Simon trusted their genuine commitment (heart) for this work, and worked on developing helpful tasks that are within their capacity (hands). As a partner, we need to walk with them and give them an opportunity to demonstrate their desire and commitment to serve the Lord and God's children, and then provide assistance to develop their capacity to carry out the work. We also know that we should be careful not to ask of them tasks that are far beyond their capacity, lest it kill their commitment out of despair. We need to be patient and share hope that through hard work, and with God's help, that our capacity will grow to match our commitment.

Last month we shared our concern for the Church's world mission work, specifically the decline in the mission force, which will be allowed to stabilize at the end of 2006 at about 240, which represents one missionary for every 10,000 members of the PC(USA). When Simon explains his work as a global missionary providing assistance around the world wherever the needs are, he is often asked whether that is the future of doing mission. Yes and no. These days, sound management, accountability, and transparency are necessary for all organizations, especially for the churches in developing countries.

Many of our mission personnel working for these institutions do not possess professional skills in administration and financial management.

Simon is frequently invited to come and help. It is precisely because we have missionaries who are culturally sensitive and who have earned the trust of our partners that Simon is able to work effectively with the partners during short visits.

In between visits, the resident missionaries are able to assist our partners with routine matters and help in communications. The answer is yes: We try to provide professional help in administration, just as we do in medical, education, and evangelical ministries. The answer is also no: We need long-term missionaries in place, because doing God's mission is being in relationship, not doing our heroic acts.

Just as the boy's act of sharing his loaves and fishes was necessary to feed the thousands, so was the spirit of sharing among the thousands for Jesus to minister to the multitudes. There's no doubt that Stan's generous gift will be a spark for the revival of the Church, but without sharing and broad participation of the members in the pews it will just be a good campaign or an event. In order to use the expected $30 million for mission that the Loaves and Fishes Church Growth Fund is expected to generate, we need dedicated and capable mission force in greater numbers than we currently have.

Mission is not a campaign, but a life commitment. Mission cannot sustain the ministries with large one-time gifts but requires small but continuing support from many. Let us dream big and plan to double the current mission force of 240. What additional financial support would it take to make this possible? It costs approximately $50,000 per year to support one mission co-worker, including salary, transportation, housing, and other benefits. For 2.4 million members of PC(USA) it means $5 per year per member, or $0.10 per week. Unfortunately for the Presbyterians, "everyone" means only a small percentage. Let's be very conservative and say that 10 percent will participate. They need to give $1.00 per week for missionary support. That's a cup of bad coffee, or a can of soda from a vending machine, one copy of the New York Times (weekday) or the downloading of one song for an iPod. This is a question of commitment, not capacity. If motivating and mobilizing 10 percent of the members is a monumental task, let us start with the young adults among us.

If 4 percent of PC(USA) members would give up one cup of Starbuck's coffee each week and send the money saved to support the mission force, we would have the $12 million to double the current force. To affirm that Presbyterians are missional and connected people, commitment is necessary, as we already have the (financial) capacity. Life-long commitment is required, not only during a campaign.

We are entering the part of the General Assembly when we make decisions and commitments. Orderly and dignified examinations of overtures and resolutions in various committees are over, and now we need to make commitments. May God bless our representatives with wisdom, compassion, and humility to listen to the voice of God and make life-long commitments to live as forgiven children of God to witness Jesus to the world.

We will write again in July from the triannual Women's Gathering in Louisville, Kentucky.

Haejung and Simon

Dear Friends and Family

Our journey continues. The Presbyterian Women had their tri-annual gathering earlier this month in Louisville. Simon was again asked to provide translation for Korean speaking participants - Korean Americans, guests from Korea and one Korean Japanese participant. This assignment coming so soon after the General Assembly, it was quite a challenge. Simon feels God is giving him repeated opportunities until he does a good job of translating, almost like Hindu reincarnation. If that is the standard, Simon will never get out of translation circuit.

Although both meetings were church-wide meetings and centered on discerning God's will, the meetings were so different and so were the translating experiences. During the General Assembly, it was critical that the translation was precise, and the logical arguments understood. As such, it was important to explain Robert's rules and regurgitate the key points before the votes. On the other hand, the presentations at the PW gathering were mostly poetic, metaphoric and emotion evoking, which presented unique challenges. It was gratifying to find those who participated through translations were discussing the speakers' true intentions just as those who heard in English.

Both of these meetings were God-centered, and both were celebrating God's ministries among us, yet the "feel" was so different. Simon believes in the General Assembly, God of truth, justice, knowledge and power worked amongst our deliberations, while in the other gathering loving, forgiving and embracing God revealed himself and encouraged us to do the same. It was another occasion to humbly acknowledge God is certainly bigger than our imaginations.

Simon wishes this powerful God would do something about the cancelled and delayed flights. During the last three trips, at least one leg had significant disruptions. In late May, returning from Cameroon the flight from Paris to Chicago was delayed by four hours which necessitated rescheduling the Chicago-Indianapolis sector. Once Simon arrived in Chicago, the final flight was delayed by fifteen minutes at a time for four and one-half hours and was finally cancelled at 10:30 p.m. Simon exercised his leadership skills and organized six other stranded travelers for a vanpool to Indianapolis, arriving home at 5:00 a.m. the following morning. In an effort to keep the driver awake we were telling stories and Simon had a lot to share about our partner churches in Africa.

Then coming home after the General Assembly meetings in Birmingham, the flight to Chicago was cancelled and we had to spend an extra night. Once again Simon had an opportunity to make mission interpretation to stranded Presbyterians with nothing to do at the Holiday Inn.

On July 13 Simon got up at 3:00 a.m. to make a day trip for a meeting in Durham, North Carolina. Checking in at the Greensboro airport for return flight, Simon learned the flight to Washington Dulles was to be delayed and would cause him to miss the connection to Indianapolis. Fortunately, another airline had a flight going through Charlotte. Simon arrived in Charlotte on time just to learn that the flight from New York that continued onto Indianapolis was delayed. The best estimate is for the plane to arrive at 11:15 p.m., giving an arrival time in Indianapolis at 1:30 a.m. The earliest Simon could hope to arrive home was 3:30 a.m. Mission is exciting, but this schedule is not sustainable! As you may have figured, this long paragraph is written while waiting for the plane in Charlotte. Simon made it home at 2:30 a.m.

Now back to the big God. We are beginning to see that we box in God to fit our own imagination and our personal needs. We heard impassioned pleas for loving and accepting God during the business meetings of General Assembly, and the grumblings about the just and righteous God being forgotten during the Gathering. It is clear to us that God is all of these and more. As missionaries we need to help others to experience these undefined, complex and sometimes conflicting personalities of God. Some of us are so certain of the God we personally experience, we are not as open to God's creative ministries tailored to specific needs of others. We are often reminded that God made us a couple and a team to share different aspects of God to each other and to others.

We pray God uses us to help others stretch their imagination and experience God's heretofore-unknown personality. In this role, our lives are necessarily chaotic and unpredictable, very un-Presbyterian. We find this service also stretches our relationship with God. As we begin to contemplate our overseas base again, we are determined not to shy away from the challenges of new culture, relationships and assignments.

At the end of July, we will be spending a week at the New Wilmington Missionary Conference in Pennsylvania. Imagine 101 continuous years of gathering to hear and experience Presbyterian mission. Our primary responsibility is to share the stories of God's ministry with small groups of high school students. We will also have opportunities to share with young adults about their careers and mission involvement as well.

Our journey continues. We do not know where, when and what of our next call, but are not anxious, just curious. In the meantime, we walk in the woods every morning and enjoy God's nature.

Haejung and Simon

See, I am the Lord, the God of all flesh; is anything too hard for me?
(*Jeremiah 32:27*)

Dear friends and family

Days of oppressive heat and humidity seem to have passed, at least here in the Northern Hemisphere. We spent the last week in July at the New Wilmington Missionary Conference in Pennsylvania. This gathering marked one hundred one years of gathering for God's mission in the Presbyterian Church. There were close to a thousand young and old spending a week immersed in "mission" and we met with high school youth daily and shared the stories of our missionary journey. We thank God and the organizers for the precocious opportunity to hear from leaders and to share with the young.

Many participants have been coming to the conference for years, many for longer than fifty years and a few even longer than seventy years! We wanted to learn about the drawing power of the conference. The old timers were putting out extra efforts to make newcomers like us feel welcome. Our queries put to the families returning year after year confirmed the attraction. They feel safe, comfortable, and experience the warmth of Christian community at the conference. This high return rate not only enhances the quality of participant experience, but also is a proven marketing concept.

Assume we start with one hundred new participants. If half of the participants were satisfied enough to return the following year, 50 will return and 25 the next and so on. Out of the original one hundred, there will be 200 participations for the conference. However, if 75 percent return for the subsequent conference, eventually they would have participated 400 times. Double the impact of the previous situation. Trust me on the math. It is difficult to increase the return rate from 50 percent to 75 percent. True, but the quantitative impact is identical to recruiting additional 100 participants at 50 percent return rate, in addition to more satisfied participants. Which path would you rather pursue? Airlines, hotels, restaurants, and rental car companies all understand the principle very well. The table below shows the power of loyal participants.

Initial Participants	Return Rate	Total Participation	Equivalent Initial Participants at Return Rate 50%
100	50%	200	100
100	75%	400	200
100	90%	1,000	500

When we first arrived at the conference, we were concerned whether we had anything to contribute to a conference so rich with history and dedicated and experienced leaders. As the week went by, we had many discussions with young professionals in secular professions (non-pastoral) discussing ways to live as faithful Christians. We also had time to hear from retired and active missionaries of the church. Their commitments to God's mission and to the church remain solid and clear, as well as their concerns for the current state of mission in the Presbyterian Church

(USA). Each also held strong beliefs in what our mission should be and how they should be carried out. Not surprisingly we are partial to our personal ministries, perhaps because we experience God's hand in the lives of the people we work with and we grow comfortable in the space we occupy in the ministry. Since we are so certain of our call, we are at times skeptical of others who do not share the same ideals.

We noticed we do this subconsciously. Allow us to share an example. When we find colleagues, who are completely dedicated to bringing the Gospel to the unreached people, those of us who are working in social justice and human development area complain that they are ignoring the most urgent needs of the people. They in turn charge that what we do does not require the death and resurrection Jesus Christ, which is the non-negotiable truth in Christianity. In our opinion both types of ministries are necessary parts of Christian mission, yet they can become the source of schism. We judge each other based on our perception of others, rather than spending time and efforts to get to know each other. With the Spirit of Christ, we should be able to build each other up rather than picking on the limitations.

We believe all mission work is bridge building across different communities of faith, culture, and socio-economic classes sharing the abundant life God wants for all His children. Any bridge must be firmly anchored on both sides of the gap. As comforting and supporting as the home community is, one must venture out into new and unfamiliar surroundings, and become a part of the new community. Otherwise, it is a one-sided project where "more" is giving to the "less". On the other hand, complete dedication to the new community without engaging the home community risks running out of gas when our initial energies run out. For all Christian mis-

Sharing stories with high school aged participants at the mission conference.

sions, the spirit of Jesus and its manifestations is a large part of the home community and the pillars to support the span of the bridge. Also, the bridge serves the purpose only when it is walked over connecting the two communities.

We find it ironic that those of us who give our lives to become bridges linking with the people who have little in common with us are not very good at building bridges among us. We pray for the spirit of Jesus to permeate among our relationships. This mutual support is more necessary than ever when our denominational level mission is negatively affected by financial difficulties as well as disagreements in other parts of church life. We should be able to work together in one diverse tent of mission for the church, rather than setting up several tents of narrowly focused missions. This has been our confession, repentance, and intercession. We ask for your prayers for healthy growth of mission in all parts of our Church. Please join us in prayer; it is within God's power.

We are having a quiet August. Simon will travel to Haiti for a few days later this month. But our visits pick up in September and beyond. We have plans to visit Denver, northern New Jersey, Detroit, Bloomington, Indiana, and Champaign, Illinois; Simon will also make a trip to Korea and Pakistan. A lot of flying with no toothpaste for in flight brushing!

May you stay healthy and relaxed during the hot weather and the never-ending violence around the world. May the spirit of Jesus control your daily lives.

September 2006

Dear friends and family

The hot summer seems to have passed. We are seeing some leaves beginning to change color and the mornings in the woods are nippy for short sleeves. Today, almost every channel of American television is broadcasting programs on 9/11.

We add our personal memory of that day. Haejung's return flight to Chicago from Korea was redirected to Minneapolis and Simon's cardiovascular bypass surgery was rescheduled due to all elective surgeries in Louisville hospitals being put on hold in anticipation of the care needed for New York victims. We have recovered and Simon is healthier than before, but the world is still hurting from the experience and the hatred continues. The wisdom and love of God and the obedient servants as humble peace-makers are what we need today more than political speeches and sensational television programs. Lord have mercy upon us.

During August, Simon made a short return visit to the Holy Cross Hospital in Leogane, Haiti, with the team from PC(USA) who are deeply committed to ministries in Haiti. Simon's specific responsibility was to objectively examine the difficulties the hospital is having and make some recommendations. In one sense Simon had the most clearly defined task of the contingent but speaking the truth in love is always difficult. Especially in this case, the messages were directed not only to the management of the hospital but also to the faithful supporters of the hospital.

Simon found two major problems with the hospital, which are very similar to the problems affecting many mission hospitals. The hospital was originally started as a small clinic to provide basic care to the people of Leogane, a city two hours away from Port au Price. Over the years many supporters from the United States helped the hospital deliver "more and better" care to the people by providing more sophisticated (expensive) care. This development meant more complex equipment, specialist clinics, and even an air-conditioned guesthouse to support many visiting teams from the United States. For the local management each of these additions meant more funds coming in and the institution growing in structure and manpower. It is not surprising that the original vision of providing compassionate quality care became secondary to the excitement of new and more. In addition to losing "founding spirit," the management capacity fell far short of the sophistication needed to handle the diverse programs.

U.S. based supporters were sincere and approached their work carefully. They examined whether the people of Leogane would benefit from adding the service to the existing ones. In all cases they were satisfied that their ministry is for the people. Many went further to ensure that their financial support was properly used for the intended purposes, competently carried out and accounted for. Many programs exercised operational and personnel control and agreed to provide salary and program cost support not to burden the hospital. Programs mushroomed, in part due to the close proximity of Haiti to United States, allowing for frequent visits. These programs contributed significantly to the serious difficulties the hospital is having. How can adding good programs lead to a bad situation?

When a program was added, the management and administrative responsibilities also increased. Unfortunately, these well-intentioned programs taxed the administrative and operational capacities of the hospital. Each program's unique purpose and desires of the supporters made these additions more like grafts rather than building on the common foundation. It reached a point where most of the senior staff members were compensated at least partly by the outside programs. The hospital added new wings without fortifying the foundation. Unfortunately, the problems and their side effects did not surface until the situation became dire. Imagine a church where all the pastoral and administrative staff members have divided loyalty between the church and the outside sources helping pay for their program costs and salaries. What would happen to the core mission of the church? Would the sessions be able to govern effectively?

My recommendation was to put all the "non-essential" services on hold and reconfigure the hospital facilities and personnel, for the basic mission of primary care to the poor. All the "nice to have" programs should operate independently or become tenant in the hospital paying for the services provided. Is this doable? We have hope. We have to have hope for the hospital and the people in order to stay the difficult course of rebirth. We have hope for the hospital, not because we can see exactly how the revival will happen, but because we trust that God will provide necessary care for the people. We believe the obedient Haitians and American helpers will put aside their narrow personal interests in specific projects and will come together to serve the people. With hope, humility and compassion we will assist Haitian leaders in this difficult task. Christ have mercy upon us.

During the Labor Day weekend both of us went to Colorado to be with the friends from Central Presbyterian Church in Denver, where we are still members. We met at the Highlands Presbyterian Camp and Retreat Center in the Rocky Mountains, sharing our stories, catching up on times and meeting new friends. We have visited many congregations and shared our mission stories, but the sharing had to always fit into the very Presbyterian time limits. This was the first opportunity in nine years to share without looking at the clock all the time. Since many campers did not know us when we were at Central, we went back in time and talked about our first assignment in Congo. It was a time to experience God's faithfulness and the unfathomable compassion. We were truly blessed to spend the weekend among loving friends in God's nature.

A friend whose entire family has been praying for us for many years shared a story you might find amusing. Noah and Matthew were only four and six years old when they started to pray for us with their parents. They prayed daily for the "Parks in Africa" for three years. When we came back from Congo in 2001, we had a dinner with their parents, Jack and Audrey. When Jack told them their parents will be gone for the evening to be with the Parks, they looked puzzled. Finally, it dawned on them and they

moaned, "Oh, Parks are people! We thought we were praying for the parks in Africa, the animals and all." We appreciate all prayers.

We will continue to make interpretation visits until Simon leaves on visits to Korea and Pakistan on October 9. We look forward to seeing John and Kevin again when we make a visit to New York later this month.

Haejung and Simon

Friends

We failed to write our monthly letter for October. A lot has happened since the beginning of October, and we are just settling in on this eve of Thanksgiving.

We started October by celebrating World Communion Sunday with new friends in Michigan. Simon went to Port Huron while Haejung worshipped with Gross Ile Presbyterian Church. On the following Sunday we bid au revoir to our friends at First Church in Bloomington, Indiana, by sharing during the adult Sunday school.

Simon and Haejung have been in different continents since then. Haejung took the responsibility of closing on the sale of our home, finding temporary housing, and packing and shipping the few items we will be taking to Korea.

"Korea?" you might ask.

Beginning in January 2007, we will be based in Daejeon, Korea, until the end of our current assignment in December 2009. Haejung will serve as a missionary associate in the chaplain's office at Hannam University, which was founded by the Presbyterian Church (U.S.A.) in 1956. The university has grown in physical and academic dimensions, but the distinct Christian spirit is not as strong as it was at the beginning. Haejung will be a symbolic presence as well as a bridge that connects the students and staff to our church. Specific tasks are yet to be determined, but we pray God will strengthen all of us to carry out this vital task. Simon's responsibility of providing managerial assistance to partners remain the same, but now he will travel from a base in Korea and assist Hannam University when he is not on the road.

We will be living in one of the original houses in the mission station built in early 1950s. These houses look very Korean from the outside, complete with the Korean tiled roof, but inside the design is very Western. They have been designated as cultural heritage houses by the city of Daejeon. We hope to live out the rich heritage of the mission, but in ways befitting today's world and its needs. After almost ten years of mission service, we have finally managed not to put anything into storage. We are taking the essentials, a comfortable bed that will outlast us, and the dining table to serve as the gathering table around the Word. The rest we gave away to family and friends. It feels good to be free of many material possessions. The joy is not in having less, but in gaining the lifestyle of needing less.

We sold our house in the woods of beautiful Brown County, Indiana. We will miss the walks in the woods, the family of four deers who came daily to graze in our front yard, the flowers, trees, and birds. But we also know there are new joys waiting in Daejeon for us to find and we know we will enjoy the history of mission, the new community, and new challenges.

While Haejung was doing all the packing, Simon went on a long trip. He went first to Korea to discuss plans with Hannam University leaders and even managed to speak to students about missionary life during their chapel services. He also preached in English at a local church for the expatriate students and the workers in the research park. For a visit without any specific agenda, it was quite an activity-filled three weeks.

Then Simon made a two-day visit to Cambodia. A large Presbyterian congregation in Seoul was making a visit to the country to explore appropriate ways to support the Christian community in Cambodia, and they asked Simon to join them and provide yet another perspective. It was a special opportunity to pray together, learn of challenges, and share hope in God. For a Korean congregation to carefully plan their mission work to build up the local church in the long run is quite unusual, and Simon was blessed to share some ideas along the way.

In spite of the busy meeting schedules, we made time to visit the monuments to the victims of genocides that happened under Pol Pot. During a five-year span (1975 to 1979), Ultra Communist Khmer Rouge Regime (UCKRR) went on a rampage of killing real or imagined oppositions. In one area alone, Cheoung Ek, twenty thousand people were killed from 1976 to 1978. Today, the site holds the memorial for millions murdered throughout the country during the period. Many thoughts went through my mind during the two hours or so we spent at the sites, but two stand out.

The first is that the blood Jesus shed for the victims and the perpetrators of this unimaginable violence is exactly the same blood he shed for me, Haejung, and the rest of us. The second realization is that the seed of such violence and hatred is also in me. We are certain that the people who carried out this evil deed were also capable of loving their own children. It is only with the daily renewal of our relationship with God we are able to live as God's children. Without this constant nurturing of God, our sinful nature reveals its ugly side in our words and thoughts. God forgive us, and we are grateful for your forgiveness.

Then, Simon continued onto Pakistan to participate in the board meeting of the Forman Christian College, which is a hope and pride of the Christian community in Pakistan. The only way to explain the miraculous resurrection of this institution, after its return to the church after thirty years of descending into ruin while in the government's hands, is "in God anything is possible."

Three days after returning from Pakistan, we participated in the mission fair at First Presbyterian Church in Champaign, Illinois. We made it to the Stony Point Center in southern New York to spend Thanksgiving with John, Kevin, and Sariah, Kevin's fiancée. We are grateful for the opportunity to spend some time together with our children before our posting in Korea. May you also have blessed and abundant holidays.

Haejung and Simon

Friends and Family

Greetings of joy and hope as we anticipate a new beginning with the birth of Christ in all of our lives. As we briefly mentioned in our earlier letter, we are preparing for yet another new chapter in our lives in Korea.

Haejung will start her role as a missionary associate in the chaplain's office of Hannam University in Daejeon, Korea. Ever since we answered the call to mission service nine years ago, it was always Simon who received the primary assignment and Haejung found proper ministry once we arrived at the community. This time, she has a specific responsibility of assisting the chaplains and the staff as they nurture the university community in the Spirit of Christ. Haejung and Simon are to be the visible presence of the Presbyterian Church (U.S.A.) on the campus and help develop closer ties between the PC(USA) and the university community. We do not know what specific tasks await Haejung, but she trusts that God will enable her to carry out the mission and will guide her.

In preparation for our move to Korea, we sold our house in Indiana. We are finally houseless and are thankful for that. Perhaps the greatest blessing we received through our mission service is learning to appreciate a simple lifestyle. During the time we spent in financially poor communities such as Congo and Nepal, it was necessary to maintain a simple lifestyle in order to be part of the communities.

During the last two years in Indiana, we coveted the creature comforts and pursued the American virtue of "control" over our own lives. We were excited to buy a log cabin two years ago and have dreamed of keeping the house when we move overseas again for the security of having a place to call "home." But as we prepared to move our base to Korea, we realized the house would be a distraction from becoming fully engaged in the new community. We admit that when we sold our house and other possessions in 1997, we could not let go of the anxiety over the uncertain and unfamiliar future. We stored furniture and purchased a small condominium-not as much for practical reasons but as a "security blanket." This is the first time we do not feel the urge to prepare a safety net ourselves, and we are actually enjoying the freedom of being houseless but not homeless.

What's this have to do with Christmas? We believe God's primary purpose in sending His son was to give all His children a new opportunity for abundant life. He disappointed many by not living up to the expectations, even to this day. Many expected to receive more of the same things: maximum possessions, maximum power, and absolute security. Instead, Jesus offered an alternative model based on sufficiency. He told us God's grace is sufficient for all our needs. We learned in many ways that it was the management of our needs rather than our possessions that balanced the sufficiency equation. Many tell us that they admire all the sacrifices we made. We have gained so much more: learning to manage our needs, the ability to join the poor communities of this world, forging new relationships with friends who carry out their ministries through us, and experiencing firsthand that God provides for our needs. Yes, there are times we still yearn for things we want rather than what we need, but little by little we are learning to be thankful for what we have and value the relationships we can build with God, neighbors, and nature. Blessed are the peacemakers!

We look forward to the joyous occasion of Kevin and Sariah's union in January. We pray their relationship will grow into true commitment to each other and that they find joy in supporting each other. John and Kevin will spend Christmas with us at the Stony Point Center, which is our home for now. Stony Point Center used to be the missionary training center for Presbyterian and other denominations. We are the first active missionaries to live on the grounds for some time. We are using our presence here to share the mission stories in this area, and Simon is assisting the administration of the Center as they plan for next year. In other words, we are called to do the same things we have been doing although we did not know that when we came here.

In January, we will move into our new home on the campus of Hannam University. As we move into the tradition-rich mission station in Daejeon, God will guide us to live as members of the community, hopefully sharing the abundant life Jesus brought us.

May you also be blessed with God's version of abundant life and be a source of blessing for all of God's creation.

Dear Friends

If two letters in one month were ever appropriate, then two letters are appropriate this month. We leave for Korea on January 15 and are expecting the story of our lives in the second half of the month to be quite different from the first. So, we've decided to share our hopes and prayers before we depart.

Tomorrow, Kevin and Sariah will exchange their vows in a very small wedding ceremony here in New York. The celebration will continue in Dallas with more family members and friends. We thank God for the opportunity to be able to participate fully in this event. Simon is going to share a charge to the new couple on behalf of all four parents and to give a parental pledge of love and support. We leave for Korea directly from Dallas.

As we share our plans to move to Korea, friends often ask why Korea would need missionaries from the United States these days. After all, Korea has had a phenomenal growth in Christianity and sends more missionaries overseas than any country other than the United States. True, in all the countries we have visited in our travels on behalf of the church, we have met more Korean Presbyterian missionaries than PC(USA) missionaries. Yet, companionship is not only for the weak. The love and presence of aging parents makes life complete, even for someone at the peak of life's success and full of vitality. It helps one to appreciate the care received when young and the humility of finite human life before the God of infinite grace and power. We would like to share what it means to commit to mission with our "hearts" while at the same time we carefully and deliberately walk the path with our "heads." So often, we approach mission with compassion and zeal, but do not have the knowledge and discipline to lift up and enrich the lives of the people we work with.

Simon's work in Niger for famine relief taught him a few things. To provide a million dollars' worth of food sounds like a big project. But if the goal is for food security for this country of 14 million people, then it has no impact. The emergency distribution is to keep the people alive and keep the families and villages together while longer-term solutions are implemented. This is where we must evaluate our "competitive advantages" and determine where and how we can contribute to the entire process. Even a casual analysis suggests that there are three major components: food production, distribution, and consumption.

Securing improved seeds and improving soil conservation and farming methods is usually beyond the expertise of faith-based organizations, at least for PC(USA). It would make more sense for the Rockefeller Foundation and Gates Foundation, working with agricultural research centers, to take on such a task. Even if they were to succeed producing more grains, then in order to achieve food security, they'd still have to find an equitable and efficient distribution system. Is this our area of expertise? Haejung and I believe the church should advocate equitable policies and help citizens to demand responsible government, but the church has a limited ability to impact political decisions.

Properly storing grains to minimize spoilage and loss to pests, proper planning for the entire growing cycle, and nutritional preparation of the available food stuff are all important issues at the village level. We believe this last area is where those who maintain long-term relationships with local communities can contribute the most, working in cooperation with local religious, governmental, and civic institutions. We need to have competence in nutrition, community organizing, and non-traditional education, or we need to work with partners who do. When the church chooses mission projects, what our hearts want to do must be supported by clear and capable heads.

Do this explanation sound too technical, without heart and spirit? In fact, it has been suggested that we have a "corporate mentality" and are engaged in development activities that do not require the death and resurrection of Jesus Christ, the gold test of Christian mission.

We serve with heart and mind, but we know in all we do the death and resurrection of Jesus Christ and our life in him is the necessary foundation of our work. We do not question the sincerity of our friends in mission. We share here only what we learned in Congo during the period when we were the only PC(USA) mission co-workers in the country. As neophytes, we were really struggling with work, daily living, and keeping our spirits up. We prayed in earnest and complained to God at times. We were ready to give up. Had we been in a place where exodus was easy, we would have. Then one morning it seemed that we heard God's voice. The message was clear. God said, "Simon and Haejung, the command I give you and the work assignment are not for you, but for my son who abides in you. Your responsibility is to obey and let my son to do my will." Friends, that was the moment of assurance and great relief. We serve with heart and mind, but we know in all we do the death and resurrection of Jesus Christ and our life in him is the necessary foundation of our work.

God has given us a gift of the passion for mission and the ability for financial stewardship, which is sometimes sorely lacking in faith communities. With Christ in our hearts, we believe that applying these

Simon's outdoor bedroom while working in a village in Niger. Without electricity an indoor room does not provide proper air circulation.

gifts at the highest level of competence is our calling. As we go to work in and from Korea, we do not know what specific tasks await us, but we believe in God, whose grace is sufficient for all of our needs. We pray for his compassion (heart) and his wisdom (head) and the humility of Christ in us. Pray for us.

In our next letter we will share the stories of Kevin's wedding, our long plane ride, and the settling-in experience in Korea.

God bless,

Haejung and Simon

chapter IV

Letters
from Korea

January 27, 2007

We are now in Korea. We've had a very busy January. On January 9, Sariah and Kevin exchanged their wedding vows in front of 14 family and friends at the Stony Point Center in New York. We moved to Dallas, and 80 people crammed into Richard and Patricia Carson's house for a meaningful and fun celebration on the January 13. The celebration continued another day due to the Dallas/Ft. Worth airport's storm-related closing. Our departure for Korea was also delayed by a day, allowing us to see all the guests off before we left on a long trip to Korea, our new base.

The trip itself was unremarkable except for the length: We left the hotel on Tuesday morning at 6:00 and arrived in Daejeon at 11:30 at night on Wednesday, 26 and a half hours (time change may confuse your math). We spent the first night in Talmage House, which is named after the second president of this university, a PC(US) missionary who served for many years in Korea. The house was built in the 1950s and recently renovated for use as the guest house for the university. We have the fortune and honor to be the first occupants.

We look forward to continuing the missionary tradition of opening the house for visitors and the local community. During our travels around the world, fellow missionaries have welcomed us into their homes and shared their family's lives. This was much more than just providing room and board—they shared the riches of God's blessing. We learned how to thankfully receive the hospitality, and now we have the opportunity to share what we have with God's children whose journeys through life intersect with ours. While we rejoice in the new joys and challenges, we also have to complete the mundane tasks of setting up house again. The few pieces of furniture we shipped should get here next week at the same time the new pieces purchased by the university arrive. We know where we can buy grocery items, but for now have to depend on the generosity of friends for transportation.

We received our residency visa without much difficulty and began our lives as members of this community. Through the experience of settling into a new community every two to three years, we have learned that joining a new community requires a journey through three stages. The first is the euphoric early days, with the joy of finally arriving at our destination when the new culture is interesting and exotic. Even the inconveniences are interesting experiences; many of you experienced this as tourists in foreign countries.

Then comes the second period, which is characterized by depression, in which nothing works, unfinished business back home requires attention and the new community is putting up more obstacles than we knew existed. That's when we question the decision to come, believe the local folks are purposefully ganging up on us, and God is on vacation. This time around, we knew better than to argue with the phone company when they refused to sell us cellular phones because we are foreigners. We simply borrowed the name of a colleague and friend who now has three cellular phones to his name. We have not solved the problem of not having a credit card, also refused by the bank, but learned not to get upset. We have not even touched upon getting driver's license and finding a car properly registered with insurance coverage. There will be many things that make us regret that we ever came here. But this time we know that the period of despondency will also pass.

Finally, in time we will understand, accept, and appreciate the local

▲ *Simon shared the blessings among family and friends.*
▼ *Wedding reception at the Carson's.*

values, cultures, and practices. We still go through these phases but we are less anxious than before because we know now that we must go through these growing phases, and know God is with us through all of our travails. We also learned that a healthy dose of humility and a sense of humor is the oil that makes the transition bearable.

Haejung is getting to know many people whose efforts have made our life more comfortable, and in turn she is exploring ways to make their lives more abundant. Haejung will introduce herself to the students during a chapel service inviting students to her ministry of compassion and care. Simon is also scheduled to share the story of commitment with the youth of this city, some so young their grandparents might be younger than Simon. This is truly a new challenge. Imagine giving a children's sermon for half an hour and holding their attention throughout. Pray for us, that we may be equipped to share God's love in the spirit of Christ.

It has been an activity-filled ten days. Much was accomplished and there is still a lot to be done. At times we feel we are spending too much time on ourselves rather than doing the work for which we are sent. Then again, we know proper preparation is necessary for a long journey.

From Daejeon, Korea

March 2, 2007

Dear Friends

We are well into our first Lent in Korea. Our ministry here has also started in earnest, as we write this letter from Gumi Youngrak Presbyterian Church in the southern industrial city of Gumi. We are here accompanying college students at their new-school-year retreat. They are all about ten years younger than our children, and we have little in common in life experiences. We came with the trust that God will inspire us to love, share, and enjoy each other. Simon is finding his stories tend to be too preachy, but Haejung's stories resonate well with the students. We thank God for calling us into a true team ministry.

Our settling in efforts are almost complete; we have our driver's licenses, we bought a car and put it to good use by bringing a load of students to this retreat. The house is almost complete inside, and we have our

"stuff" with us including a few baby pictures of John and Kevin. The Rev. Insik Kim, area coordinator for Asia and the Pacific, inaugurated our guest room by being the first overnight guest. We pray that the space will be used often to share the grace of God and the good will of Hannam University, which provides housing for us.

Not knowing the road system and traffic regulations, we invested in a good navigation system to guide us. Simon would not dare venture out to an unknown destination without confidence in the ability of the machine to show the directions (as well as the hidden speed traps). Simon finds the navigation system shares many similarities with God, but with one important difference. Once we set the destination, the navigation system shows the way, and even when we veer off the course it forgives and continues patiently to guide us from where we are, not from where we should be. When we think we know better and take our own initiatives, we generally end up paying the price, such as a dead-end, but it guides us out of the trouble. We don't follow the directions perfectly. Even as the machine warns us of speed limit violations, we tend to follow other faster vehicles. We think or wish that the fact that there are other cars traveling faster than we are justifies our misdeeds. We know in our heart that no cop will buy that lame excuse, but we continue to behave that way. Forgive us Lord.

The other day, we found a major shortfall of the machine. Simon entered the wrong coordinates for our destination and confidently set out. Only when we arrived at the "destination" did we realize that it was not where we should be but a place we didn't recognize. The machine can't tell us whether the destination entered is where we really should go, and because we are following one instruction at a time, we tend not to pay any attention to sights along the route. When we arrived at "nowhere" we realized that we felt uneasy at the strange passing scenes, but our trust in the machine suppressed our concern. When we entered the correct coordinates, the machine again took us to the right destination some five miles away. Unlike the machine, our God guides us to set proper destinations in our journey and also shows us the way there. We pray God will help us fix our eyes on the correct destination, set proper intermediate stops during our stay here in Korea, and follow the directions well.

Kevin and Sariah made their first business trip to India as husband and wife, and they plan to come to Korea in late May. We do not know when John will come to visit, but we hope soon. The invitation goes out to all of you as we have a room especially set aside for guests. One of our main talking points is that our mission is to have fellowship, and our lives are open for intrusion.

During this season of Lent, we want to follow the path of suffering and rejection that Jesus took to make Easter possible. We have several speaking engagements this month and we ask for your prayers.

Grace and peace,

May 3, 2007

Dear Friends,

We are in May already, and the unpredictable weather of spring is beginning to yield to warm weather. Here in Daejeon we've had some truly wonderful sunny days with the trees filled with flowers and leaves. On Easter Sunday we did not have lilies, but enjoyed forsythias and cherry blossoms. These days the campus is full of white dogwood blossoms contrasting with pink and red blankets of azalea.

We have been here for more than three months already, and we are greeted by many smiling faces belonging to students who know us from chapel services and Bible studies. Haejung earned the endearing title "imo," maternal aunt, from the students, and consequently Simon is called a "imobu," the husband of imo. As we assimilate into the community, we realize our tourist or honeymoon period is ending, and the differences in culture and values begin to bother us. We know that this is a crucial period for us to rely on the wisdom and compassion of God, as we walk with the

people we came to serve, sharing Jesus Christ without being judgmental or accepting what's wrong as culture. It is always a struggle when we start again in a new culture, but we know eventually we will be able to find our role and place with God's help.

Talmage house is one of the six houses remaining in the original mission station and the only one currently occupied by PC (USA) missionaries, us. Others are being used as of-

fices and housing for other organizations. Daejeon has grown, and this one-time pear orchard is full of high-rise apartment buildings. The mission station is a designated site for cultural preservation, with green spaces and a stretch of unpaved road.

As Spring came and the grasses and weeds began to grow, the grounds around our house were invaded daily by neighborhood ladies harvesting herbs and edible greens. At first, they were hesitant, unsure whether we would be offended by their presence. Trying to put them at ease, we struck up conversations asking what types of greens they are harvesting. When we learned the list included dandelions, we assured them that they are not taking any valuable resources from us and encouraged them to take all the dandelions from us, roots and all. One lady thanked us and showed how earth-friendly she was. She said "We only take the leaves and leave the roots alone. This way the dandelions will all grow back next year!"

Our work here at Hannam is mostly the "ministry of presence." We are not here to do anything of our own but to be helpful in any way we can in the ministries of Hannam University. One niche we found is the "inn-keeper ministry." We have three bedrooms in the house, and most of the time there are only two of us. We want to offer hospitality to the visitors who come to take part in the programs of the chaplain's office. It is a good stewardship to save hotel charges and also an opportunity to meet people serving in different ways. It frees up the staff from providing limousine service to the visitors since we live on campus. For English-speaking guests, it is a time for them to converse freely in English without wondering whether they were understood correctly. It has been a blessing for us. For night-owl guests, we bid them good night at our bedtime and leave the whole house to them. We have not had any complaints yet.

The "innkeeper ministry" has another dimension to it. As we all know, the innkeeper in the parable of the Good Samaritan (Luke 10:25-37) has only a non-speaking minor part, yet the story is not complete without the

Since the house has been sitting empty, the grounds around our house has become a smoking area. Cigarette butts and trashes are thrown about. Our gentle encouragement to be mindful mostly worked!

innkeeper's obedient service. We want our work here in Korea to be exactly like the role of the innkeeper. We pray to faithfully assist in the ministry of mercy the Samaritan shows. We want to be faithful innkeepers, starting with the ones who spend a night in our guest room.

At the end of this month, Kevin and Sariah plan to come to Korea, their delayed honeymoon. We plan to travel in Japan with them, extending our time together. Simon, however, will travel to the States for ten days, leaving Haejung more time to be with the kids.

Take care of yourselves in this season of change.

Haejung and Simon

Martharization

It has been a while, hasn't it? We kept putting off the letter, waiting for an event worth a letter to happen, but nothing came up. During the past three months our days were occupied with mostly routine things that demand our time and attention. We completed our first semester at Hannam University without major incident and Haejung is getting to know more students.

Kevin and Sariah came to visit us as their delayed honeymoon and a market survey for Sariah's fashion line. Did we tell you that Sariah is an up-and-coming fashion designer who has her own label? It was a joy to see her designs on display at high fashion houses in Tokyo. While Kevin and Sariah enjoyed their time in Korea with Haejung, Simon accompanied a team of administrative staff at Hannam on their study trip to the States. They took a few days of their trip to do volunteer services with the South Louisiana Presbytery's "Project Homecoming," the Church's Katrina recovery effort.

The unskilled team of nine could not do much practical work in three days, but the message of solidarity was powerfully delivered across the Pacific. It was a moving and meaningful experience for the people of Louisiana and the visiting team alike. On his way back from New Orleans, Simon joined the rest of the family in Tokyo and spent a week touring Japan.

Among the historic and scenic sites, we visited Hiroshima, the city where the first atomic bomb was exploded in August 1945. We spent a day at the site of the explosion and the museum among many primary and middle school students on their school field trip. Our prayer is that the children would learn to denounce violence and mass killing under any circumstances and renounce hatred and revenge. We will never forget the images of destruction and suffering, and we pray that these images will push us towards God's grace and peace in moments of crucial decision.

Since last week, all Korea is in shock at the taking of 23 members of a "short-term mission" group from a Korean church by the Taliban in Afghanistan. The subsequent cold-blooded slaying of the group's leader increased the already hot emotions of the Koreans, especially the Korean Christians. The hostage situation has brought to the surface the strong undercurrent of a negative attitude towards the Christians on the part of the non-Christian population (70 percent), which borders on overt hatred. While we are not comfortable with the "occupying force" aggressiveness of Korean Christians in world mission, we are saddened to see the video footage of the sacrilegious activities towards another religion and culture. The overwhelming majority of the postings on the discussion boards on the Internet puts the blame squarely on the hostages and the church who sent them as well as the lager Christian community.

How have the Korean churches, well known for their devotion and zeal, who send more missionaries overseas than any country other than the United States, come to be despised and ridiculed by so many? We certainly do not have insights into the causes of the current situation. Last Sunday's lectionary readings (Luke 10: 38- 42) spoke to our hearts and at least partly addressed the question. In a well-known story, Martha invites Jesus and his followers into her house for a meal and goes to prepare a meal.

While working hard in the kitchen, she finds that her sister Mary is sitting at the feet of Jesus and neglecting the work in the kitchen. Being resentful, Martha complaints to Jesus that Mary is not helping. Instead, Jesus rebukes Martha for being distracted and praises Mary for finding the important thing. Jesus probably knew that Martha was seeking "recognition" from Jesus for her dedication to him, but he warns against the "works" running ahead of the "relationship." We cannot purchase the close relationship with Jesus with our works no matter how eager and capable we are. Jesus tells us to keep our focus on a solid relationship with Jesus, and draw energy from that relationship, not vice versa. We believe some of the Korean Christians run ahead of their energy supply line due to their desire to "serve Christ"; Simon calls this syndrome "Martharization."

The miraculous growth of the Korean churches during the last 50 years parallels the economic miracle of the country. Simon remembers a lecture he gave about 20 years ago to a group of seminary students. The economic miracle of Korea was like instead of waiting for a baby to mature in the mother's womb over nine months, the leaders are asking nine women to produce a baby in one month. The miracle is that it was happening.

As many of us know, the miracle did not happen according to the natural law of economics but relied on a few large corporations to lead the export drive of products and human resources. The distribution of benefits was not fair, and many in power fell victim to the temptations of converting the public wealth to personal gains. About ten years ago, the country went through a painful correction at a cost of many ruined lives. To this day, the enmity between the haves and have-nots pains the society.

In the same way, the growth of Korean churches gave birth to many powerful megachurches, and they led the "export drive" of Korean Christianity to new markets, and many of these new markets were majority-Muslim countries. This export strategy became a growth path for local congregations and a sign that they have "arrived." We do not suggest that this is all bad, and we note that not all churches are doing this. But this growth pattern is easily recognizable, and it's often associated with a kind of mission that pays no regard to churches that Jesus Christ has already planted in the mission field. Even within Korea, establishing a satellite congregation of a megachurch in a community leads to closure of many smaller congregations in that community, for the brand name of the mega-church draws members from smaller churches rather than reaching the unchurched. Small-town merchants facing the encroachment of mega-stores understand this situation well.

During our short missionary career, we've learned that we should never go into a mission field with the attitude that we are "bringing God" into the darkness, for God has been there since the beginning, is there now, and will be there long after we are gone. Those who think that they are "bringing God" can often act like God themselves.

We pray for the family of the victim and the 22 remaining in Afghanistan. We also pray that this be the seminal event that brings all of us believers on our knees and helps us to become mature in our relationships with Jesus and other children of God, avoiding Martharization. We ask you to pray for the grieving and also for the Korean churches.

Grace and peace to you all.

Dear Friends

No news is good news, right? Well, to a point. We have not written for almost three months! We started several times and got pulled away to meet more pressing deadlines, and some of the work we are engaged in should not be discussed prematurely. We are already half finished with the fall semester, and Simon has been on the road a lot. Simon made two trips to the States, is preparing for the third, and squeezed in trips to Pakistan and Japan in-between.

No complaints, just glad to be serving where the church needs us. On October 20 we had the honor of greeting the Executive Director Linda Valentine (of the Presbyterian Church (U.S.A.)'s General Assembly Council) at the Inchon International Airport as she entered Korea, the final stop of her Asian tour. It was a joy to meet Chris Valentine, who came to Korea as the "trailing spouse" just as Simon is staying in Korea thanks to Haejung's appointment at Hannam University. Chris and Linda's trip was guided by the expert hands of our area coordinator, the Rev. Dr. Insik Kim. Since all other PC(USA) missionaries who serve in Korea are in the States visiting churches as a part of the Mission Challenge '07, our bid to come to the airport was successful.

Simon had met Linda before, but it was the first opportunity to spend some time together and discuss topics of our mutual interest, mission. One of Linda's questions was what should the role of a missionary from PC(USA) be in places like Korea where the church is so strong and the economy is vibrant. Simon's answer was that his mission is to be a lubricant to help many of our historical partners to cooperate and work together in mission—not lubricating, but being lubricant. Linda asked, "Being a diplomat, rather than exercising authority?" Simon replied, "Perhaps more like being a doormat."

We remember our good friend and the past moderator of our church, Syngman Rhee, telling us that mission is building bridges between people and Christ and between believers and non-believers. Simon's mission is shoring up the bridge among believers, our partners. Syngman continued to say that in order for a bridge to function it must be firmly anchored on both sides of the divide, and the bridge must be walked all over to serve its purpose. We pray a doormat serves a similar purpose. Linda's visit was a visible support of our partners in Korea.

President Lee of Hannam thanked the Church for opening of the school 51 years ago and for continuing to support the university with prayer to this day.

Simon has been assisting the leadership in Louisville as they study ways to deliver relief and development ministries effectively and efficiently while helping our partners to strengthen themselves so that they can eventually handle the challenges themselves. At the same time, the folks at PC(USA) headquarters realize the desire of its members for hands-on mission at home and abroad. The challenge that faces the leadership is to design and carry out the denomination level mission in such a way as to encourage and support both grassroots, hands-on mission of PC(USA) members and our partners.

Simon learned during the past several months that the true and only way to support our partners is to address the root causes of the pain: poverty and injustice. Being cured of a sickness is only the first step in the jour-

With Moderator Syngman Rhee at the General Assembly 2001 in Louisville, Kentucky.

ney to an abundant life. The journey starts with the hope of abundant life and seeing the possibilities. Next come physical and spiritual nourishment, harmonious relationships with other people and the environment, and the ability to chart and walk the path towards the abundant life. There is a place for everyone to help. The local partners themselves, individual members, congregations of our church, mission fellowships, and the denominational staff all have their place to serve. At the end of the day, we must seek ways for the children of God to manage their own pain with the grace of God. Our work is only to assist in the journey. Many of our fellow missionaries visiting churches around the country during this month are telling their own versions of this story.

We want to be the lubricant for the dynamic relationship among the parts of our church to bring love and peace to suffering communities, including parts of our own Presbyterian Church (USA). We shall start in the immediate community where God put us for now. Pray that we would be the faithful and humble servants to bring peace into our immediate neighborhood.

Hannam University had the honor of hosting the entourage with a welcome dinner.

Beginning on December 11 we will be spending about five weeks at the Stony Point Center in New York. We will be a part of a team to transform several mission visions put forward for the Center into specific operational plans. These plans will be presented to the mission decision-making body, the General Assembly Council, for review and approval. Stony Point is a national conference center of the PC(USA), with a rich mission history. It used to be the primary missionary training center and home for many missionaries on home assignment, including us. It is an honor to be a part of the team to envision and shape the new mission for the Center. We hope to see some of you during the time of our stay at the Stony Point Center.

Perhaps next year, we can share more details of our work in Korea and elsewhere. We hope to write again before Thanksgiving.

Grace and peace,

Haejung and Simon

For there is one God and one mediator between God and men, the man Christ Jesus, who gave himself as a ransom for all men (1 Timothy 2:5-6).

We have just arrived at Stony Point Center in New York. We left here exactly eleven month ago to start our assignment at Hannam University in Korea. We are now back for a month-long assignment to explore what God has planned for this conference center and for us. We will be able to see John, Sariah, and Kevin during our stay here as an added bonus.

As we celebrate Advent and await the Prince of Peace, we are especially mindful of Jesus as the mediator. Our work in Korea is mostly a ministry of presence rather than getting things done. It does not require skilled time management, eloquent persuasion, and unlimited physical energy. But the ministry requires confidence in God borrowing from his patience and Christ's spirit and humility. One must find peace with the role given by God and the feeling of going around in circles, not making the progress we all want.

In our weekly Bible study we have been studying the life of Moses, and how God molded him as his representative to the Hebrew nation. We were also invited to relate our role to Moses' responsibilities and experiences and grow together. At first the members of the study group were uneasy for not having the "correct answer" presented to them, but as the sessions progressed and we learned to trust each other to share our uncertainties and our personal desires that are at variance with what we know to be God's desire. As we learned to admit our selfishness and began to support each other's journey to become more compatible with God, we all began our journey of being mediators, Christ's disciples.

We do not want to review the Exodus in this missive; most of you are already familiar with the story. Moses wanted to be the leader on his own right at age 40 and had to spend 40 more years undoing what he had done. God called him to be his "messenger" to the Hebrew people and to Pharaoh. He only had to obey God, which he did reluctantly. We can also be God's messengers without genuine concern for the people, like Moses before the Pharaoh, like Jonah to the people of Nineveh. Haejung and I, as missionaries or fellow members of the Church, at one time or another spoke the word of God without the spirit of a mediator but one of a judge. We were calling on the authority of God to support our actions and thoughts. It may have given the appearance of good servants, and it may have helped us to experience the power and love of God ourselves but did not bring others closer to being in harmony with God.

Then when God's anger burned against the rebellious people of Israel, Moses uses his close relationship with God to plead for the people, even asking that his own name be stricken from the book of life if God were to refuse to forgive. Clearly Moses grew in his relationship with God and with the people. We wondered whether there were moments like this in our life as missionaries during the past ten years. Yes, we started as mission co-workers for the Presbyterian Church (USA) on January 1, 1998. Towards the end of the Bible study sessions we began to seek God's true will rather than bending God's will to fit ours. We hope this is not just a temporary change, but a new direction for us; being intercessors for the people rather than just messengers to the people.

Our work in Korea requires us to be active peacemakers. We have had no formal training in mediation, bringing people in dispute to a harmonious coexistence. Hannam University is a Christian university, but Christians are a minority in the student body, which is approximately 30 percent Christian, and this is about the same as the Korean population in general. Therefore, distinctive Christian activities such as mandatory chapel services create dissatisfaction and tension among the members of the school community. What is our place in this situation? How can we help start a dialogue and help develop mutual respect? I have also learned that the consulting work on management issues that I have been doing for our partners over the last few years mostly consists of closing the gaps between our desires and expectations rather than providing technical solutions. The work calls for our genuine concern for the people rather than problem-solving expertise. Why should that have taken ten years for us to learn? I'm not sure, but better late than never.

As we spend Christmas here at Stony Point, we hope to welcome the mediator Jesus into our midst. We learned the Spirit of Christ is the only true bridge that can close the gap between God and us and among us. May you also be a mediator in your own family, church, and the community in the coming year. Most of all, may you welcome the baby Jesus into your lives as the mediator between you and our God.

Merry Christmas and a happy New Year.

Dear Friends ·

Where were you on January 2, 1998? Not many will remember this day as clearly as the day President Kennedy was assassinated or when our country was attacked by terrorists on September 11, 2001. On January 2, 1998, Haejung and I reported to our mission personnel orientation in Santa Fe and learned that our appointment with the South African Council of Churches has been withdrawn. That's how we started the ten years of our amazing journey as mission co-workers with the Presbyterian Church (U.S.A.).

On January 2, 2008, I was introduced to the staff of Presbyterian Disaster Assistance (PDA) as the new interim coordinator. I don't dare to think about what the news on January 2, 2018 will be. We can never "figure out" God's sense of humor and the power of the Spirit to guide us through experiences never imagined possible. My new assignment with PDA is a surprise. It's both sudden and temporary, and I pray very temporary at that. Some have already asked whether we have left the mission service. No, I am "on loan," and Haejung will return to her duties at Hannam University later this month.

I probably should explain what "PDA" and "interim" mean for those of you who are not familiar with the ministries and structure of the PC(USA). For those who find my simplistic explanation to be alarming, I ask for your prayers. Presbyterian Disaster Assistance is the ministry program that helps people suffering from the effects of disastrous events such as tornados and hurricanes, as well as man-made events such as war, famine, and other violence. PDA is usually the church's first responder and the primary channel for church members to share their expression of compassion and solidarity with the "poor and weak" as God's children. I am too new on the job to give you a good overview of PDA. I am grateful to have assisted in the field activities of PDA over the years and have seen the responses of church members and those we assisted. I invite you to visit PDA's Web site to learn more about our ministries.

The term "interim" may be foreign to many of you. When there is a leadership change in our Church we appoint an "interim" to guide the members through the process. My role as the interim coordinator is to ensure that the core ministries of PDA continue with little disruption while preparing for PDA's future. It is like moving into a new house. There are so many fond memories that we would like to carry to the new house, but one must evaluate items based on how useful they are and how they will fit into the new house, rather than how it was in the old house. While we must choose carefully and discard the unnecessary ones, we also must identify the new items we will need in the new house. We have begun to identify the mission and vision of PDA and examine the things we do.

We are evaluating our current programs based on our competence, the capabilities of our partners, and the needs and wants of people affected by disasters. As I write this letter, I am on my way back to Louisville after an all-day meeting with our PC(USA) partners serving together for the restoration of lives affected by the hurricanes in 2005 (Katrina, Wilma, and Rita). All the partners were encouraging and very kind to the new kid on the block. I need to respond in kind. As an "interim," I will be preparing the foundation for the permanent coordinator to build a house of service. I pray the day will come soon.

Pray for Haejung and me, that we would have the energy and wisdom to know what God is asking from us and the courage and humility to obey with the faith that he is with us. It will be a period of much travel for me and our staying connected with each other through phone (Skype). I will write more when I learn a bit more.

Grace and peace,

Simon

nt village to house volunteers helping at a disaster site. Usually church facilities se the volunteers. Major disasters such as Katrina makes the church building abitable..

Dear Friends and Family

This month Simon and I have to write our letters separately.

While we were in New York at Christmas assisting the Stony Point Center with their business plan for 2008, we were asked to make a special trip to Louisville. Simon was asked to serve as the interim coordinator for Presbyterian Disaster Assistance (PDA) starting immediately, that is, January 2, 2008. That was the day ten years ago that we started our first appointment as mission co-workers. We discussed and prayed about our living arrangement. After a month of discernment, we came back to Daejeon together, but Simon went back to Louisville after a week.

During the last 10 years we told our friends that being together 24/7 was the most difficult part and also our favorite part of missionary life. Care to guess who said it was difficult? I was called to be with my husband and support him during the 33 years of our marriage. I have not had any responsibility other than being a loving mother and supportive wife. Now I have a clear sense of my own call here at Hannam University.

East Asia mission personnel retreat was held here on the Hannam campus from February 19 to 25. Forty PC(USA) missionaries from China, Hong Kong, Philippines, Japan, and Korea, and five staff members from the World Mission office in Louisville attended. During the time when we shared about our ministries, I told everyone that "graceful presence" is my ministry. My role is to be here at the chaplain's office and be available when someone needs me. Doesn't it sound like being a mom? Many students call me "aunt" or "mom." Once a student introduced me to his friends as a person with whom he can meet and talk easily. That's when I was sure that this was my call. I have always been serving in that role, but I expected something greater than just being a mom. Now I am proud of myself as a mom to 13,000 students and staff. I thank God for giving me a task that I so love.

This week was a very busy one for me. The new school year just started. About 3,000 students entered a new stage of their life with hope and also with a lot of anxiety. I was one of those. I also started my studies in the master's program in Christian counseling at this university.

As a team, Simon and I have always said that mission has two parts: "being" and "doing." Over the last 10 years, my part has always been "being" and Simon's has been "doing." As a solo, I have to do more "doing," and I need more professional skills. That is why I started in the program. I have to do well in my studies as a role model for my own children and for other missionary-kids. I have confidence in Christ, but hon-

The caretaker of the mission station lived in this house.
I will be the sole caretaker of our mission here until Simon returns.

estly, I am scared.

During the first class I learned that Jesus was the best counselor. It is interesting to hear good stories about Jesus and our fellow missionaries as good counselors. After all, missionary life is to imitate Jesus.

I do not know how long Simon and I will live separately. Thanks to Skype, a free Internet phone service, we talk with each other every day. We share stories of our daily lives and encourage each other. The time difference is about 13 hours, so we tell each other to "have a good day" and "have a good night."

I am doing fine so far. Thanks be to God that he uses me and trains me in his unique and loving ways. I will let you know how it goes. Meanwhile, pray for me and Simon.

In Christ,

Haejung

... what does the Lord require of you but to do justice, and to love kindness, and to walk humbly with your God? (*Micah 6:8*)

I am back in Korea in mission service after six months of staff assignment in Louisville. I'm with Haejung in the same house and the same time zone. We are back at the same table sharing meals, and we can share stories face to face rather than through the Internet using headsets.

My assignment as interim coordinator for the Presbyterian Disaster Assistance ended with the conclusion of the biannual General Assembly of the Presbyterian Church (U.S.A.) in San Jose. I am grateful for the opportunity to have served the church in a different role during the past six months but am also grateful for the freedom to return to my field assignment. I pray what I learned during the time working in the office will make me a better servant of Jesus.

Presbyterian Disaster Assistance (PDA) is a ministry of the Presbyterian Church (USA). It is the main arm of the Church reaching out with the compassion of Jesus to those who are suffering the effect of natural and man-made disasters. PDA relies on the gifts of Church members and friends for its ministry—not only on financial gifts but also on their labor of love and their mission networks. As a part of the body, PDA's responsibilities include helping Presbyterians to share their compassion in appropriate ways, including volunteer services.

I supported PDA in the field for several years, but I was only at the field level and in one disaster site at a time. Being at the hot seat for all disaster responses was a quite different experience. Thanks to the dedicated staff and our partners in and out of the Church we were able to respond to an unprecedented season of disasters: tornadoes, wildfires, record-breaking flooding, mass killings in the United States, the Myanmar cyclone, the Chinese earthquake, and there were also food security issues and continuing responses to Katrina and the tsunami. It certainly was not a picnic, but by the grace of God we were able to respond to the urgent needs. Most of these responses are continuing, and I was able to leave the office relying on the faithfulness of God.

There were moments when Haejung and I were convinced, with the encouragement of others, that now is the time for us to come in from the field and serve the Church from its headquarters in Louisville. We even made some arrangements to make my living arrangements in Louisville a more permanent one. But events beyond our control prompted us to evaluate the opportunities again, and we concluded that God has us exactly where he wants us: in Daejeon, Korea. It was a discernment process that yielded a very positive confirmation of our current call. My experience with PDA during the past six months and the experience of living apart will improve our personal and working relationships with other children of God. I learned that I do not have in me the necessary ingredients to "to do justice, and to love kindness," but I trust that anything is possible when I walk humbly with the Lord. While we lift up justice and love much, we pray that we walk with God in humility.

My first priority is to get back into the rhythm of missionary life and write regular letters sharing our lives rather than multitudes of office memos. In the office had to put emphasis on completing the tasks at hand but hope that I now bring a clearer perspective on relationships and partnership. We may not always have the luxury of moving at our own pace, but we hope to slow down enough to hear God's voice and to feel the needs of our neighbors.

It is extremely hot here in Daejeon, but many trees surrounding our house provide welcome relief, a special privilege in a city where most people live in the concrete jungle. It is indeed good to be home and enjoy a few days of inactivity without feeling guilty.

I am ready to get back to regular letter writing. Talk to you soon.

Simon

Dear Friends and Family

Based on the frequency of email queries regarding Simon's where-abouts, we believe it is about time for us to write. Simon wrote in early July that he returned to Daejeon, Korea, trying to get back into the rhythm of missionary life.

Several months have now passed since I (Simon) was interim coor-dinator of Presbyterian Disaster Assistance (PDA), giving me sufficient time for rest and reflection on that work. Now I am back in my assigned role of assisting partners as needed. The six-month detour as a staff person responsible for a part of the church's ministry was a growing experience in many ways. I learned the necessity of humility when others needed our help. Cyclone Nargis in Myanmar/Burma, the earthquake in China, the flood in the Midwest, the famine in North Korea—all these were only a few events that called upon PDA to respond.

PDA has to provide help not only to the survivors the disasters, but also help members of the Presbyterian Church (USA) to effectively and appro-priately share their compassion. Humility was needed to quietly serve as a part of an ecumenical body rather than raising the PDA logo too high. This attitude was easier to maintain as a missionary whose task was to assist, not lead, partners in their ministries, but PDA was the visible lead office to re-spond on behalf of the larger Presbyterian Church community. We always tried to look to God for confidence and humility when the needs were great, and the people looked to us for help.

Working in a large office setting in Louisville, where I did not have much prior experience, the priorities for many tasks were affected by events and others' schedules. While my assignment as a mission co-worker has me wearing many hats, depending on the partner needs, the work for PDA required continual multi-tasking. There was paperwork with deadlines, reports to committees, and responses to urgent requests for help. In many ways, the items that rose to the top of the pile were the ones with visible consequences and short deadlines. It was difficult to concentrate on the items that will be truly important in the long run, such as building relationships and the basic system of sharing God's love.

I have no regrets that I worked hard and to the best of my ability to communicate the urgent needs of God's children who survived various disasters to fellow Presbyterians and then deliver their compassionate care to God's children in need. Of course, questions remain whether our efforts have been effective and or even sufficient, but I have no doubt that the dedicated staff at PDA did their best. As Barak Obama said, the President needs to multitask, but so do PDA staffers who need to respond to many disasters concurrently.

I did learn a lesson in the process of multitasking. It is the priority thing again. Since Haejung and I were living in two different cities 13 time zones apart, I could devote most of my waking hours to the tasks. When I needed to travel across the oceans, the time differences allowed me to avoid missing many workdays. For example, if I were to leave Louisville on a Saturday I would arrive in Korea, Thailand or Indonesia on Sunday evening and I could work with others on Monday. On the return trip, I would leave an Asian city early on Sunday arriving in Louisville late on the same day. On Monday. I would show up in the office very early in the morning. I crossed the Pacific or the Atlantic twice and did not miss a day in the office. During the six months working for PDA, I did this seven times. However, not missing a day in the office meant missing two Sundays of worshiping God with fellow Christian brothers and sisters. What is the cost of missing fourteen Sundays in six months?

I now know the plain truth that my time with God is not one of the tasks in the multi-tasking, but one that sits apart as a "non-negotiable" foundation for my spiritual and physical health. I probably was the only one who was blind to this truth, so I will not elaborate on this. I thank God for helping me see this after six months and return me to the task of humbly assisting and waiting.

We have a few items to share on the family front. John and Laurie (Bohler) became husband and wife on September 29, 2008. While we wish we could have been there at the wedding, we are grateful to God for keeping them in his arms and blessing their union. We plan a special celebration in May 2009 when all the family members can get together in Clearwater, Florida. In the meantime, we thank you for your prayers for the couple and the family.

Kevin and Sariah have launched their women's fashion line, SARIAH, and Sariah is getting good press coverage. It is a struggle for young designers to establish themselves, but the SARIAH brand is showing encouraging signs. Kevin is busy putting their work online.

Haejung is planning to spend a few weeks with the children during the Christmas and New Year holidays. It will be a good time for her to have quality time with daughters-in-law without Simon itching for different activities.

We are doing well, learning to appreciate God's blessings in routine life, enjoying his presence and sharing our presence with the Hannam

University community.

God bless.

Haejung and Simon

Used clothing are often a big problem. Remember the victims do not have a closet to keep the donations. For Pakistanis to survive in the mountains, a warm parka is much more useful than multiple t-shirts.

Disaster site is not a place for a turf war. A muslim doctor caring for an injured using the Christian donated medical supply is a norm as it should be.

Mission station to bus station

We came to Korea in January 2007, the day after our son Kevin married Sariah. We were in Florida at the end of May to celebrate our first son John's marriage to Laurie. Having completed our first term in Korea, it's time for us to return to the States for a while. Our usual six-month interpretation period will be cut to two months due to our personal needs and also Simon needs to be in the region for mission service during the final quarter of 2009. Many friends have been concerned and have asked whether we are having difficulties since we haven't been writing letters. Please accept our most sincere apology. We started many times, but never completed any, either due to other urgent demands or the sensitive nature of the tasks we were engaged in. Perhaps the biggest reason was that we did not feel our daily work would be interesting to you.

Nevertheless, during this term we've had our share of challenges and God's blessings through friends and colleagues. The biggest difference between this assignment and our assignments in Congo and Nepal is that here we are living with the people. Haejung serves as a surrogate mother to many young folks at Hannam University, and she made many friends studying Christian counseling at Hannam University. She may not have the answers, but she understands the concerns of Korean people beyond the news coverage of the popular press.

Except for teaching an introductory accounting class—for the first time in 20 years—Simon had little direct contact with the students. Simon spent most of his time assisting in the background, flying under the radar. The exception to this was the six months he spent in Louisville as the interim coordinator for the Presbyterian Disaster Assistance. While Simon believes his assignments during the term were meaningful and necessary for the church, he doesn't think it would be interesting or proper to share the details.

One insight we've gained during our time here in Korea is that once we venture out of the "mission station" and join the crowd at the "bus station" our view of society and people changes. During our current assignment, Simon has used public transportation in Korea as well as in Japan and other countries. As much as we try to open ourselves to everything and everyone, the people we come in contact with in the course of our ministries are limited and often self-selected.

As we ride the bus through different neighborhoods, we get to know the economic and demographic picture of the communities. People riding the bus also vary by the hour of the day. Simon now carries bus and train passes for several cities in three countries and uses public transportation whenever possible. This difference in perspectives also reflects our changing view of mission. For safety and other conveniences, missionaries lived compounds called "mission stations." We stayed in a house on a mission station in Congo, and we are also living in a mission compound in Korea. We try to open our house to welcome overnight guests and visitors. But during the last two years we've learned that there is an invisible barrier that stops the local folks from visiting as friends.

These barriers tend to come down when we meet in a setting that is natural to them. When I see them in a bus or at a market, their manner towards me is much more relaxed and open. The main barrier to opening relationships was probably our uneasiness in functioning outside of our "mission station," physically and metaphorically. We have found the setting in Korea comfortable and familiar enough to venture out and share lives, and we have felt safe to engage people in their natural settings. Of course, this was taught to us during our orientation twelve years ago. It only took ten years for us to find the joy of "bus station" ministry.

We thought about "retiring" from mission service and settling down, but it seems God calls us to another term of service in Korea. Haejung often reminds Simon that he is not 36 but 63. Pursuing a schedule for a 36-year-old sometimes lands Simon in trouble, but Simon is under good medical care, complete with nagging doctors. Haejung and I are planning to host PC(USA) Young Adult Volunteers starting in 2010. We hope to share the joy of bus station ministry with these young people, yet guide them not to take unnecessary risks and to be patient while the Spirit works through them. Simon expects to continue his mundane bureaucratic duties for the church, and he is grateful for the opportunity to put his gifts into service.

During our six weeks in Louisville, Simon will be working mostly in the World Mission office, although we hope to visit as many churches in the area on the few Sundays we have. We promise to write more often.

Grace and peace,

September 2009

Dear Friends

After spending six weeks working at PC(USA)'s national offices in Louisville, we came to Stony Point Center to spend a week with Young Adult Volunteers preparing to leave for their one-year service to the church in various places.

Most of them are fresh out of college and are asking the proverbial question, "What am I going to do with my life?" Rather than giving an answer, our church provides an opportunity for them to extend the boundaries of their lives by serving in a volunteer position for one year and touch other lives in the process. It is a risky endeavor; they may not find what they are looking for after giving a year of their young lives. They will be sharing lives with people who have little in common with them, and they may even face some harsh living conditions. Why do they do it? And why does the church spend resources to encourage our young people to take these risks?

A short and clear answer in my mind is that "mission is risk taking."

Since 9/11 and the global financial meltdown in 2008, the word risk has become a disease to avoid at all costs. True, many of us take foolish risks due to ignorance, a sense of our own invincibility, blind faith, and even because of the love of adventure. Through training, supervision, and close communication with people who have more experience, we try to minimize the avoidable risks. This, however, does not mean we will let the risk assessments dictate whether we engage in mission or not.

Mission is offering our lives into the lives of others. There is always the

Young Adult Volunteers and the orientation facilitators at Stony Point Center. Note the stretched arms make "hearts," which signals their love for one another and for God's children...

risk of rejection, misunderstanding others, being misunderstood, and many other consequences we did not anticipate or want. But that is the very nature of reaching out.

We are blessed to be a part of the efforts to help our young people step out of their comfort zone and explore the unknown. Sixty-seven 20-somethings with idealism, hope, and resolve (mixed with anxiety and trepidation) are going out to change the world. The world may not change much, but surely 67 lives will be changed, along with the lives of their families. May God's blessings and peace go with them.

You can learn more about this best kept secret in the Presbyterian Church (USA) at the Young Adult Volunteer Web site. May we ask for your prayer support as well as financial support of this wonderful program of the church?

Another reason for us to be here is that the World Mission chose Korea as a new site for the YAV program, and Haejung will be the site coordinator, supervisor, and mother to the YAVs. It also means that we will be based in Korea for three more years, until the end of 2012. This is the first time we return to the same place of service for another three-year term. Our first term in Korea has been a period of learning and growth, building mutual respect and trust with the partners. We will be relying on the partners to open doors and opportunities for our young adults to serve God's children together with the Korean young adults. If you want to know more about this opportunity to serve in Korea, please let us know.

We will be posting information about the YAV site in Korea on PC(USA)'s Mission Service Recruitment Web site soon. For the first year, we hope to find four young servants. We hope to have a mix of men and women, Korean-Americans and those with no prior Korean connection, but all with huge hearts for God and His children. We believe we will be able to find and design good work assignments, respond to individual needs, and work out teething problems. We do not know how exactly things will work out; we just trust that they will.

Simon continues to travel on church business, combining his heart for mission with his gifts for organizational and funds management. Twelve years ago, when Simon answered the call to mission, he was deeply ambivalent about leaving the profession of accounting and education. Little did we know that God uses every bit of our skills and fortifies us with a vision for mission at the same time. It is tiring, emotionally taxing, and sometimes discouraging work. But the occasional success is enough to re-energize and to remember why we are in this business. Risk of failure is much bigger than a batter in baseball games, but the rewards of experiencing God's word coming true sustain us. Seeing young people committing their lives gives us strength, although watching and participating in 14-hour-a-day programs for a week leaves us exhausted.

We return to Korea during the first week of September, Haejung to continue her studies in Christian counseling and Simon to continue his travels to work with colleagues in many countries. We promise to share the news of preparation for YAV service, which will start in 2010.

During our short two-month stay in the States, Simon worked in the national office assisting the finance and the Asia office, and Haejung was able to participate in the missionary sharing conference for mission workers on home assignment during the summer. We managed to fit in short visits to the churches that have adopted us as their missionaries for many years. It was good to see old friends and to affirm our common ministries.

John and Laurie have settled back in Boston after their wedding reception in Tampa, Florida. Kevin and Sariah have completed the manufacturing of their fall 2009 collection, and are working hard to get buyers interested in their spring 2010 line. Sariah's beautiful clothes are shown at Sariah's Web site.

Simon is returning to Japan in mid-September to work with our partners there, then goes on to Louisville for an important item of action at the upcoming General Assembly Mission Council meeting. More on this in our next letter.

mmitting to a service in a foreign setting is taking a bus into a new world. The YAV gram provides a loose boundary and a basic safety net in which the young people e a leap of faith.

May you enjoy the abundance of harvest season and experience the joy of sharing the abundance with our neighbors.

Simon and Haejung

This is not a return of the gift, but a gift that keeps on giving.

Dear Friends

During the General Assembly Mission Council meeting of the Presbyterian Church (USA) in Louisville, the delegation from the Yodogawa Christian Hospital (YCH) in Osaka, Japan made a gift of $208,577 to PC(USA)'s World Mission.

In 1955, Presbyterian Women gave their Birthday Offering to a clinic that had just been opened by a Presbyterian missionary doctor, Frank Brown. The Birthday Offering was started in 1922 to celebrate the blessings in the lives of Presbyterian women. The entire sum of the offering in 1955 went to a project to help poor people without adequate healthcare living near the banks of Yodogawa River. $208,577 was the seed money for the 76-bed hospital, which opened in 1956. Fifty-three years later, YCH is planning a entirely new campus less than half a mile from the current site. In the midst of planning for the new campus, leaders from the YCH traveled to Louisville to make their presentation to the GAMC.

Throughout their history, Presbyterians started and developed medical and educational institutions in every country that God sent them to. Many of these institutions went on to become renowned institutions. Very few of these institutions, however, maintained their mission roots. As they became large and successful, they drifted away from the church, partly to

compete with secular institutions and partly because the church did not provide the best management structure for these institutions. Yodogawa Christian Hospital, however, stayed within the mission structure, and the Christian witness of its motto, "Care for the whole person," is an important principle. It is obvious that their decision to stick with their Christian roots did not hurt them in secular measurements: this year's survey of medical institutions ranked YCH as one of three top private hospitals in Japan. Deep faith does not have to compete with quality, even in the secular world.

As part of my work with the Japan Mission, I have been working with the leaders of YCH, and I have seen the truth of the often-heard phrase "A Christian lives in the world, but is not of the world." Such Christians do exist and indeed serve as the salt and light of the world. I have the honor and joy of working with them during the next three years as they build the new campus.

When a journalist asked why the gift was given to Presbyterian World Mission rather than, say, to the Presbyterian Women, the answer came back quickly and with clarity. "This is not a return of the gift," said Dr.

Mukubo, the superintendent of YCH, "but a gift that keeps on giving. Presbyterian Women planted a seed in Japan, it grew and is bearing fruit. The best way to thank PW and honor God is to replant the seed in another place of need and nurture it to healthy growth." I can only say amen to that.

Later this month, Simon is traveling to the Democratic Republic of Congo (Kinshasa) to work with the office and local partners. His yellow card (record of vaccinations) shows that some of his immunization shots are over ten years old, which means he'll need a fresh round of shots. It also means our initial journey to Congo was more than ten years ago. Malaria prophylaxis pills are back in the regimen. This trip will once again remind us how easy living conditions are in Korea.

The call for Young Adult Volunteers (YAVs) in Korea for next year just went live on PC(USA)'s "One Door" Web site. We hope to be answering many inquiries, and we ask you to share the opportunity with young adults in discernment. Haejung is back in school and plans to complete her graduate work before the young folks arrive in Korea next September. Pray for her as she prepares to serve as the site coordinator for the YAV program in Korea.

November 2009

Friends

It is November already and the trees in our yard are all lit up with colors only God can create. One maple tree is very healthy and situated at a perfect place to receive and reflect the sun's rays. Each year about this time, students, faculty and town folks come to take pictures under the tree. We pray that we do not hide from God's grace and stay healthy to reflect what we receive to others.

I (Simon) traveled to Kinshasa, Congo, in October. It was my first trip there since 2005; it was good to see old friends. I do not know why, but I hoped and expected to see a different country than the one we left behind in 2001. My hopes faded at the immigration counter. Unlike last time, there were landing forms to fill out for the immigration office. The problem was that they ran out of the form. Caught between the window that insisted on the completed form and the officer who simply repeated "Non plus!" we simply went back and forth. In the meantime, I saw other agents running special errands for some of the passengers. They were acting as substitute landing forms at a price! I chose to wait it out. Eventually the officer at the window decided to take the information verbally, while continuing to process the "substitute landing forms."

It was only during the long ride to the hostel that I had enough presence of mind to process the experience. We come only once in a while, what about the people who live here? How difficult would it be to have hope for their children? Yet hope is the only thing they have, and how am I adding to their hope? I had come to evaluate the need and work of the office the

PC(USA) keeps here to support partners, mission personnel, and projects. Presbyterian World Mission (PWM) tries to be faithful stewards by assessing whether the funds to run the office would be better spent in ministry projects. DR Congo has been a challenge for many years due to continuing civil war, non-functioning banking and communication systems, and corrupt and inept government at all levels. The church, in effect, had to establish a private banking network of importers, wholesalers, and others to handle money around the country. I had hoped, without any reason to hope, that the situation had improved enough to allow us to concentrate on helping people, and that we could stop spending energy and resources on the administrative structure. This concern is not limited to Congo, but it is here where we have the most difficulty.

As funds for mission projects diminish, a fixed amount for administrative expenses use up a greater portion of the funds, making this issue more important. Sometimes, because we are a church and not a business, we need to look beyond finances and be compassionate for the welfare of our colleagues. At the same time, we need to be frugal and minimize administrative expenses so we can channel more funds to program activities. For the denominational office, this question is even more complex because many of the programs run by individual members and congregations function without our administrative support. In short, we not only need to examine program goals and activities from God's perspective but also our administrative decisions. Another challenge is to build up our local Congolese partners until they can take leadership for mission programs, including the administrative affairs.

I'm off to Lahore, Pakistan, this week to work with PC(USA)'s office there. Many challenges await, but our partners are truly making a big difference in that troubled society. Medical and educational institutions witness Christ's love without forcing religious beliefs on those they serve, a necessity in that Islamic society. Simon's visit to Lahore is to assist the Presbyterian Church of Pakistan and other partners as they move towards greater ownership of mission and mission resources.

There were times we wondered why we left the life of teaching and consulting just to do the same things in the mission field—away from family and with economic sacrifices. Twelve years has passed already since we entered mission service, and now we are comfortable with our supporting roles, assisting others to serve in ministries of more direct service. We are thankful that the PC(USA) asked us to serve another three-year term beginning in January. Recently we read one of our early letters from

Armed guards protecting Christians during Sunday mornings in Gujranwala, Pakistan.

Congo where Simon said that we feel as if we are "beta version" missionaries, seasoned enough to be tested in the real world, yet not stable enough for general release. We now feel that we will always be beta missionaries, but hopefully for version 5 (fifth term).

We will spend a few days at Thanksgiving with John and Laurie and Kevin and Sariah in New York. Then we will return to Daejeon to host Dr. Sue Makin, who just retired from mission service after 20 years in DR Congo and Malawi. Sue is this year's Linton Award recipient named after the first dean of Hannam University. The award is bestowed on a person or organization who has given dedicated humanitarian service to God's children, just like the first leaders at Hannam University. Sue's missionary service resembles that of Dr. William Linton, and Sue was the very first real-life missionary who gave us hope that we might be able to serve. We look forward to having Sue spend a few days with us in a different mission field.

So went another month of travels and learning.

See you next month.

Haejung and Simon

March 2010

Friends

It's been so long since we have written, that I don't even remember the exact month we last wrote. Put your mind at ease — we are well, healthy and quite engaged in mission. Nevertheless, we offer our apology for not writing more often.

Now that you have accepted our apology, allow us to bring you up to date, at least the first steps. Unlike our past terms, we have been re-appointed to Korea for another three-year term that ends in 2012. Haejung now has an additional duty of being the site coordinator for the brand-new Young Adult Volunteer (YAV) site in Korea. The YAV program was started sixteen years ago to offer a one-year mission experience to the twenty something members in the Presbyterian Church. They serve in many social witness programs during the period of discernment for their career and life journey. They serve in the United States and internationally, and we are offering opportunities in Korea for the first time this year.

Each site has a theme and in Korea, it is to "shine God's light and warmth into the shadows of globalization." Everyone knows the story of Korea's phenomenal economic growth during the past two decades and its prominent placement in the global markets. During the past several years we became keenly aware that global markets fall short of developing global communities for all. Migrant workers, brides from Southeast Asia living in rural areas, their children are all who suffer in the shadows. Our YAVs will be working in partnership with Korean YAVs to share God's love with these children of God. We are certain that Haejung and Simon, the

YAVs and the children we minister to, and our partners will all grow closer to God through the experiences we share. The Presbyterian Church of Korea and Hannam University are institutional partners, and we will be working with local congregations, after school programs, and community service programs.

Haejung and Simon participated in the placement event for the YAVs and are delighted to share with you that the young face of the Presbyterian Church (USA) will be represented by Becky Francisco, Jennifer McArdle, and Katie Patterson beginning in September. They are all very different from each other, but together they make a wonderful team of disciples. They will live together in the mission station on the Hannam campus, continuing the mission started 56 years ago. We ask for your prayers for them and the program. Each YAV serving in the international sites is required to raise $9,000 to help defray the cost and to share the story of mission. We will share the ways you can help in our future letters. If your congregation has any uncommitted funds in your mission budget, may we ask that you save some for these young missionaries?

Haejung is in her final semester of the Christian counseling masters program and working hard to keep her perfect grade in the program. She wishes that being mentor and mother to the YAVs would be as easy as studying for the examinations, but she knows that she will be blessed in many ways through her struggles. When we went to northern Quebec for French language study when Simon was 52, we controlled our fear by claiming "anything is possible in God." Nine months later we went to Congo still claiming a slightly modified version, "ALMOST anything is possible in God." A dozen years have passed and we know the same God helps us when we attempt things beyond our own abilities in his name for his children. Thanks be to God.

Simon continues to serve as a management and financial consultant for the Church. Much of his effort is to help restructure mission offices to function under new partner relationships and with reduced number of field missionaries. Whenever possible we support in-country partners rather than leading the programs. In countries like Korea and Japan, we work with partners to expand our common vision. We are developing mission strategies to include "mission from" these countries in addition to "mission in" the country in ways to pool our resources and capacities for God's mission. Of course, Korea and Japan partners have been active in overseas missions, but not together with PC(USA). It requires high trust levels and good deal of coordination, but the result is well worth the efforts.

In our next letters we will share more details on many of the topics, we just wanted to let you know that we are well and still in the field. We promise to write more often. Wishing you a meaningful Holy week and a truly Happy Easter.

Friends

After we wrote to you last month, several of you asked us the specific ways you can support the Young Adult Volunteers, especially who will serve in Korea. Now we have the information and wanted to share it with you. We are beginning to work with partners to assign specific service sites to the volunteers. They will be arriving in Korea on the last day of August and will start their service activities towards the end of September, after a period of settling in and orientation. We all need your prayer support for wisdom, courage, energy and humility.

We hope you would also consider supporting the program financially.

Hi, nice to meet you! I'm Becky Francisco. Just a few basic things about me ... I am 21 years old and soon to finish up my senior year at Smith College, where I am majoring in language studies. I am the daughter of a Presbyterian minister and a carpenter-turned-computer-specialist, and I

Rebecca (Becky) Fransisco.

also have an adorably sarcastic video-game-addicted little brother. I am so excited to be participating in the YAV program this year, especially in Korea! This upcoming year will surely hold challenges as I adjust to a different culture and confront the demands of mission and what it

Jennifer (Jenny) McArdle.

means to serve God, but I trust that God has a plan for me and will make it a wonderful eye-opening experience, helping me grow as I work alongside my brothers and sisters in Christ.

I am finishing up my Master's degree in International Development at Ohio University. At OU, I have focused on women and gender studies, sport-for-development, and African studies. My undergraduate degree was from Coe College in Cedar Rapids, IA, where I completed a self-designed major titled Global Development that focused primarily on the economics of growth, development, and globalization. Previously, I spent a few weeks in Seoul, South Korea, in a study abroad program, and also spent a month last summer in the southern African nation of Botswana. I love traveling, meeting new people, and especially trying new foods!

My name is Katie Patterson, I am about to graduate from Ohio State University with degrees in Psychology and Sociology. I am also the president of Presbyterian Campus Ministry. My church family is very important to me and they have taught me the importance of sharing my talents with others. Also I enjoy traveling because I meet people from different cultures with different beliefs, and I can learn so much by understanding different perspectives. I enjoy taking the time to get to know people and help them in whatever way they need it. I look forward to coming to South

Katherine (Katie) Patterson.

Korea and getting to know all of you.

International Young Adult Volunteers experience a year of developing Christian community through spiritual formation and volunteer service. Serving at several sites internationally, international young adult volunteers live together in Christian community and serve neighborhood ministries. Funds will be used for programmatic site support or to directly support young adult volunteers through reimbursement of outstanding student loans, housing and food allowance and/or a travel subsidy.

Grace and peace,

Haejung and Simon

Presbyterian mission is alive and growing daily!!

This is not a line we hear often these days. After we shared the news about the Young Adult Volunteers, Simon traveled again to participate in the lives of our partners in Korea and Japan. The seeds planted by God many years ago through the Presbyterian Church continue to grow and bear fruit.

Japan is not known as a Christian nation, in fact Christians number less than 1 percent of the population. The Presbyterian Church (USA) stopped sending new missionaries to Japan many years ago, and the numbers are down so much that we have a difficult time filling committee seats traditionally filled by mission personnel. We have made a decision to invite Japanese partners into our governing structure as true colleagues in mission. During the short period Simon has been involved in the change process, he has seen a remarkable transformation. Our Japanese partners were able to tap into many talents the missionary community did not have such as the administrative skills to navigate through the legal and bureaucratic rules of the land. In addition, our Japanese partners brought a great love for God's children and a new energy and enthusiasm, which is often associated with the young.

The most important change we noticed is that of the mission perspective. Often the North American perspective has been "mission to" Japan and the boundary of that work was Japan. When we joined forces with Japanese Christians, the focus became both mission in Japan and also "mission from" Japan. We became more aware of the priorities of mission

from Japanese perspectives, the desire to share what they received with the others, especially in developing countries in Asia. The partnership developed further to plan activities together and even to pool resources together.

On April 10, Simon joined in the dedication service of the new mission office and represented PC(USA) at the dinner to thank Dr. Ishida for his retirement from the Yodogawa Christian Hospital (YCH) and to welcome Dr. Mukubo in as the new Superintendent.

YCH is an important part of Japan Mission and their leadership is also in the leadership of Japan Mission, working together for the Whole Person Healing mission of tomorrow.

During the latter part of April, we visited the fruits of mission work in Korea. We went to Jeonju, about 60 miles south of Daejeon, to see and learn about the medical mission work at the Jesus Hospital (Presbyterian Medical Center). Dr. Min-Chul Kim, the hospital director, showed us the newly opened Mission Museum displaying the selfless services of the missionaries who shared God's love in the hospital. Of course, the hospital itself is the living museum of the continuing ministry. As an aside, we were told that the name for the hospital came from the local folks who neither

understood the official name of Presbyterian Medical Center nor could they pronounce it, thus the simple name Jesus Hospital.

Simon also visited the Honam Theological University and Seminary (HTUS) in the southern city of Kwangju. It is a school for over a thousand students, all preparing to serve God in one capacity or another including contemporary Christian music. The president of the university, the Rev. Dr. Chong-Soon Cha, shared the history, work and vision of the University and the special project with the city government to present the history of Presbyterian mission as a cultural heritage site for educational and cultural tours. Many of the significant programs for the ordinary people of the last century originated from the residences of the missionaries, and HTUS is helping to share the story as an important sign of God's ministry.

Presbyterian mission is alive and growing. Not necessarily in the traditional way of God's servants fanning out into the far corners of the world to share his love, but by the fruits of earlier efforts replanting seeds from the same root. As we hear and experience challenges in the world of great needs and the limited resources of the Church, we remember God's assurance and find new energy in every turn.

Praise God for his works are forever.

Simon and Haejung

Missionary cemetery on the campus of Honam Theological University and Seminary. Many buildings from the original mission stations remain.

This area serves as a Christian historic site in the Kwangju city.

Dear friends and family

It's already the middle of June and very hot and humid here in Daejeon. At Hanman University the spring semester is over. Many students have started to move out from the dormitory for summer vacation. I turned my last paper in and finished the master's program in Christian Counseling. (I wrote our newsletter in March 2008 when I started the program at Hannam University.) I enjoyed meeting many fellow students and faculty members with life experiences very different from mine. I realize I have changed a lot since I left Korea when I was young. I learned a lot while we studied together. As a Christian and as a counselor I need to respect others without judging. I practiced my learned counseling skill on Simon. While I know he must have been very irritated at being a test case, I thank him for his much patience and encouragement. Having finished this program, I pray for more self-confidence and humility.

As you know, we signed up for another three-year term of mission service, starting in January this year. Unlike the first assignment period, I have fewer responsibilities in the chaplain's office. This semester the most important task for us was the chapel service in English for the students. There were two sessions, with more than a thousand students in each, which met every week. It's not that they are extremely religious or the chapel services are so popular, four semesters' chapel service is required of all students.

In order to make the service valuable even to non-Christian students, we pick a theme relevant to all. This semester it was 'To Be a Global

Citizen in the 21st Century." Chapel service has been the tradition since the Hannam community was founded in 1956 by the Presbyterian Church, and the Christian faith was the requirement for admission at that time. But times have changed and now fewer than 30 percent of the students are Christians. We hope and try to have students touched by the Word as a seed that is planted. We presented the "fruit of the Spirit" in Galatians 5:22 as the personal qualities of a global citizen. We asked the speakers to choose one among the qualities — love, joy, peace, patience, kindness, goodness, faithfulness, gentleness and self-control — as their main topic. The favorite, most often chosen, was love. Next semester's theme will be "Global Citizens in Action" or "Walk the Talk."

During our second term in Korea I have the additional responsibility of being the site coordinator for the Young Adult Volunteer (YAV) program in Korea. We are looking forward to working with three young ladies — Jenny, Katie and Becky. They will arrive on the 31st of August and stay until the end of July 2011. They will be living in one of the houses on the mission station. As soon as we receive their diplomas and other documents we will start on their religious visas, which will allow them to live and serve in Korea for a full year. Through our chaplain's office we are trying to recruit many Hannam students to work with these three YAVs as partners. We believe they can learn from each other and help those who are in the shadows of globalization. Korea is growing economically but there are large gaps between haves and have-nots.

Our children are doing fine. John and Laurie are living in Boston. John works as a senior copywriter at Digital Influence Group. Laurie is studying at Boston Architectural College and working as an interior designer. Kevin and Sariah are living in New York. Kevin has many talents, especially in music, and is working as a piano tuner. Sariah is a fashion designer and has her own label, SARIAH. They both are working hard to make the SARIAH business grow and become profitable.

I pray for you to have healthy and happy life in God's presence and hope. We pray together for all who read this letter.

Haejung

It's new every morning

Several events at the end of the summer stretched us in many ways. As we were preparing for the arrival of three young brand-new missionaries, we heard the news that Simon's brother-in-law passed away in Champaign, IL. We lived in the same town for many years and although we have not seen each other very often after we entered the mission service, Kee had been an important part of our lives. Simon got on the plane to be with Eunhee, the widow, and three daughters and many friends. It was a long trip but was an occasion to experience again what it means to be with loved ones and to share the memories of a brother who lived a short life of 64 years. But he lived it fully by giving his love to all around him. He was an ordinary pharmacist, but the hundreds who came to his memorial service shared how he shared God's love with all in need through his limitless hospitality, and what a big hole he left in their lives.

Is that what he did, leave a hole? I knew that our lives would have to be reconfigured without daily interactions with Kee. Eunhee and her daughters would need to adjust and redirect the time and energy spent to care for Kee to creating a new life while keeping Kee in healthy remembrance. To a lesser degree, all of us who loved Kee would have to do the same. Then it dawned on me that following Jesus also requires these transitions.

When we enter into a new mission assignment, we are filled with the surge of energy for a new beginning along with the fear and trepidations of the unknown world. These are confusing times; being calm, collected and brave while being irritable, short-tempered and irrational at the same time.

New missionaries (YAV) introduced to Hannam students at a chapel service.

Remarkably, when we leave the field after several years we go through the same experience for "going home." Yes, there is a big culture shock when we re-enter the American culture and lifestyle. But soon we adjust and get enough energy and courage for another "new life." I can understand why the disciples of Jesus acted cowardly when Jesus was arrested, and the same people could so calmly give their lives to sharing the Good News.

The reason I had to hurry back was to greet the three Young Adult Volunteers arriving the last day of August to begin their new lives after campus life. What a change and challenge it is for these young lives to enter into a period of service in a strange culture thousands of miles away from home and familiar surroundings. They all arrived safely 10 days ago and took the initial steps of their lives here in Korea. Instead of me telling you about them, I would invite you to read the blog postings by Jenny, Becky and Katie. Of course, I could not let them twist my good intentions as being controlling (just kidding), so I started a parallel blog for their parents and you. Hope you find time and interest to follow our journey. The real grind will start in two weeks when everyone will have work assignments along with their four-hours-per-day language study.

May this day bring you a renewed life with God.

Simon

Dear friends and family

Jenny, one of the Young Adult Volunteers (YAVs) in Korea, reminded me that the half-point of the YAVs' term will be reached soon. I noticed that our last letter was sent in September announcing the arrival of the first class of YAVs in Korea. Simon posted many stories on his blog since then.

This first group of YAVs have adjusted well to a different environment and the culture and they are learning the Korean language. They have also carried out many tasks assigned to them, and the workload will increase during the second half of their term.

The contingent at the Hiroshima Peace Park. The skeletal remains of

The contingent at the Hiroshima Peace Park. The skeletal remains of the building was, and is, the only remaining structure after the atomic bomb was detonated.

the building was, and is, the only remaining structure after the atomic bomb was detonated.

We just finished a 10-day study trip to Japan. In addition to the YAVs, three Hannam students and a chaplain joined Simon and me for the trip. We visited three Christian colleges and participated in short forums. Each

It was an opportunity for young people of U.S., Korea and Japan discussing issues of common interest; peacemaking, environmental protection and discrimination.

one was very unique and interesting. American, Korean and Japanese young folks shared their thoughts on an assigned topics: environmental issues, discrimination and peacemaking. Once the formal sessions were done, they found many more items of common interest among them. It was a pleasure to watch them making friends, overcoming the language barrier and culture differences.

Since the YAVs arrived in Korea my role has been one of on-site mom. It is not easy being a mom to three grown up daughters, but it has been fun and meaningful. I often wondered what it would be like to have a daughter, because I have two sons. Now I know! By the way, in May our older son John will become a father. Simon and I will be grandparents for the first time.

In a few weeks Simon and I will go to Louisville to interview and invite the second YAV class. I pray and trust God will be with us during the interviews and call the young servants who can give and receive most from the experience.

With this short letter I want to let you know that we are doing fine.

Thanks for your continuing prayers for us. I also am praying that God be with you wherever you may be.

chapter V

Report on
North Korea

You thought we vanished from the face of the earth, didn't you? We started to write several times, failing to complete the letter each time for several reasons.

We can't wait any longer to share some of the personal news as well as happenings on our mission front.

At dawn of May 9 healthy Henry Augustus Johan Bohler-Park came into this world, our very first grandson, in Boston. Haejung was able to make a short visit in June and held him in her arms.

While Johan's arrival is the big happening for Haejung and me, other parts of our life in mission continued. I have been working hard on important but mundane task of preparing our mission offices in Japan and Korea for the new era of mission. In essence, our mission is not to run our ministries for others in foreign countries, but to assist our partners in

mission. Our resource and personnel deployment must also fit this pattern. My role is to get the resources and system ready for others to enter into the new phase.

Our Young Adult Volunteers are finishing their year of service at the end of July and returning home. It will be a while before they can fully process the impact they had on others as well as the impact of the past 11 months in their own lives. I cannot begin to share their stories, but invite you to hear from Jenny, Becky and Katie directly.

They all had very challenging times, but their commitment, faith in God and love for the children and the help of their work supervisors enabled each of them to build true relationship with others. We have learned a lot through unexpected joys, sorrows and mistakes. Through the year we learned again the wisdom from Africa, "If you want to go fast, go alone. If you want to go far, go together." May we always go together with God and God's children! They pass their torches to the 2011 class of YAVs, who will be arriving at the end of August. Soon you will be hearing from them as well.

I have been traveling a lot this year as well, and it will probably continue until we retire next year. But not all travels are the same. I traveled to Pyongyang in early July for a site and program assessment visit to the Pyongyang University of Science and Technology (PUST). This was the first visit to the country where both of my parents were born before the country was divided in 1945.

PUST is the first private school funded with gifts from overseas supporters, educating the very best of the country in science, technology and management. I was impressed with the vision, dedication and the quality of the students, faculty and the administration. There is no question that the university operates within the tight domain allowed by the government au-

Simon with Presidents of the university, representing North Korea (right) and the international communities (left), under the auspices of the Kims.

thorities, but genuine care and education happens. Currently there are 500 graduate and undergraduate students learning English and technical subjects throughout the calendar year. Qualified teachers in electrical engineering, computer science, management and English are urgently needed. All instructors and staff serve as volunteers without financial compensation. I pray that these interactions with the future leaders of the country continue to grow. I hope to be able to share more stories in the future letters. The photos below are of the group arriving at the Pyongyang airport, and the special lecture I delivered under special permission.

So went our few months; a lot happened but not a lot to write about. For that we are grateful.

Simon & Haejung

Arrival at Pyongyang airport. Anticipation and anxiety filled.

Unplanned but welcome opportunity to address the students. Always be prepared to share the hope in you.

Next nine letters form our report of the time we spent in Pyongyang University of Science and Technology.

December 2011

We are back safely!

It was a once-in-a-lifetime experience. Six weeks in North Korea! Actually, only on the campus of Pyongyang University of Science and Technology (PUST). We returned from Pyongyang only yesterday (December 23, 2011) after six weeks of teaching, sightseeing, shopping and getting to know some people at a personal level. All of this happened within the context tightly drawn by the North Korean authorities, and always with a minder or two with us. Nevertheless, the encounters were real and we were able to overcome the caricature image of North Koreans and their society.

Two days before our departure from Pyongyang, the death of Kim Jong Il became public. We were in town until around 11 a.m. and saw many university students marching with flags. We knew there was going to be an important announcement at noon, but we had no idea as to the content of the announcement. t was only after the formal announcement that most people on campus, like most North Koreans, became aware of his death. As one can imagine, the students and the staff of the DPRK (Democratic People's Republic of Korea, North Korea) were in shock and in deep sorrow. We maintained our respectful postures and offered condolences. We have no insight into what is ahead for this country and the people— probably neither do the people of DPRK. We pray and hope for peaceful developments of more abundant life in the country. Our final two days is worth a separate letter, so we return to the subject of this letter.

Some poverty situations are beyond our imagination, but we were able to talk about family members and our common history before the Korean War. With some we shared stories, meals and personal opinions, but not comments about politics and religion. The closest we got to those subjects was when one minder said that "while we differ on politics and religion, that should not preclude us from working on the unifying of our motherland." Even that was quoting Great Leader Kim Il Sung, whose name must always be in bold letters (so is the name Kim Jong Il since December 19, and their sayings are printed in red).

While we had to obtain permission whenever we left the campus and had to be with minders, we managed to visit the cities of Kaesung (110 miles from Pyongyang) and Nampo (60 miles) and numerous sites near Pyongyang. We also had weekly grocery shopping trips and were able to eat out at restaurants, mostly combined with other outings.

As said before, the greatest reward of this visit was the opportunity to relate to students, staff and people in the shops and markets as fellow Koreans, unlike the impersonal interactions at the airport security check and the immigration kiosk.

There is so much to tell, we can't do it all in one letter. We will send a series of letters in the near future. Let us do only the shopping experiences this time.

Every Saturday morning we went shopping in a group of 15 or so. We would go to several stores in the morning. Generally, the first store is the Botong-gang department store, where North Korean currency is used. It has three floors and the first floor carried household goods while the third floor displayed electric goods such as refrigerators and air conditioners.

We went only to the second floor, which carried food items. One can buy some fruits, bread, and packaged goods, but few fresh vegetables. Since we did not have cooking facilities at the guest apartment, we did not look carefully at the green groceries, but rather searched for locally made items that could serve as gifts, more like souvenirs. We bought candies, cookies and teas for friends back home. One item that caught Simon's interest was whole pheasants frozen in a freezer. During the final visit Simon found courage to ask for permission to take a picture. The clerk sought out a supervisor who granted permission for one shot after quizzing me as to the reason for wanting to take the picture. The minders went to the money change office for us, as we were not allowed to go to the moneychangers, to change Euro or U.S. dollars or Chinese RMB into Chosun won. The exchange rate in November was 3,800 won to a dollar, compared to 2,500 won in July. Rumor had it that the black-market rate was over 5,000 won to a dollar—imagine the inflation in local currency.

We then continued on to two hard-currency shops, where mostly imported goods were sold but only for hard currency. It did not seem to limit the North Koreans as long as they had the requisite money. One store had mostly Japanese food items and no fresh groceries, but boxed ones. When we paid in dollars and the changes less than a dollar were paid in small packets of cookies. Another store was called an "Argentine store," where they had some refrigerated food items in addition to canned and boxed goods. We were told that the store names come from the source of investments in the store rather than the products, though no one knew for sure. Then we went to the final stop—the diplomat store with the formal name Pyongyang Shop. It is located in the diplomatic enclave, complete with guards who collected our minder's ID when we entered the zone. The store is located in a small compound that housed a spa, restaurant and other general goods store in addition to the grocery store. We got bottled water, fresh dairy products, cheese and crackers. They sold fresh vegetables and fruits but we did not buy them there. At the sole checkout counter one person adds up the charges and another collects the money in three different currencies and often returns the change in a combination of different currencies. This store also accepts debit cards (also a new development since September), which helps speed up the checkout process, but only when the electricity is on.

We returned to the PUST campus for lunch and at 2:30 in the afternoon a different mix of shoppers left for Tongil Market in the middle of a housing complex. This is a large one-story warehouse, a building where they sell everything from building materials and tools to clothing and fresh meat. It is also the only market where foreigners are allowed to shop with the local citizens. We never passed up the opportunity to go to Tongil Market, at first out of curiosity but later on to buy fruits and nuts and for encounters with ordinary citizens working for their daily living. Surprisingly, they never stared at us or other colleagues but only wanted to sell their goods, at good prices. Well, one child stared at us but would not accept our offer to share some roasted pumpkin seeds.

The market is arranged in long columns of tables, some tables with shelves behind them. Sellers in each section wore different colored vests. The purpose of the vests was not explained to us, but Simon suspected it was to keep unauthorized people from doing business in the market. Many vendors wrote down their transactions in a notebook and there were many people roaming about, also in some sort of uniforms. There were often three or four vendors for each table, each vendor having no more than one and a half feet of counter space. Even when we bought from the same table we had to make

Frozen pheasants at Botong-gang store.

I needed a special permission from the store manager to take this photo of the birds in the frozen section. Be assured that NO artificial ingredients are added!!

separate payments. We also saw people in the aisles and in the parking lot with things to sell, obviously people without a license but overlooked. Some also had goods under the counter that may have been homegrown. We tried to buy as many things in this market as possible since some portion of the payments would go to the vendors directly. When we haggled with a price it was more for the opportunity to carry on conversation than to save money. After a few weeks they remembered our faces and we were able to share good-natured laughs, and they even remembered our favorite fruits. The parking lot was filled with buses like ours, cars with diplomat plates, and taxis—yes, taxis. Too bad we were not allowed to take pictures.

Beyond the students, we got to know the minders as friends with whom to share our joys and concerns, more than givers and keepers of rules of conduct. We will share the life at PUST in our next letter.

It is good to be back. The YAVs are glad to have us back also. Merry Christmas and a Happy New Year to all.

Haejung & Simon

Teaching at the Pyongyang University of Science and Technology

Simon went to Pyongyang at the invitation of PUST to teach an intensive course in financial management. Spouse visas are only a recent development and Haejung went to keep an eye on Simon and the other eye on North Korea. (Just a joke, Haejung.) A brief introduction to PUST is borrowed from a faculty recruitment letter:

Pyongyang University of Science & Technology (PUST), located in Pyongyang, DPRK (Democratic People's Republic of Korea), is jointly operated by the DPRK and an international foundation (the Northeast Asia Foundation for Education and Culture). PUST offers both undergraduate and graduate programs to DPRK students in a fully English-speaking environment in the fields of Electrical and Computer Engineering (ECE), Agriculture and Life Sciences (ALS) and International Finance and Management (IFM). Qualified applicants should hold a Ph.D. or an equivalent degree with a proven record of teaching and research experience. In addition, qualified and experienced English teachers are needed to provide general English courses, which all students are required to take prior to starting their major courses.

PUST was specifically requested and endorsed by Kim Jong Il and enjoys special privileges as the only "international university" in North Korea. But this letter is about our personal experiences on the academic side. Apparently, my intensive course was not pre-approved by the North Korea authorities and we found that a series of non-credit special lectures were the best we could do. It turned out to be a blessing for us as we had

free time to visit places (in another letter, we promise).

I was to give a series of six lectures to graduate students in the International Financial Management track. These students are graduates of the most prestigious universities in DPRK, most of them from the Kim IL Sung University in Pyongyang. I asked what subjects or topics they would like to cover during the six lectures. Knowing that they grew up in a socialist economy and their understanding of market economy would not be well rounded, I wanted to fill in the gaps. The students were alert and co-operative but did not offer any suggestions. After a while it dawned on me that the students did not know what they did not know. It was natural that they would not know where the holes in their studies were. And since their studies were so uniform, so were the gaps. We worked together to lay a sounder foundation for their studies, but it may not have made any mean-ingful difference. At the invitation of the DPRK academic vice president, I shared the following evaluation of the students.

"All the students were highly motivated and participated eagerly. They learned quickly and were well prepared in specific areas but were lacking in their ability to build bridges across the gaps for which they had little exposure. That is, they were not able to draw inferences by connecting dots they knew and make educated guesses as to the missing dots. As a consequence, they made statements and conclusions that are not internally consistent. Students everywhere make these mistakes but given the raw caliber of PUST students this kind of mistakes should be rare. Furthermore, the ability to apply and extend their knowledge beyond what they know already is an important ingredient of independent research in the field, perhaps more than most. Building on their high motivation and superior intellect, a course or two covering the macro view of the field and key analytical tools would greatly enhance their ability to absorb new information and to do quality research."

I also noticed that they had difficulty in searching for and using information to formulate loosely defined questions into research questions. PUST graduate students have one major tool that their colleagues at other institutions do not have: access to Internet. I wanted to demonstrate using the search engines to find information to formulate and answer questions. I requested, through the proper channels, to do a live Internet demonstration during class. To the surprise of many, the authorities granted permission. Since the classroom was not wired for the Internet, I set up the equipment in my office and had a successful dry run. In the morning of the final lecture, I invited the students into my office for this history-making session. As usual, the students were early for the 8 a.m. class, but just before we got started the electricity went out at 7:56. The light came back on for three minutes during the 90-minute session. We worked with screenshot handouts I had prepared and a blank screen. But all was not in vain.

Imagine what might happen next semester, if the Internet use in class is routinely requested and granted. Perhaps the session was indeed history-making.

These changes do not come often. PUST is peeling back the heavy curtain on the window to the world, an inch at a time to a few selected eyes. I hope and pray that in 15 years the students I worked with will be leading the country and interacting with the world. They have the desire and the raw capacity. I hope I added a bit to their journey, personally as well as for their society. PUST has many obstacles to overcome, but the journey is too important to give up, both for us who are helping and for the people of North Korea. Kim Jong Il knew that; I hope his successor does as well.

Graduate students at PUST enjoy the rare privilege of internet access. However, the sites visited by them are recorded by the ever-present room monitor.

Death of Kim Jong Il

Our final week in Pyongyang started with 6:30 breakfast in the cafeteria. Students are through with their final examinations and the teachers are beginning to leave the country in large numbers. This morning most of the foreign professors are absent from the cafeteria, perhaps finishing up all their food items before they leave for the long winter vacation. The students will stay on campus until December 26 finishing up the semester, including studies of Kim Il Sung ideology.

For me it is time to return the office key and hand over the printer, a notebook computer, and a projector I brought as gifts to the school. Then we joined the final souvenir-shopping outing at 9:30, remembering the need to return to campus by 11:30 for the "Christmas lunch" among the foreign staff. We were interested in a painting by a highly decorated artist. It turned out to be a disappointment, so we stood outside the store and watched a large number of students marching behind large flags with their school names. We thought they were going to their work site or going to the assembly for the important announcement scheduled for noon that day. We simply followed the group along and got back to campus just in time for the lunch. We visited and wished safe travels for all and returned to our room around 12:30. That is when we learned of the death of Kim Jong Il, and ran to share the news with colleagues still at lunch. Then the following happened during the next 48 hours.

Dec 19, 1:30 - 1:50

Informal meeting of the expatriate staff The students and DPRK (Democratic People's Republic of Korea, North Korea) staff have begun paying their respects at the Kim Il Sung Ideology Center on campus.

Cancel all festivities and refrain from singing or loud laughter.

Wreaths have been ordered and those who wish may join the group to offer condolences.

Dec 19, 5:30

Final meeting of the expatriate staff for the semester The wreaths have not arrived yet and the visit would probably be in the morning of the following day.

The cafeteria has been closed for the evening. It will probably reopen in the morning. We should respect the sorrow of the North Koreans and behave accordingly.

Dec 20, 10:00 a.m.

We gathered in the lobby of the main building There are three wreaths; one each from the president and the vice president of PUST (Pyongyang University of Science and Technology) and one from the foreign staff. Simon is to help carry the third wreath into the room set for the visitation.

We were the second group for that day and the DPRK president of the University and other leaders were receiving the visitors.

Comrade Lee, the leader of the group who processed our permits and guided us in our outings, thanked us for paying respect and for the service at the University. He was saying how much the dear general valued PUST and he would do his utmost to make the University a success for the country. I am filling in the end of his remarks as he could not finish his talk but left weeping.

We came back to our room and packed my only white shirt together with the only suit I had brought. Only thing to do was to wait for our departure the following day. At 12:45 we received a call that there would be another visitation outside the campus and the bus would leave at 1:20. Haejung helped me to "un-wrinkle" the shirt as best we could and out came the suit again.

1:20

We got on the bus and there were four guides, rather than usual two, with us, and they would not tell us exactly where we were going except that the first destination is Haebang-san Hotel in downtown Pyongyang.

1:50

Haebang-san Hotel parking lot—we stayed on the bus while the guides attended the briefing for guides of many other groups.

We were told that we will need to leave all metallic objects including keys, pens and non-essential items like cigarettes and candies in the car. Basically, empty all pockets. We collected the items and put them all in one purse.

Guides were even paying attention to our attires and made some suggestions.

We are told the hotel would be the final opportunity for using the facilities. As soon as our group returned the bus departed at 2:10.

2:30

The bus traveled to the Peoples Cultural Palace.

We were led into a very large auditorium; we remembered seeing the hall on television where Kim Jong Il was greeted with great adoration.

We were told to sit and try not to talk loudly while waiting.

After a long silent wait, a lady came in and told us that PUST would be the third group to be processed.

We followed the crowd and waited in line. The PUST group was called out and then individual names were called for a security check. We went through a metal detector, were patted down by hand, and then a soldier worked a hand-held detector over our bodies again.

We went back to our bus and waited a while longer.

The bus left at 3:30 with a military police riding in our bus.

On the road we saw large groups of people walking to pay respect at places set up within walking distances. The largest crowds were at the Pyongyang Stadium and the 4.25 Memorial Cultural Center, numbering in many thousands.

4:00

The bus traveled for a while and turned into a manicured six-lane boulevard that led to a large stone structure and a vast parking lot.

Before we could figure out where we were, we were told to leave any outerwear and bags on the bus and move quickly. Other buses were unloading people and they were also moving quickly.

When we reached the building we climbed up through a very narrow staircase that only one person could go through at a time.

As we entered the lobby and edged closer to the person in front of us, we could hear the military band playing somber music continuously.

While we stood in waiting I recognized ambassadors from European nations as well as leaders of international organizations leaving the hall.

After the dignitaries left, our line started moving forward in good speed as people were going up on the stage in groups of 30 or so. Then it dawned on us that we may be in the group viewing the body of Kim Jong Il.

Suddenly it was our turn to be on the raised platform and I stood at the rear of the three rows of people bowing deeply. Though I could not see the body, I bowed my head slightly and offered a silent prayer for the people of North Korea. Haejung had been clinging to me for the previous 10 minutes or so and she was at my right.

After 30 seconds, the front line was asked to move out to the left. As the people moved in single file, I saw Kim Jong Un standing a few meters away shaking hands with some of the visitors. Prime ministers and other high officials were standing a few steps to his right and rear.

When my turn came, I offered my hand of condolences and he reached up with both hands, which surprised me.

I quickly walked on and moved to the head of the glass coffin and saw Kim Jong Il clearly. Lingering in the area would not have been proper, and I moved on out to the waiting bus. When I got to the bus, it was 4:35.

We rode in silence and the bus arrived back at the PUST campus at 5:00.

Only then we learned that we had been at the Kumsusan Memorial Palace where they keep the body of Kim Il Sung as well.

Dec 21 10:00

Nine of us left on a bus to the airport for the short flight to Shenyang,

China.

At noon, exactly 48 hours after the announcement of the death, the plane left the ground.

As the cabin crew distributed copies of Rodong Shinmun, the official newspaper of the ruling Workers' Party, it was not surprising to see that all six pages of the paper were devoted to the coverage of mourning.

It was a shock nevertheless to see a picture of me on page 4 accompanying the article about overseas Koreans paying respect to Kim Jong Il and offering condolences to Kim Jong Un. Difficult to believe, isn't it?

We pray for wisdom and compassion of the leaders to bring a lasting peace and hope for the people of North Korea.

Simon, back row third from left, paying respect at Kim Jong Il's viewing.
*This photo is taken from Rodong Shinmun, the official party organ of the Worker's Party. (December 21, 2011 page 4)

Where do we go from here?

The most common question I hear these days is whether I plan to go back to PUST (Pyongyang University of Science and Technology). A short answer is, "I don't think so." It is not because I do not believe in the mission of PUST or that I lost interest. It is precisely because I believe in the importance of the mission and I am not able to fulfill the need.

Having spent some time at PUST, two things became very clear to me. First, PUST may be the best opportunity for a long-term collaborative endeavor with the North Koreans. This is a project where neither side just gives or takes; each side needs to give their best and depend on the efforts of the other. This mutual dependency makes a good framework for a sustainable mission project. In my personal opinion, when a project is started with mutual dependency, the eventual transfer of control for the project to the local partner is more acceptable and smoother than in other cases.

What Christians provide to PUST at this time is the qualified faculty and the linkage to the Western academic community. This effort requires a far more qualified academic than I am. I have not published any scholarly research papers in accounting and finance for the past 15 years. As much I tried to prepare for the lectures, I was never completely satisfied, although the students probably did not know that. If PUST were an ordinary institution of higher education, I could find a niche teaching introductory survey courses, but for North Korea, this is the place they consider a very important window to the outside world.

Prior to the collapse of the Soviet Union, much of higher-level training for the North Koreans in science and technology was done in Russia and in Eastern European countries. North Koreans returning from their education overseas and their family members not only brought back technical abilities but also the experiences to interact with other societies. After the collapse, Russia had neither the economic resources nor the reserve energy to train large numbers of North Koreans, and the Eastern bloc demanded payments for educating North Koreans in their universities. North Korea did not have the money and had the urgent task of building up the Kim Il Sung regime to survive without the backing of the Soviet Union. China was preoccupied with building up their economic infrastructure and was not in a position to step in and fill the gap. Thus, North Korea experienced 20 years of intellectual drought along with economic disasters. Kim Jong Il must have envisioned PUST providing the avenue to the world, at least for some selected people in a controlled way.

Some may complain that good-willed, but naïve, folks are playing into the hands of the North Korean regime. Perhaps true, but is that necessarily bad? Couldn't both sides gain from the partnership, each learning a bit more about their counterpart in the process? I believe in conversation over shouting matches or brinkmanship. PUST offers a wonderful setting where both sides have incentives to stay engaged although their short-term goals may not match completely. In the long run, capable mid-level leaders who are able to interact with the outside world are key resources for the North Korean society, and we all value that. PUST is one, perhaps the only one, institution that requires daily collaboration of North Korean students and staff with the volunteers from outside. This may lead to other opportunities for meaningful engagement.

The second point is that the work must be done well. For the North

Korean leaders this is a very important experiment and they are putting in efforts and resources to make it a success. The volunteer teachers at the university are among the most dedicated people I know. What concerns me is that there are not enough academic professionals to lead and develop the students in world-class research. As stated earlier, I do not have the technical ability to contribute fully in this endeavor. It requires persons with top-notch academic abilities and true discipleship commitments.

Presbyterian World Mission is currently seeking a mission co-worker who would commit to this program. I hope many academic professionals would consider this position carefully. If you would drop me a note, I would be delighted to share my thoughts with you in more detail.

Grace and peace,

Simon

North Korea's One Percent

The fact is that Haejung and I lived as the "one percent" class in North Korea, and our experiences do not represent the lives of the ordinary citizens of the country. In some respects, we lived in lifestyles much closer to the people when we were in Congo and Nepal. We could argue that we were not allowed to, in North Korea, but I am not sure whether we would have voluntarily lived the lives of the 99 percent, even 50 percent. This is to simply remind you that the experiences we share in our letters are those of the privileged.

We were privileged in two dimensions. We worked and lived at PUST, not much different from living in a diplomatic compound and, second, we had the economic means and the currency to eat and shop in the "hard currency" world.

PUST sits on a 216-acre piece of land just south of Pyongyang inner city near the inter-province highway connecting to Kaesung. There are many groups of people living and working on the campus, starting with 60 or so expatriate faculty members, administrators and operations staff. Faculty members come from many English-speaking countries, the majority of them having Korean heritage. Many of the operations and maintenance staff are ethnic Korean-Chinese from Yanbian Province in China, and some are ethnic Koreans with citizenships of other countries such as Australia, Canada and the United States.

There are currently 200 undergraduate and 70 graduate students on campus. All male and selected by the North Korean government based on their academic ability and family background (I assume). Approximately 70 percent are from Pyongyang and 30 percent are from other parts of the country.1 They all live on campus and are not allowed to go home during the school term, although that may take less than 30 minutes by car for the students from Pyongyang. Nonetheless, they clearly belong in the top 1 percent of the NK students, both in their abilities and the special privilege they enjoy.

There are also 25 or so professors on research appointments at PUST from Kim Il Sung University. They are designated as the future professors to teach side by side with the foreign professors and perhaps lead PUST in the near future. They study English and monitor teaching materials presently used, and they also reside on campus.

There is a North Korean team of academic administrators, starting from the president, vice president and others, who do not seem to be on campus at night. Then there is a team of eight very important External Relations officers who process our visa, make arrangements for our visits to the outside, and accompany us to all outings. We cannot go anywhere without them—both by the regulations and for practical reasons they are our minders and guides.

There are also 65 women soldiers who guard the grounds. They keep uninvited persons from entering the campus as well as keeping the members of PUST in. In addition, there are administrative, kitchen staff, and cleaning crew who commute daily via a PUST bus. All members of these groups belong in the "1 percent" in that they have been selected by the North Korean government and are parts of the experiment to prepare the society for eventual opening. PUST is a very high-stake experiment for

North Korea.

During the drive to complete the construction of the promised world to unveil in April 2012, (Kim Il Sung's 100th birthday) all universities in North Korea are closed and the students work on construction projects. PUST students, however, continue their studies as the only international university in the country. Members of the university community also eat three square meals a day—all they want though the fares are simple. Their sleeping quarters are heated, and they have easy access to communal bath and sauna. Yes, these are all privileges of being in the 1 percent. We were even more privileged than the students in that we had water heaters in our bathrooms and did not have to participate in snow removal.

There are many others in the one percent club. One percent of 25 million people, estimated to be the population of North Korea, comes to 250,000. These high-level officials and military officers enjoy some special perks as in other societies. These people have the power and the money to shop in hard-currency stores and dine in hotel restaurants, and they have cars to take them where they want to go, and most of them must be living in Pyongyang. So did we.

In our earlier letter, we shared our shopping experiences. In this one we

want to share the life-
style that is possible
only if one has hard
currencies, both the
money itself and the
privilege to use them.
Stores and hotels in

North Korea accessible to foreign nationals accept the Euro, U.S. dollar, and Chinese yuan. Prices are posted in a virtual currency that closely tracks U.S. dollars times 100—that is, one unit of this currency is approximately one cent. When the prices are quoted verbally, it is most often done in Euro and the exchange rate into dollars is mostly very bad. Once we paid $1.70 per Euro. At hotels they posted rates and those were more reasonable.

In short, you can find almost anything in these stores: imported goods and North Korean-made goods for export as well as medicinal herbs popular in East Asia. One shop that surprised us most was the three-story consumer electronics shop near the Japanese shop. On the first floor they had all the popular electronic goods—notebook computers (Asus, Toshiba, Dell and Sony brands), rice cookers, hot water pots, digital cameras, including current model DSLRs, and espresso machines. The most expensive home-use espresso machine was priced around $4,700. On the second floor they displayed air conditioners, refrigerators, freezers, stoves, filtered-water dispensers, and Italian brand water heaters. More expensive ones matched in size and features any you would find in stores in South Korea, Japan and the United States, though the prices seemed a bit higher than what we have seen in other countries. The third floor was completely dedicated to flat panel televisions and karaoke machines. Again,

they ranged from 32 inches to beyond 55-inch models. We are convinced that the store was not simply for propaganda, but a store meeting genuine demand. Many of the restaurants we visited had flat panel displays and karaoke machines.

Most of the shops and restaurants in North Korea specialize and offer very limited selections. Given the economy based on government allocations, there are neither many items available for purchase nor the money. Even restaurants specialize in one line of dishes, noodles, meat, etc. We saw many large-scale restaurants with the sign "Dahngogi" (dog meat). This arrangement may increase the efficiency of the store operations but does not offer consumer choices. Haebangsan Hotel restaurant is well known for their Galbi-tang (rib soup) and Kori-gomtang (oxtail soup). When we ordered these dishes, and only these dishes, they were served efficiently, and the dishes were served together. This was true in other specialty restaurants for Naengmyun (cold noodles) and pizza and pasta. Yes, we went to a pizza restaurant. Why? We were overruled. Actually, the pizza was more suitable to our taste than the ones we find in Daejeon.

Some hard-currency restaurants are the exception. They offer a full line of cuisine much like the restaurants we are used to. However, when we ordered different dishes that must be prepared separately, we invariably caused a logistics nightmare for the kitchen and the service staff. The servers are very attractive and polite, but the service would be enough to downgrade the restaurants. Almost every time we ordered a variety of dishes, they came out one at a time in a serial fashion with enough time lag between the dishes to make us suspect that they are cooking dishes one at a time. Once a broiled fish was served without rice. It turned out that the kitchen learned that they were out of cooked rice only when they were ready to serve the fish. Thus our friend had to wait while a fresh pot of rice was prepared. Of course, she was through with the fish when the steaming bowl of rice was served. Luckily her husband's dish was served around the same time and she could pinch off some and did not have to eat just the rice. The same scene repeated itself whenever we went as a group and ordered a variety of dishes from the menu.

The quality of food at these restaurants was generally very good. After all, the clientele are the upper crusts of the 1 percent group. In a society where uniformity is valued and insisted upon, and where standing in line for anything, including waiting for their turn in a public bath house, is the norm, good food served one at a time with long intervals must be perfectly acceptable. When we came out of our private dining room at the Haebangsan restaurant, the hall was full of North Koreans dining. In the parking lot we saw more than a dozen Mercedes Benz and Lexus vehicles waiting for their owners, clearly top 1 percent of the 1 percent.

Compared to July 2011, we saw many more cars on the streets and at a bridge even experienced a sort of a traffic jam. Individuals are not allowed to own cars, so the vehicles are registered in the name of institutions. Many more institutions these days must be able to afford vehicles and the fuel. Gasoline costs approximately $20 per ticket, good enough for 19.4

liters (about 5 gallons). At the Tongil market we saw a long line of taxis waiting for their fares. Since foreigners are not allowed to ride in taxis, there must be sufficient North Koreans riders with money. The 1 percent apart from the 99 percent exists even in this society.

It is our hope and prayer that the day will come soon when the ordinary people may take their children to the restaurants we dined in and each order their favorite dishes. The day may come sooner than we think!

Simon Park

Life in a five-star prison, Pyongyang University of Science and Technology (PUST)

Time to return to the life of and life at PUST, since an important reason for these letters is to introduce PUST and solicit support for it. Allow me to veer off for a moment and share my reasons for supporting PUST even in the face of strong objections of some friends for anything that would aid North Korea. I firmly believe that we never win by running our opponents, even enemies, into the ground. I have been in hopeless situations but resisted humiliating submissions at any cost. I believe running the North Korean society into the ground hoping for an implosion would not work and also is not a proper Christian approach. Instead, I pray for them to see the possibility of a better world and help them gain confidence that they will survive the change and thrive. This is also the motivation and goal of my small effort—not that I expect my efforts would make any tangible difference, but there are more capable and dedicated people working toward the same goal.

We received a visa as a faculty member and accompanying spouse at

PUST. Since North Korea and the United States do not have diplomatic relations, the visa was not attached to the passport but a very official-looking piece

of paper is issued and the entry and exit are stamped on the paper.

Of course, we paid hefty visa fees and the authorities kept the paper when we left. (What a disappointment!) We also had to surrender the passport to the External Relations Department at PUST, not only for control but also for obtaining permits and confirmations from other government offices. Our identity during our stay in North Korea thus depended upon the presence and words of the guides.

Our movement while on campus was not hindered or controlled in any fashion, though I am certain was monitored discreetly. Within the wire-fenced 230 acres, we were free citizens and our lives were not much different from what they would be in South Korea or in the U.S. However, we refrained from religious activities in the presence of North Koreans and did not talk aloud when the subject was North Korea or life in North Korea. Religion was off topic because the NK authorities do not allow any thought system that would challenge or compete with their own ideology. Life in NK was off limits because they did not want any discussion of failures or shortfalls in their society, I believe. Some of the limits were self-imposed, for fear of running afoul of them, not imposed on us by the NK authorities. Perhaps this self-imposition of limits explains our frame of mind while in NK very well.

Physically 65 women soldiers guard the premises. They live on campus, eat meals at the cafeteria, have two days a week allocated for them at the communal bath; in a word, they are fully part of the PUST family. But they do not socialize with any other group. Simon tried very hard to take a photo with them without success. They were polite and smiled back when greeted but would not agree to take a picture with Simon or have their pictures taken during "duty hours." We could not find them when they were not on duty.

Simon and Haejung shared experiences most of the time, as is common in the mission field, but also had some unique experiences. Simon's with the students in the classrooms, and Haejung's with the staff and students in the store are unique experiences for us. Students are carefully selected by the NK government, and we suspect that they were chosen for their academic performance, competency in English, and their loyalty to the party. Rumor had it that even their heights were considered to show the very best of North Korea. The students were very motivated, extremely capable, and overly polite. Simon could not walk the hallway carrying teaching equipment without students offering to help; most of them did not know him. They never pass us without greeting us, in English. All this made us to wonder whether they are behaving according to a script that came from above. That is always a possibility, but we think it is more of a result from years of living under strict behavioral norm rather than a conscious act for being at PUST and in the presence of foreign people. Haejung shared her experience with the students in the shop: PUST has a shop for daily neces-

sities and snacks on campus and the students are given approximately $10 in credit each month. They are to manage their funds and purchase what they need. I was hoping that this would turn into a lesson for budgeting and for making personal choices rather than the system making all the decisions for its people. We also learned another lesson. I observed three different behaviors. One group spent all their funds as soon as the credits were given, often sharing with their friends. Another group was very cautious and saved their funds for future needs, some wanting to buy gifts for their siblings when they go home after the semester is over. Yet another group would use up their allowance and badger their friends for the rest of the month with varying success. See, no system can change the basic human nature.

Then there are NK staff working in various roles, from administration or cooking to cleaning. They are employees of the NK government, as all North Koreans are, and PUST is not directly responsible for their work. Those who are commuting by bus, furnished by PUST, punch in at a machine with a camera, not sure of face recognition capability, when they come in. I am told that the work they perform officially may be less important than the responsibility given by the internal security apparatus. They are to report on the activities of others that they can observe. For example, a cleaner in an office may report on the section chief. There may be another reporting on the same subject, thus the cleaner may not choose to ignore a questionable behavior. No doubt there would be someone reporting on the cleaner herself, perhaps more than one. The system is most effective when people do not know who is watching them. We had to assume that the same system applies to the PUST faculty. Now you get the picture of a mental prison?

One sad consequence of this system is the impossibility of opening one's heart to anyone, especially on the topics of faith, economic and political systems. I had to be very careful not to compare market economy to the socialist system of NK. They were keenly interested in learning about the market system, banking and financial markets, but I was not able to learn more about the systems in NK. It would have been more interesting for all of us, and to you, had we been able to "compare and contrast." I am hopeful that a day when we could freely argue for competing social, economic and political systems would come to the Koreas. How else will they ever try different systems or even know that the current system is the one they want? Mental prisons of their own making! It seems we are in a pit that we cannot dig out of, but faith means believing in things that we cannot figure out and continue to put energy into the things hoped for.

As I write these intimate letters I fear I might inadvertently place someone in harm's way. It is a delicate dance to share and reveal as much as possible while keeping the discussions general enough to avoid misunderstanding and finger pointing. Even among the foreign faculty we all have different views of the world and Christianity. A collateral con-

North Korean Trinity —prominently displayed on a wall at the main building at PUST extols the blessings by Kim Il Sung, Kim Jong Il and Kim Jong Un. This is another sign of the religious cult like system of North Korean society.

sequence of the environment is that open and honest discussions and debates among the people who serve at PUST do not exist, for fear of hurting individuals and the institution. It may be that active discussions take place, but just that I was not a part of them. Still, it was possible for me to share with the people we came into close contact with on issues devoid of politics, religion and socioeconomic systems. We talked about our common economy, culture, and the joy and travails of raising children. I believe these interactions still lowered barriers between us and built up a small measure of trust. I do not know whether I will be going back, but we exchanged plans and hopes for the "next time."

Summing it all up, the real prison-like effect is in the inability to pursue one's passion without worrying that our actions, speeches and thoughts might violate some unspecified rules. It is a serious problem in any setting but becomes lethal when in pursuit of academic creativity and socioeconomic development. But one must always have hope and I find it in the experiment NK is carrying out at PUST. Allowing Internet access to graduate students and real-time access to Internet during classes, and allowing foreign journalists to come. I pray that it is just the beginning and that the experiments will expand to other venues and additional topics. I keep hoping, based on the belief that the truth will free us all! The course of the long march PUST is on perhaps is the only "Get out of jail" card for the North Koreans and for those of us hoping and working for a different tomorrow.

Simon & Haejung

Mankyungdae and Keumsan Academy

One day four of us went out, with a driver and two minders, to see sites around Pyongyang. We went to see the Juche (self-reliance) Tower and other standards sites. We also rode the subway for one stop, paying the tourist fare, and had a wonderful lunch at our favorite restaurant, Haebangsan. Then we went to Mankyungdae, in the outskirts of Pyongyang, to the birthplace of Kim Il Sung. It is now a large park of reverence with only the house originally built by Kim Il Sung's grandfather. A large group of North Koreans were being briefed with the aid of a bullhorn, but we were ushered directly into the house. An attractive guide came from the nearby guide waiting room and led us through the tour. She emphasized the humble beginnings of the family and how the grandfather refused to personally benefit when his grandson became the head of the country. The message is that the grandfather instilled the love for ordinary people of North Korea in Kim Il Sung and that that love continued through the generations of the Kims. Curiously, not much was said about his parents.

Our guide must have been a very experienced one as she easily engaged us in conversations and asked us for the English word for the gazebo-like structure built above ground by five feet or so. When I asked whether she guides in English as well, she said no, but in order to keep the honored position of guiding at this revered place, she needs to show that she is continually working to improve herself. She continued with us on foot onto the Mansubong, a low hill where a panoramic view of Pyongyang can be seen.

Then we rushed off to the nearby Keumsan Academy with another small contingent of three. Our guide told us earlier in the day that he had planned all along to show us a regular children's performance in the Children's Palace, but unfortunately the season had ended. He called the academy for a sampling of performances the day before. The academy was hesitant because of lack of time for preparation, but they agreed to present a few students "in practice."

Keumsan Academy is one of the two main training grounds for performing artists in Pyongyang. It includes primary school, high school and college level programs for the performing arts as well as a science stream through high school. There are about 3,000 students in the academy, and 30 percent of these live on campus as they come from other parts of the country. When we arrived in the afternoon, we were met by the principal of the school and a lady guide who took us to a hall showing the history and accomplishments of the school. The fact that the school received the Kim Il Sung Medal for Excellence left no doubt as to the status of the academy. Although the regular academic classes had finished, the students were engaged in extracurricular programs and some of the performing arts students were taking private lessons. We visited two computer technology classes briefly and continued to the performing arts wing.

As we walked down the hall, a staff person walked ahead of us, opening doors to the private-lesson rooms, and the vocal sounds and instruments rushed out into the hallway. We peeked into the rooms where stu-

Accordion quintet who is also a YouTube sensation.

Like all public performances, the finale was an ode to Kim Jong Il.

dents in stage costumes were practicing under the guidance of teachers in colorful Korean dresses. Their talents were remarkable as was their ability to concentrate with the strangers looking in and their fellow students' sounds. It almost seemed that the sounds were in perfect harmony. After the brief tour of the private lessons we turned around and were led through a narrow door into sudden sounds and sights from the main stage of a large auditorium. We had entered through a side door and were led to a row of chairs set in the middle where the rows to the front were empty and the rows behind were filled with an audience of a couple of hundred students.

The orchestra of Western and traditional Korean instruments was accompanying six young ladies singing a welcoming song (ban-gap-se-up-ni-da). The next 45 minutes went like a military honor drill. They sang traditional Korean folk songs and patriotic songs honoring and pledging allegiance to Kim Jong Il. They danced a drum dance and a musical interpretation of acrobatics. They also presented the beautiful harmony of an accordion quintet. All this happened without a word of explanation or a second of gap or hesitation. After an ode to Kim Jong Il, the entire group of performers sang the song of a great country to come. It really was a remarkable presentation by high school students. It would have been a remarkable one by professionals as well.

Later at the PUST campus I thanked our North Korean colleagues and shared what an inspiring and beautiful performance that was. He said the performance wanted to highlight the culture of the country and the artistic level of the people as well as the physical beauty and grace of their youth. As I suspected, this was not a performance put together overnight.

Two weeks later another visit to the Academy was announced, and I joined in again since I was not prepared to take photos and videos the first

time and I really wanted to record them to share with friends later. So we visited the Academy one very cold afternoon and went through the routine. The program was almost identical to the previous one but added a piano on stage and one or two new performances. The quality of performance, organization, and the patriotic spirit were all very high as before. The director of the Academy showed modesty in response to the congratulatory remarks by everyone, saying that the students are far short of professional standards, but he hoped that some of the students would make it into the next level.

I remain impressed with the presentation, but I couldn't shake the feeling that not only the stage performances but also the private lessons and the computer classes were scripted performances for us.

Why else the same students would take lessons in the same rooms with the same teachers on different days of the week and at different times? They did not expect the same guy to come back in such a short period, I suspect.

Then, I do not fault them for trying to show the best products of their system to outsiders though they went further than I would have. Think about the poor students in the audience who have to attend whenever an outside group comes and applaud at the proper times. They tried and accomplished for the most part the three objectives our guide explained earlier. I hope the pressure and the system's demands do not rob the youngsters of their youth and innocence.

Chilgol Church

We were hoping to attend Sunday services at several churches around Pyongyang. We were able to do that only one Sunday, at Chilgol Church located near Kim Il Sung's birthplace. According to an unverified story, Kim Il Sung's mother (Kang Ban Suk) used to attend this church and she had had quite an influence on Kim Il Sung. The story continues that initially Kim Il Sung was favorably disposed to Christianity until his ideology could not afford to have any "competition."

We heard about Bongsu Church, which was rebuilt with the donations from South Korean churches and was the church visited most often by foreign visitors. Instead, we went to the Chilgol Church—I do not know whether it was the choice of our side or was assigned to us. Six of us went to the church for the 10 o'clock service on Sunday morning of December 4. It was a very cold morning and two lady elders of the church waiting for us at the outside entrance welcomed us.

As we entered the smallish sanctuary, we found the members of the congregation and the choir already seated. We thought we might have arrived late, but found it was five minutes to 10. The first four rows of the pews on the right side were reserved for foreign visitors. A big surprise to us was that Sue Kinsler, recently retired from Presbyterian Church (U.S.A.) mission service, was visiting as the chair of the newly formed Green Tree Foundation, together with the Executive Director. Behind us sat members of the Nigerian Embassy, and some visiting American missionaries from the past were seated on the fourth row.

The service was in a very "Presbyterian" order of worship. The pastor preached from John 14, exhorting people to keep hope alive and live as God's people until the return of Jesus. Although there was a passing remark on the wrongness of the Free Trade Agreement between the U.S. and South Korea, it was a sermon that could have been delivered anywhere without much controversy. A very unusual part, for us, were very loud "Amen" responses from the congregation throughout the service; a man's voice stood out as he was shouting! Although the demand must not be very large, the hymnals and Bibles were printed in Korean.

There were anthems by the choir, an offertory solo, and a voice ensemble. It was obvious the members of the choir were professionally trained musicians. The service ended in exactly one hour. Then the greetings by the visitors went on for an hour. We were surprised again when Rev. Insik Kim, Presbyterian Church (U.S.A.)'s longtime coordinator for Asia who retired three years ago, came to the pulpit and greeted the congregation. It would have been a surprise to see both Sue and Insik in the same worship service in South Korea or in the States, but in North Korea! With others, the greetings lasted another 30 minutes. Then we went outside to greet the leaders and took some photos. During the time we were in the church, our minders and the driver had to wait in the cold car outside. The warmth inside would have been a good incentive for them to join in the service, but they did not.

While we greeted each other and took photos, the pastor (Rev. Whang MinWoo) and four leaders of the Chilgol Church joined the visitors for fel-

All the forms are there, but the substance(?)

lowship and to bid us journey mercies, the members of the church stayed inside, waiting until our departure.

We all had to go back to our respective locations with our minders, according to the schedule for each group. We could not invite others to the PUST campus since we did not know whether it was possible.

We are also told that there are house churches not exposed to the outside. It is not surprising that there would be these communities of faith, as they existed in China during the Mao's rule. After all, Pyongyang was known as the Jerusalem of Asia for its role in bringing and nurturing Christianity in Korea and beyond.

We heard conflicting opinions about whether the Christian churches sanctioned by the government are real or just for show. We couldn't tell you for certain. We want to believe that they are real Christians living their faith in God and Christ within the 333 bounds of their society. The state, however, does not want uncontrolled contact between the North Korean Christians and us. Our role is not to convert North Koreans into Christians but to share Christ's love with them without our own designs. God will do the necessary in God's time and way.

May God bless all his children, wherever they may be.

Simon & Haejung

Visits to Monuments and Historical Sites

During our short stay we visited many historical sites and recent monuments built since 1950s. All the sites are designed to emphasize the main theme of the Kim regime, which I will share with you all at the end of this note. Anyone arriving in Pyongyang cannot avoid the sights of ubiquitous towers, gates and plazas in grand scale. Every monument is to demonstrate the superiority of their society and the infallible wisdom of the leaders, namely Kim Il Sung and Kim Jong Il. Allow me to share a few with you.

A mandatory stop for every visitor to Pyongyang is the Juche Tower. This tower is built to commemorate the work of Kim Il Sung and to remember him eternally. This white granite tower is 150 meters tall and topped with a 20 meter high torch, and the guides take pains to point out that this is the tallest stone tower in the world. The tower is flanked with statues and fountains as well as the Daedong River.

One of the statues is the ruling Labor Party (Rodong-dang) symbol. Unlike the communist party symbols of China and Soviet blocs, the North Korean symbol has a calligraphy brush standing in between the hammer and sickle. The guide pointed out that Kim Il Sung did not consider the intelligentsia as enemies of the people but were those to lead the construction of a

strong motherland.

They point to the Great People's Library across the Daedong River as proof of the respect for knowledge the Great Leader had. They add that Kim Il Sung rejected many site recommendations for the library and instructed that the library must be located in the heart of great buildings commemorating the revolution, which shows how much the Great Leader valued knowledge, they add. The Arch of Triumph to commemorate Kim Il Sung's triumphant return in 1945 was officially dedicated at the April 1982 celebration of his 70th birthday. The guides never forget to mention that this gate is taller than the one in Paris.

We traveled a good distance one day to Nampo on the west coast and at the estuary of the Daedong River. There we visited the five-mile-long dyke with several locks, each capable of handling ships of 2,000 tons to 50,000 tons. They pointed out that this civil engineering feat was completed in 1985 and they built it in only five years. Just another proof that a great leadership with eager followers can accomplish great things for the motherland!!

We visited several historical sites, mostly tombs of kings of ancient dynasties. The tombs we visited are those of Dangun (a mythical figure

who founded the ancient Korean kingdom), King Dongmyung (founder of Koguryoh), Wang-gun (first king of Koryuh) and King Gongmin (the last king of Koryuh).

Dangun's tomb was particularly interesting to us since we learned during our school days that Dangun was born between a bear and a women and this superhuman being founded the ancient kingdom (Ko-chosun). North Koreans claim, however, that an archeological dig and subsequent testing proved that Dangun was born 5,011 years ago (as of 1993), and Kim Il Sung ordered his tomb rebuilt in a scale befitting his historical importance. Thus, they built this massive white granite edifice in only eight months, on a hill 30 miles to the northwest of the city center.

Then 16 miles to the northeast of Pyongyang we find the tomb of King Dongmyung, who started the Kokuryeo sometime after the demise of Ko-chosun. NK claims that Kokuryeo is the rightful successor to Ko-chosun, and this site was rebuilt in 1993. History tells us that the Shilla kingdom from the south unified the Korean peninsula but is ignored by the NK authorities. We are told the legitimate heir to Kokuryeo is the kingdom of Koryeo, founded by Wangun around 900 AD. His tomb was moved to

Kaesung and was rebuilt in 1995.

Koryeo established its capital in the city of Kaeseong further to the south and was toppled by the coup instigated by Lee Sung-gye about 600 years ago. Then several hundred years of chaos and invasions by foreign forces devastated the country until, as the story goes, Kim Il Sung ended the Japanese occupation in 1945.

You may have noticed that many of these sites were restored or rebuilt during the 1990s while the country was suffering from economic failures and South Korea was making remarkable progress in the world markets. I suspect that the regime felt a need to shore up their claim to leadership, not only for NK but also for the entire Korean peninsula, especially after the collapse of the Soviet Union in the late 1980s and they could not rely on the Soviet support. I do not have any scholarly proof of this, just my suspicion.

They built up historical sites around Pyongyang as the authentic lineage of Korean people, which also connects to the "Kim dynasty." That is one reason why each of the sites contains some signage crediting Kim Il Sung and Kim Jong Il for bringing the site to proper recognition and physical improvements. For those of you without knowledge or interest in Korean history it may be of little interest, but it helped us to understand why the North Korean people hold the Kims as not only their political but also their spiritual leaders, appointed for them by heavenly authority.

We came away with a feeling that the entire North Korean society is like a religious sect completely sold on the manufactured story of their leader being the promised messiah. They are unable and perhaps unwilling to examine the story line regardless of harsh realities; they have no other alternative to believing that the next in line would be the true one—that is Kim Jong Un for now.

Some additional photographs from North Korea

e were allowed to ride the subway for
e stop in Pyongyang. Pyongyang
izens seemed to know how to ignore
e tourist.

Do you notice absence of people in the
heart of Pyongyang at mid-morning?

e Christianity, Buddhism has a token representation in North Korea.

◀ *Notice the remarkable resemblance between the king and Simon? Should they ever want to make a movie about the king, I am available.*

▼1 *Professors from Kim Il Sung University learning English at PUST. It is expected that they will eventually take faculty positions at PUST.*

▼2 *Another example of 1% life, part of a table setting for one.*

At a children's hospital in Pyongyang, listing the value of "free" healthcare the government provided since 1953.

A large display at PUST extolling the success and accomplishments, including underground nuclear bomb tests, guided by the Juche ideology.

Though little known outside the circles, both in North Korea and elsewhere, aid programs such as UNDP, WFP, WHO and others are active in North Korea.
Many NGOs who run afoul of the regime makes news often.

At the "claimed" Dangun tomb with the guide. Being a guide at a historic site is a very high honor. To defend the veracity of seemingly wild tales, they simply state that "Kim Il Sung said…."

The arch on the highway leading to Pyongyang. Kim Il Sung calls on the unity around Korean ethnic identity to overcome ideological, political and religious differences for Korean unification. Left out of this statement, in my opinion, is the non-negotiable condition that the North Korean structure or regime be maintained.

chapter VI

Farewell
to Mission Service

Friends,

We are in transition. So, what's new? Transition has been the story of our life for the past 15 years since we transitioned from academic life into mission service. Unlike many missionaries, we received new assignments every three years. Now we are transitioning into a yet another phase of our lives, RETIREMENT. On August 21 we will be leaving Daejeon, Korea, for southern Indiana to begin our "private life." It is not completely true as we will be on our interpretation assignment until the end of 2012, but Simon's frequent trips to airports will stop, or at least slow down significantly.

We purchased a house in Nashville, Indiana (55 Pine Hills Drive, POB 2013, Nashville, IN 47448-2013), to enjoy serenity and the beautiful surroundings of Brown County! We have been looking forward to this transition, but there will be moments of awkwardness for a while. We are blessed to be able to choose the time and place of retirement on our own terms.

As always, we leave many things unfinished, trusting that God and his servants will bring them to good closure and also take them way beyond what we could have done. We left Nepal at the end of 2004 and returned for the first time in January this year with the Young Adult Volunteers who served in Korea. Simon had worked with several projects of the United Mission to Nepal (UMN). When UMN went into Nepal, they planned to turn over all projects (hospitals, schools and community service programs) to the Nepali nationals and their organizations. It was Simon's main duty

to prepare them for leadership, including external communications and fund raising. Experience has shown that many, if not most, NGOs are very poor in outcome evaluation and accountability reporting compared to their ability to prepare good-sounding proposals. Simon worked hard and was quite demanding that the NGOs go beyond articulating the needs and demonstrate their ability to be effective and accountable implementers in partnership with foreign supporters. This was new and difficult to those who mainly followed what missionaries asked.

One particular NGO in Pokhara, Nepal, proved to be quite a challenge as they enjoyed more than ten years of generous support from an overseas church and they were not as demanding as Simon. They went through a restructuring and leadership change before we left in 2004. When we visited the UMN headquarters in Kathmandu in January 2012, our old friends could not wait to tell us what a success story the Pokhara NGO turned out to be. The new leadership had decided to take Simon's suggestions and worked hard to make it their own. When other international NGOs came to Nepal seeking to find capable and trustworthy local partners, this NGO stood out and within five years they were partnering with six international institutions and grew beyond anyone's imagination. Since we were scheduled to visit Pokhara six days hence, we were all very excited to visit them and share the joy.

As we were traveling through Lumbini (Buddha's birth place) and Tansen (hospital whose tag line is We Serve and Jesus Heals) it seemed as if God was speaking to us: "Simon, I am glad that my Nepali children are running the NGO well to serve my children in need and I know that was your goal when you worked with them. Be happy and be thankful. How would your visit help them do their work better? I am happy to leave them to write their own story." We realized that we don't have to be a part of every story being written. We only need to rejoice in the stories of God's love in their new lives. The main purpose of our service has been to help others write new life stories, and we need not play a speaking part in them.

Many friends ask what we plan to do after leaving the field. We honestly don't know, but Haejung is clear about her role. She wants to be a gracious host to the visitors to our home and share God's grace and peace. Her role model is the innkeeper in the story of the Good Samaritan. The innkeeper did not go out and find the victim in need, but when he was brought to the inn, she gladly gave her best to care for the person in need.

The innkeeper did not have a speaking part, but the story would not end well without her. Haejung wants to "be" the innkeeper.

We will be visiting churches after we get settled in our new home. Our official itineration period ends at the end of this year, but we would probably continue as long as there is demand and our health holds up. Let us know if you want us to visit; we will come whenever we can.

At Tansen Hospital where a PC(USA) missionary built the hospital with the tag line - "We serve, Jesus heals."

Friends, our 15 years as PC(USA) mission co-workers have given us life experiences no other life path would have given, and we got to experience God in most intimate ways. We know God will be with us in our retirement life as well. Thank you for your prayers and your support all these years. We will write again when we are settled in Indiana and ready to come visit you, and when we are ready to play the innkeeper. Come see us —we will leave the porch light on.

Grace and peace,

Haejung & Simon

Farewell to mission service

Already a year has passed since we left the mission field and started our new life here in Brown County, Indiana. We want to share the joys and challenges of transitioning into retirement after fifteen years of "cared for" life we lived as missionaries.

Our ongoing transition faced quite a few adjustments; cultural, financial and relationships in broad categories.

We used to take pride in saying that we entered missionary life without regards to the financial issues as the Lord provides what we need. Upon entering the retirement phase we had to face some realities.

We entered mission service when Simon was fifty-one and ended at age sixty-six. For most people, these are the years to enjoy peak earnings and to save for retirement. Faced with small savings and anemic return on bank deposits, we wondered whether we would ever be able to retire without financial anxiety. Then we realized that God has indeed provided. We've had fifteen years of training in living simply. We learned to appreciate quality rather than quantity, not only in material things but also in relationships. We learned to save and not waste on frivolous things. Most people place "travel" high on retirement wish list, but we have done more than enough exotic travels during our mission service. We wish for visits by friends and family instead, we even have a very comfortable space for the guests. Please come visit us, whenever.

Since our return to the stateside, we've had two Thanksgivings with John and Kevin's families at our home already. We dreamed of picking up where we left off fifteen years ago. Haejung and I imagined Norman Rockwell portrait family gathering, while the children dreamed of the home they grew up in. We knew we changed a lot in fifteen years, but did not appreciate that John and Kevin also developed in different paths from ours and from each other. It took us a couple of gatherings to figure out that we are to celebrate and give thanks for our relationships, not the ceremony of the Thanksgiving dinner. When Haejung started the prayer for all of us with "thank you Lord for the bountiful table before us⋯", our two-year-old grandson Johan replied in a loud voice "You're welcome!"

Thank you Lord for the rich presence of all in our lives. Haejung continues her daily prayer giving thanks for the blessings in our children's lives and that they would always live in close fellowship with Christ.

All in all it's been another year of transition. Adjusting from a life of visibility and action to a supportive and contemplative role is still ongoing and at times difficult, but we are becoming wiser and more positive about our current role. We shared our mission as "ministry of presence" during our overseas service, and we hear our Lord asking the same in our retirement life as well. It is a bit more challenging when the people know what we are really like.

We give thanks for all God has allowed us in our transition and look forward to another year with the incarnate Christ among us.

Unlike the time in Bethlehem two thousand years ago, we have room at our inn and we wait for your visit with us.

Merry Christmas and a Happy New Year.

Haejung & Simon

Thanksgiving 2013.

A personal dispute led to multiple church burnings in Pakistan. These burned baptismal records are often the only formal record of some low caste folks. These terrorism acts threaten to destroy human existence and their dignity.

Being blonde agrees with Simon.

Index

Letter	Page	Missionary Life	Mission/ Missiology	Faith Journey	Life of Our Neighbors	Location
November-2003	118	x		x		India, Japan, Tibet
December-2003	122			x		Nepal
January-2004	124		x	x		Nepal
March-2004	127	x		x		Nepal
April-2004	130		x			Pakistan
May-2004	133	x				DR Congo
July-2004	136		x			Malawi
August-2004	140		x			Nepal
October-2004	144		x		x	Nepal
December-2004	147			x		Nepal
May-2005	149	x				USA
July-2005	152	x	x			USA
September-2005	155	x			x	Niger
October-2005	159	x		x	x	USA
November-2005	164		x		x	Pakistan
December-2005	167	x			x	Pakistan
February-2006	170			x	x	Niger
March-2006	173	x				USA
May-2006	176	x	x			Haiti
June-2006	179	x				USA
August-2006	185		x			USA
September-2006	188	x	x		x	Haiti, USA
November-2006	192	x	x			Cambodia
December-2006	195	x				USA
January-2007	197		x			USA
January-2007	200	x				Korea
March-2007	203	x		x		Korea
May-2007	205	x	x			Korea
July-2007	208	x	x			Korea
October-2007	211	x				Korea
December-2007	214	x		x		Korea
January-2008	217		x			USA
March-2008	219	x				Korea

Letter	Page	Missionary Life	Mission/ Missiology	Faith Journey	Life of Our Neighbors	Location
July-2008	221	x				Korea
October-2008	223	x				Korea
June-2009	226	x		x		Korea
September-2009	228	x	x			Korea, USA
October-2009	232		x			Japan
November-2009	234	x	x			DR Congo, Pakistan
March-2010	237	x				Korea
May-2010	241	x			x	Japan
June-2010	244	x				Korea
September-2010	246	x		x		Korea
February-2011	248	x				Japan
July-2011	250	x				North Korea
December-2011	253	x				North Korea
December-2011	257	x				North Korea
December-2011	260	x				North Korea
March-2012	265	x	x			North Korea
March-2012	267	x				North Korea
March-2012	272	x			x	North Korea
March-2012	277	x			x	North Korea
March-2012	281	x		x		North Korea
March-2012	284	x				North Korea
March-2012	291	x	x			Nepal
December-2013	294	x				USA

Author Profile

Simon Park

Born into a Christian family, he grew up in Seoul and went to the United States shortly after high school and completed his tertiary education with a doctorate from the University of Iowa. His academic career started at the University of Illinois, Urbana-Champaign in 1976, and continued at the Korea University and the National University of Singapore among others, he also consulted for many multi-national service enterprises. Together with his wife Haejung, he began his mission service with the Presbyterian Church (U.S.A.) in January of 1998, and retired from the field service in March 2013.

He served as the Business Manager at the Hopital du Bon Berger in DR Congo, worked to enhance the Nepalese staffs' management capacities of international NGOs, and beginning in 2007, based in the mission station at the Hannam University campus, he concentrated on helping mission projects, already established by other missionaries, to continue their ministries effectively in a sustainable manner. Whenever the Church asked, he helped with disaster and famine relief efforts around the world in short-term assignments, as well as assisting in efforts to improve accountability for financial resources at the Presbyterian Mission Agency in Louisville. His quest to better understand the need for lay missionaries and how to utilize the gifts they bring to mission service continues to this day.

Haejung Shin Park

Born in a non-Christian family, she accepted Jesus Christ as her Lord and savior during her teens. After graduating from Ewha University in Seoul, she was working as a teacher when she met Simon and married him in December 1974 at

Iowa City, Iowa. During the ensuing 23 years, she dedicated her life to making a loving home for their two sons while the family crisscrossed the Pacific several times. After their children left for college, Simon and Haejung sought a new endeavor in which they could journey together as partners bringing together their respective gifts. While examining several opportunities, God reminded her pledge of long-time ago, having heard the real need for administrative professionals to serve as missionaries, that they would serve in that role when their children did not need her daily care.

The Presbyterian Church (U.S.A.) initially assigned them to the Council of Churches in South Africa, but their first field assignment was in a small village in D.R. Congo where she learned what it means to be a neighbor in a community which shares little in common in culture, economy and life experiences. Although she later earned a Master's degree in Christian Counseling, the essence of her ministry is to become a good neighbor in obedience to the Lord and to live in such a way that leads those around her to experience the love and grace of God leading to self-esteem and the fullness of God given life. She remembers the years she accompanied the young adults in their discernment period through the Young Adult Program of the Presbyterian Church as one of the most memorable in her mission service. Having retired in 2013, she lives in New York state and enjoys nurturing her grandchildren. In the spirit of her mission service, she tries to be a good neighbor to many ladies in the Over-55 community where she makes home with Simon.